THE EUROPEAN
WITCH-CRAZE OF
THE SIXTEENTH AND
SEVENTEENTH CENTURIES

and Other Essays

*the text of this book is printed
on 100% recycled paper*

'A Witches' Sabbat'

THE EUROPEAN
WITCH-CRAZE OF
THE SIXTEENTH AND
SEVENTEENTH CENTURIES

and Other Essays

H. R. Trevor-Roper

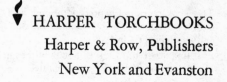

HARPER TORCHBOOKS
Harper & Row, Publishers
New York and Evanston

Contents

Illustrations

1 Religion, the Reformation and Social Change

If we look at the 300 years of European history from 1500 to 1800, we can describe it, in general, as a period of progress. It begins with the Renaissance and ends with the Enlightenment; and these two processes are, in many ways, continuous: the latter follows logically upon the former. On the other hand, this progress is far from smooth. It is uneven in both time and space. There are periods of sharp regression, and if the general progress is resumed after that regression, it is not necessarily resumed in the same areas. In the sixteenth century, indeed, the advance seems at first sight general. That is a century of almost universal expansion in Europe. But early in the seventeenth century there is a deep crisis which affects, in one way or other, most of Europe; and thereafter, when the general advance is resumed, after 1660, it is with a remarkable difference: a difference which, in the succeeding years, is only widened. The years 1620–60, it seems, mark the great, distorting gap in the otherwise orderly advance. If we were to summarize the whole period, we could say that the first long period, the 120 years 1500–1620, was the age of the European Renaissance, an age in which the economic and intellectual leadership of Europe is, or seems to be, in the south, in Italy and Spain; the period 1620–60 we could describe as the period of revolution; and the second long period, the period 1660–1800, would be the age of the Enlightenment, an age in which the great achievements of the Renaissance are resumed and continued to new heights, but from a new basis. Spain and Italy have become backwaters, both economically and intellectually: in both fields the leadership has fallen to the northern nations, and, in particular, to England, Holland and France. Just as the northern nations, in the first period, looked for ideas to the Mediterranean, so the Mediterranean nations, in the second period, looked north.

Now what is the cause of this great shift? Why was the first Enlightenment, the enlightenment of the Renaissance, which spread outwards from Italy, cut short in its original home and transferred, for its continuation, to other countries? Why was the economic advance which, in the sixteenth century, seemed so general, and in which all Europe had its share, carried to completion only in certain areas: areas which, at first, had not seemed best fitted for the purpose? This is a large question and obviously no general or easy answer can be satisfactory. In this paper I wish to consider one aspect of it: an aspect which is not, of course, easily separable, and which is admittedly controversial, but whose importance no one can deny: the religious aspect.

For religion is deeply involved in this shift. We may state the case summarily by saying that the Renaissance was a Catholic, the Enlightenment a Protestant phenomenon. Both economically and intellectually, in the seventeenth century, the Protestant countries (or some of them) captured the lead from the Catholic countries of Europe. Look at Europe in 1620: the date I have chosen for the end of the Renaissance period. With the advantage of after-knowledge we are apt to say that the shift had already taken place: that Holland and England had already usurped the place of Italy and Spain. But of course this was not so. At that time the configuration of power — to a superficial observer at least — must have seemed much the same as it had been in 1520. Spain and the Empire, Italy and the Papacy, these are still the centres of power, wealth, industry, intellectual life. Spain is still the great world power; south Germany is still the industrial heart of Europe; Italy is as rich and intellectually exciting as ever; the papacy is recovering its lost provinces one by one. Now look again in 1700, and how different it is. Politically, economically, intellectually Europe is upside down. Its dynamic centre has moved from Catholic Spain, Italy, Flanders and south Germany to Protestant England, Holland, Switzerland

and the cities of the Baltic. There is no escaping this great change. It is general fact; and although we may find special reasons applicable to this or that part of it, its generality is too huge and striking to be exorcised by any mere sum of particular explanations. The Inquisition may have ruined Spain, the blockade of the Scheldt Flanders, the loss of the Levant market Venice, the change of sartorial fashion Lombardy, the difficulties of transport south Germany, the opening of Swedish iron-mines Liège. All these events may be separately true, but together they fail to convince. A wholesale coincidence of special causes is never plausible as the explanation of a general rule.

How can we explain this extraordinary rise of certain Protestant societies and the decline of Catholic societies in the seventeenth century ? It is not enough to say that new discoveries or changed circumstances favoured north Europe as against south (for Catholic Flanders and Liège and Cologne are in the north, and yet shared the Catholic decline), or the Atlantic countries as against the Mediterranean (for Lisbon is better placed on the Atlantic than Hamburg). And even if opportunities did change, the question remains, why was it always Protestant, not Catholic societies which seized these opportunities ? Surely we must conclude that, in some way, Protestant societies were, or had become, more forward-looking than Catholic societies, both economically and intellectually. That this was so was a commonplace in the eighteenth century ; and in the nineteenth it was elevated into a dogma by those *bourgeois* propagandists — the Germanophil friend of Madame de Staël, Charles de Villers, in 1802 ; the Protestant statesman François Guizot in 1828 ; the Belgian economist, who followed his own reasoning and became a Protestant, Émile de Laveleye in 1875 — who sought to restore to their own Catholic countries the lead they had lost.[1] The

[1] See Charles de Villers, *Essai sur l'esprit et l'influence de la réformation de Luther* (Paris, 1804) ; F. P.-G. Guizot, *Histoire de la civilisation en Europe* (Paris, 1828) ; Émile de Laveleye, 'Le protestantisme et le catholicisme dans leurs rapports avec la liberté et la prospérité des peuples', in *Revue de Belgique*, 1875, and 'L'Avenir des peuples civilisés', in *Revue de Belgique*, 1876. On de Villers, see Louis Wittmer, *Charles de Villers, 1765–1815* (Geneva and Paris, 1908). Both Guizot's and Laveleye's essays were widely translated and republished and had great influence : the former

success with which largely Protestant entrepreneurs industrialized France and, through France, Europe under Louis-Philippe, Napoleon III and the Third Republic is evidence that, in their own time at least, there was some truth in their theories. In the nineteenth century, if we may trust appearances, it was by becoming 'Protestant' — that is, by accepting the rule of a 'Protestant' *élite* and a 'Protestant' ideology which convulsed the French Church, alarmed French Catholics, and brought papal thunderbolts from Rome — that France caught up, industrially, with those Protestant neighbours which, two centuries before, had outstripped it.[1] Such empirical evidence from the nineteenth century cannot be overlooked by us, even when we are looking at the seventeenth century.

But even if we admit the obvious fact that, in some way, Protestantism in the seventeenth century (and evidently in the nineteenth too) was the religion of progress, the question remains, in what way ? The nineteenth-century French propagandists did not argue the reason : as men of action they had not much time for reasons ; they merely stated the fact and pressed the consequence. It was left to the more academic German sociologists to explain the phenomenon. They explained it in several ways. Karl Marx saw Protestantism as the ideology of capitalism, the religious epiphenomenon of an economic phenomenon. Max Weber and Werner Sombart reversed the formula. Believing that the spirit preceded the letter, they postulated a creative spirit, 'the spirit of capitalism'. Both Weber and Sombart, like Marx, placed the rise of modern capitalism in

even provoked a Spanish reply from J. L. Balmes, *El protestantismo comparado con el catolicismo en sus relaciones con la civilisación europea* (Barcelona, 1844) — a reply considered by the too partial Menéndez y Pelayo as 'obra de immenso aliento . . . es para mí el primer libro de este siglo' ; the latter was introduced to the English public with a panegyric by Mr Gladstone.

[1] Propaganda in favour of Protestantism, not as being true but as being necessary to economic vitality, can be found in the works of Edgar Quinet, Ernest Renan, C. de Laboulaye, L.-A. Prévost-Paradol. See E. G. Léonard, *Le Protestant français* (Paris, 1953), pp. 220 ff., and Stuart R. Schram, *Protestantism and Politics in France* (Alençon, 1954), pp. 59–61. The alarm it caused is shown by Ernest Renauld's *Le Péril protestant* (Paris, 1899), *La Conquête protestante* (Paris, 1900). The Modernist movement in the French Church was in part a new Protestant movement and was specifically condemned as such by Pius X in the bull *Pascendi Gregis*.

the sixteenth century, and therefore both sought the origin of the new 'spirit of capitalism' in the events of that century. Weber, followed by Ernst Troeltsch, found it in the Reformation : the spirit of capitalism, he said, emerged as a direct consequence of the new 'Protestant ethic' as taught not by Luther but by Calvin. Sombart rejected Weber's thesis and indeed dealt it some heavy and telling blows. But when he came to make a positive suggestion he produced a far more vulnerable thesis. He suggested that the creators of modern capitalism were the Sephardic Jews who, in the sixteenth century, fled from Lisbon and Seville to Hamburg and Amsterdam ; and he traced the 'spirit of capitalism' to the Jewish ethic of the Talmud.[1]

Nobody, I think, would now defend Sombart's positive thesis, but much of Weber's thesis is still firm. It remains the orthodoxy of an influential school of sociologists in America. It has its defenders still in Europe. It is therefore worth while to summarize it very briefly, especially since it has often been misinterpreted. Weber did not argue that Calvin or any other Protestant teacher directly advocated capitalism or capitalist methods. He did not argue that Calvin's teaching on the subject of usury had any effect in the creation of capitalism. In fact, he explicitly repudiated such an idea. Nor did Weber deny that there had been capitalists in the Middle Ages. What he stated was that in the sixteenth century there arose a completely new form of capitalism. In the Middle Ages, as in Antiquity, men had built up great fortunes in commerce and finance ; but this, said Weber, had not created even the beginnings of a capitalist system. Such men had been 'Jewish adventurer-capitalists', 'speculative pariah capitalists', who made money because they

---

[1] Sombart's views are first given in *Der moderne Kapitalismus*, 1 (1902), i, 440, and developed in his later writings : see especially *Die Juden und das Wirtschaftsleben* (Leipzig, 1911) ; Weber's in *Die protestantische Ethik und der Geist des Kapitalismus* (1904–5), *Die protestantischen Sekten und der Geist des Kapitalismus* (1906), and *Wirtschaftsgeschichte* (Munich, 1923) ; also in numerous controversial articles published in *Archiv für Sozialwissenschaft u. Sozialpolitik*. Troeltsch, *Die Soziallehren der christlichen Kirchen und Gruppen* (1911) ; *Die Bedeutung des Protestantismus für die Entstehung der modernen Welt* (Munich, 1911), echoes Weber, of whom indeed he can hardly be considered independent (see Walther Köhler, *Ernst Troeltsch*, Tübingen, 1941, pp. 268, 358).

loved money and enjoyed making it. But the makers of modern capitalism, he said, were dedicated men who were not animated by love of money : indeed, if they made money, that was an accidental, almost an unwanted by-product of their activity. They were inspired by a moral discipline, an *innerweltliche Askese* or 'worldly asceticism', which caused them to place their religion in the methodical pursuit of their 'calling', and incidentally to pile up wealth which, since they eschewed all forms of luxury, extravagance and social ambition, they could only reinvest in that 'calling'. So, indirectly, their moral discipline created that new phenomenon, that 'rational bureaucratic capitalism', that 'rational organization of citizen labour', which was quite distinct from 'Jewish adventurer-capitalism' and which made Europe unique in world history ; and this moral discipline, according to Weber, was the Protestant, or rather the Calvinist, ethic. The Protestant ethic thus created the spirit which, when applied to economic affairs, created modern industrial capitalism. For we will not be far wrong in equating Weber's 'Jewish adventurer-capitalism' with commercial capitalism and his 'rational bureaucratic capitalism' with industrial capitalism.

Now, in spite of all that can be said against it, I believe that there is a solid, if elusive, core of truth in Weber's thesis. The Calvinist ethic did lead, in certain cases, to the formation of industrial capitalism. It is not enough to say that capitalism had a freer field in Protestant countries, because we have to explain why even in Catholic countries, like France or Austria, it was Protestants who throve and built up industry. And it is indisputable that extreme forms of Protestantism were popular among industrial workers, whether the miners of Bohemia and Saxony or the cloth-workers of Yorkshire and Lancashire. On the other hand, there are certain serious difficulties about Weber's thesis. Any general theory has to take account of exceptions. Since Weber himself limited the Protestant ethic to Calvinism, he had no need to explain the economic stagnation of Lutheran Germany ; but what about Scotland ? According to Weber's theory, Scotland, with its coal deposits and its strict Calvinist system, should have progressed faster than England, whose Anglican system was regarded by Laveleye as, economically, little better than popery. And why was it Arminian Amsterdam which created the amazing prosperity of the United Provinces, while Calvinist Gelderland remained the reserve of booby squires — that class which, according to the earliest explicit exponent of the theory, Slingsby Bethel, was always the enemy of mercantile progress ? [1]   Such notable exceptions suggest that even if Calvinism did create or fortify the capitalist spirit it did so in a very uncertain manner.

For these reasons I wish to consider the thesis anew — or rather, not the thesis but the historical facts to which Weber supposed it to apply. I think this is worth doing, because Weber himself merely described a theoretical connection : he never gave a single historical instance of the connection thus described ; and Weber's most distinguished successor, R. H. Tawney, confined himself to English examples, thus denying himself the light which may come from a comparative method. In considering the facts, I will begin by a brief glance at Europe in the years of revolution between what I have called the period of the Renaissance and the period of the Enlightenment : i.e. in the years of the Thirty Years War.

Let us start with the Protestant powers. In the late 1620s and early 1630s the political champions of the Protestant cause were not Calvinists, they were Lutherans. They were the two kings of Scandinavia : the extravagant, catholicizing aesthete, Christian IV of Denmark and, after his defeat, the severe, mystical, crusading hero, Gustavus Adolphus of Sweden. In order to intervene in Europe, both these kings found themselves obliged to mobilize new industrial and financial resources, and this meant employing great capitalists. Who were the capitalists whom they found ?

Christian IV turned first to a Calvinist firm in Amsterdam, the de Willem brothers. Jan de Willem, in Copenhagen, was one of the founders of the Danish East India Company. His brothers Paul and David sat in Amsterdam and through the international

---

[1] [Slingsby Bethel] *The Present Interest of England Stated, by a Lover of his King and Country* (1671) ; cf. also his (also anonymous) *The Interest of Princes and States* (1680).

money market provided credit for the purchase of arms. When the de Willem brothers ceased to serve him, Christian IV turned to another Calvinist family, of Flemish origin, the Marcelis family, who had already made a commercial empire in the north. At first it was a cosmopolitan empire. They sought to corner Swedish copper, handled the King of Denmark's Norwegian copper and the Czar of Russia's corn and armour. But in the end they plumped for Denmark. By the 1640s the brothers Gabriel and Celio Marcelis were the King of Denmark's economic advisers, contractors, financiers, munition merchants, timber exporters. They advanced money on the Sound tolls and the copper tithes. They raised fleets. Around them, the native Lutheran aristocracy sank into mere landownership and the native Lutheran merchants became mere agents of Dutch Calvinist merchant houses. The Dutch Calvinists became, in fact, a new capitalist aristocracy in Lutheran Denmark.[1]

The King of Sweden did likewise. What the Marcelis family was for Denmark, the firm of de Geer and Trip was for Sweden. Louis de Geer, indeed, a Calvinist from Liège, settled in Amsterdam, was to become the seventeenth-century Fugger of the north. Driving out all his rivals (also Dutch Calvinists), he became 'the indisputable master of Swedish economic life', 'the Krupp of the seventeenth century'. The whole copper and iron industries of Sweden were in his hands, and from them he supplied the armies and fleets not only of Sweden but also of Holland, France, Venice, Portugal, England, Scotland, Russia and the German princes. He also manufactured brass, steel, tin, wire, paper, cloth. He was a great shipper and shipbuilder: in 1645 he assembled, chartered and equipped a naval squadron to serve Sweden against the fleet which his kinsman Gabriel Marcelis had similarly raised for Denmark. He organized and financed the Swedish African Company. In repayment of his loans to the

[1] For the Calvinists in Denmark, see Violet Barbour, *Capitalism in Amsterdam* (Baltimore, 1949), pp. 112–14; H. Kellenbenz, *Unternehmerkräfte im Hamburger Portugal- u. Spanienhandel* (Hamburg, 1954), and 'Spanien, die nördlichen Niederlande u. der skandinavisch-baltische Raum', in *Vierteljahrschrift für Sozial- u. Wirtschaftsgeschichte*, 1954, pp. 305–6, 311, etc.; Axel Nielsen, *Dänische Wirtschaftsgeschichte* (Jena, 1927), pp. 193–6.

Swedish Crown he received yet more concessions, consignments of copper, leases of Crown lands, customs dues, privileges, exemptions, titles of honour. He was the financier of Sweden's empire abroad, the founder of its extractive industry at home. To operate it, he brought to Sweden Calvinist workers from his native Liège : 300 Walloon families who never learned Swedish but whose influence was felt in Sweden for more than 300 years.

De Geer was not the only great Calvinist financier and industrialist in Sweden in those years. Willem Usselincx founded the Swedish West India Company. The brothers Abraham and Jacob Momma opened up iron- and copper-mines in Lapland and became the personal financiers of Queen Christina. The brothers Spiering controlled the Baltic corn market and farmed the Baltic tolls. It was a Dutch Calvinist from Livonia who founded the Bank of Sweden in 1658. Other Dutch Calvinists controlled the export of iron guns, the royal brass factory at Nacka, etc.[1]

If Lutheran Denmark and Sweden were modernized and financed by Calvinist entrepreneurs, what of the other supporter of European Protestantism, the Catholic monarch of France ? Cardinal Richelieu, it is well known, like Henri IV before him, relied largely on Huguenot men of affairs. His bankers were French Calvinists, the Rambouillets and the Tallemants. To pay the French and Swedish armies he employed Jan Hoeufft, a Calvinist from Brabant who had been naturalized a Frenchman in 1601 and had been employed by Henri IV to drain the lakes and marshes of France. Through his brother Mattheus in Amsterdam, Hoeufft was in touch with the Calvinist international, with de Geer, and with the Baltic.[2] But in 1639 Richelieu found another Protestant financier, who was to dominate French

---

[1] For Calvinists in Sweden, see Eli F. Heckscher, *Economic History of Sweden* (Cambridge, Mass., 1954), pp. 101–19, and 'L'Histoire de fer : le monopole suédois', in *Annales d'histoire économique et sociale*, 1932. There are biographies of de Geer in Dutch by F. Breedvelt van Ven (Amsterdam, 1935), and in Swedish by E. W. Dahlgren (Uppsala, 1923) ; cf. also G. Edmundson, 'Louis de Geer', *English Historical Review*, 1891.

[2] For Hoeufft, see Barbour, *Capitalism in Amsterdam*, pp. 30 n., 105–6.

finance for the next quarter of a century. This was Barthélemy d'Herwarth, who, in that year, brought over to the service of France the leaderless German army of his deceased employer, Bernard of Saxe-Weimar.

Barthélemy d'Herwarth is a famous figure in French economic history.[1] By his financial ability he kept the army of Alsace loyal to France. He financed Mazarin's German policy. 'Monsieur d'Herwarth', the Cardinal once declared in the presence of the young Louis XIV, 'has saved France and preserved the crown to the King. His services should never be forgotten; the King will make them immortal by the marks of honour and recognition which he will bestow on him and his family.' The King duly made him *Intendant des Finances*, and relied on him more than once in moments of crisis. The *dévots* were outraged to see this Huguenot so powerful at Court, but they could do nothing : Herwarth 'had rendered such service to the State by means of his credit with the German army', it was explained, 'that all other considerations must yield'. As *Intendant des Finances*, Herwarth filled his office with his co-religionists. Under him, wrote Élie Bénoist, the contemporary historian of the Revocation of the Edict of Nantes, 'Public Finance became the refuge of the Reformed, to whom other employment was refused'. Upon which a modern French historian has commented, 'Herwarth after Sully, there — as far as France is concerned — is the true origin of the famous Protestant Finance ; not in the intimate connection and theological reasons invoked by Max Weber and his school.' [2]

'As far as France is concerned' — possibly ; but possibly not. Even if the French Huguenots sought to introduce each other into financial office, does that explain their competence for these offices ? And anyway, the phenomenon does not appear in France only. We have seen it in Lutheran Denmark and Lutheran Sweden. Once again, we cannot properly invoke a special reason to explain what seems to be a general rule. In order to see how

[1] For Herwarth, see G. Depping, 'Un Banquier protestant en France au 17e siècle, Barthélemy d'Herwarth', in *Revue historique*, vols. x and xi (1870).

[2] E. G. Léonard, *Le Protestant français*, p. 52.

general it is, let us now continue our survey of Europe. Let us go over to the other side in the Thirty Years War : the side of Catholic Austria and Catholic Spain.

For the Habsburg powers also needed industrialists and financiers to mobilize their resources and pay their armies : those armies that had to fight on so vast a theatre, from the Baltic to the Alps, from the Carpathians to the Pyrenees. That they were successful for a time was due, it is well known, to the genius of one man, Albert von Wallenstein. Wallenstein, greatest of *condottieri*, discovered the secret of keeping an army in being, paying it by contributions levied from conquered provinces and cities, feeding, clothing and arming it from his own workshops, factories and mines. But behind Wallenstein, we now know, stood another man whose presence, long hidden, has only recently been revealed : Hans de Witte, a Calvinist from Antwerp.

There is something incredible in the career of Hans de Witte, the solitary Calvinist who sat in Prague financing the army of the Catholic powers. He had come thither to serve the tolerant, eccentric Emperor Rudolf II, and had somehow stayed to finance his intolerant successors, who, however, tolerated him for his industrial and financial services. Already, by the beginning of the war, he controlled the silver and the tin of the empire. Thereafter his power never ceased to grow. It was he who advanced all the money to pay Wallenstein's armies, recouping himself with the taxes of loyal and the contributions and ransoms of conquered provinces. It was he who organized the supply of those armies with arms and armour, uniforms, gunpowder, salt-petre, lead, all drawn from Wallenstein's duchy of Friedland. Production, manufacture, transport down the Elbe — he managed it all. All the silver-mines, copper-mines, lead-mines on Wallenstein's estates were in his hands. The iron forges of Raspenau in Bohemia, the rival of the iron-mines of Arboga in Sweden, were under his control. He was the de Geer of the Catholic powers. Like de Geer he brought his co-religionists with him to work the mines, and secured guarantees that they would not be molested for their religion. It was a guarantee that only he could have secured : for as the Jesuits took control in Bohemia, the Calvinists had been remorselessly driven out. In the end only one remained : Hans de Witte, the greatest industrialist, greatest financier, richest subject of Bohemia, the banker of the Emperor and Empress, of the generalissimo, the nobility, the clergy, the Jesuits themselves. When the crash came — when Wallenstein fell and the banker's long-strained credit was finally ruined — it was still in Prague, still a Calvinist, that he met the end, drowning himself, bankrupt, in his garden well.[1]

So much for the Habsburgs of Vienna. What of the Habsburgs of Madrid ? It is hardly to be expected that we should find a Calvinist entrepreneur at the ear of Philip IV ; but we soon find that, to mobilize his resources, even the most Catholic king was obliged to look outside the faith. In fact, for the handling of his foreign trade and the provision of his fleets, he looked to the Lutheran merchants of Hamburg, who, if they were heretics, were at least neutrals and nominal subjects of his cousin the Emperor. For a whole generation Lutheran Hamburg became the mercantile capital of the Spanish empire. There were centralized the sugar trade of Brazil, the spice trade of the East. Through it the King of Spain drew on the industry of Germany, the commerce of the Baltic. Through it his overseas colonies were supplied with manufactures in exchange for the precious metals which financed the war. Through it were equipped the successive armadas with which he hoped to keep his colonies and reconquer northern Europe.

But when we look more closely at Hamburg, what do we find ? Numerically the Lutheran Germans are no doubt in a majority, but in quality they are eclipsed by Dutch Calvinists. It was in vain that Spain sought to avoid dependence on the hated rebels by using Hanseatic merchants : the Hanseatic merchants, on closer inspection, turn out to be Dutchmen, or Dutch agents. It was Netherlanders, not native Hamburgers, who founded the Bank of Hamburg in 1619, and formed three-quarters of its

---

[1] The character and history of Hans de Witte have been brought to light by Mr Anton Ernstberger, *Hans de Witte Finanzmann Wallensteins* (*Vierteljahrschrift für Sozial- u. Wirtschaftsgeschichte, Beiheft*, 1954).

greatest depositors. In 1623, when the Spanish government pounced on the foreign ships in its harbours, no less than 160 'Hanseatic' ships were found to be really Dutch. In using the Lutheran Hanseatic cities, Spain was only concealing its real dependence on its open enemies, the Calvinist Dutch.[1]

Meanwhile, on the Rhineland front, the Spanish armies had to be maintained. The King of Spain needed a capitalist who could mobilize the salt-mines of Franche-Comté as de Geer had mobilized the copper-mines of Sweden and de Witte the iron-mines of Bohemia. He found the man he needed. François Grenus, a Swiss Calvinist from Berne, a merchant-banker in Geneva, farmed the royal salt-mines and, by his loans, sustained the Spanish forces. The other clients of this Swiss de Witte were the other enemies of European Protestantism: the Emperor, and that Duchess of Savoy, the sister of Queen Henrietta Maria, who is chiefly remembered in history for slaughtering the saints of God, the Protestants of the valleys of Piedmont.[2]

Thus in Catholic as in Protestant countries, in the mid-seventeenth century, we find that the Calvinists are indeed the great entrepreneurs. They are an international force, the economic *élite* of Europe. They alone, it seems, can mobilize commerce and industry and, by so doing, command great sums of money, either to finance armies or to reinvest in other great economic undertakings. Faced with these facts, it is easy to assume a direct connection between their religion and their economic activity ; and yet, before we jump to such a conclusion, we would do well to look more closely at the picture we have sketched. We must apply the historical tests with which Weber, the sociologist, dispensed. In particular, we must ask, what was the common denominator of the actual Calvinist entrepreneurs whom we know ? Was it Calvinism of the type defined by Weber ? If not, what was it ?

[1] See Kellenbenz, 'Spanien, die nördlichen Niederlande', pp. 308, 315 ; E. Baasch, 'Hamburg u. Holland im 17ten u. 18ten Jahrhundert', in *Hansische Geschichtsblätter*, 1910, XVI, 55–56.

[2] For Grenus, see Baron de Grenus, *Notices biographiques sur les Grenus* (Geneva, 1849).

Now, certainly the men whom we have named were not all orthodox Calvinists in religion. Louis de Geer was : he indeed showed a firm, enlightened Calvinist piety from the time when, in La Rochelle, he took his vow to serve God with whatever he might gain in a life of virtuous commerce. He patronized Calvinist scholars, gave generously to dispossessed Calvinist ministers, and in all his career as an industrialist seems never to have supplied any enemy of the Calvinist cause. But in this uncompromising Calvinist piety Louis de Geer is an exception. His opposite number, Hans de Witte, though he professed Calvinism to the end, was as bad a Calvinist as it was possible to be. Not only did he serve the Jesuits and the Catholic powers against European Protestantism : he had his son baptized in the Catholic Church with Wallenstein, the terror of European Protestants, as godfather. The Swiss Calvinist François Grenus was not much better. As for Herwarth, it is not even certain that he was a Calvinist at all. As a naturalized French subject, he counted as a 'Huguenot'; but he was already middle-aged when he became a Frenchman. He was born a German, of a Lutheran family, and Mazarin found him in the service of a Lutheran prince. He was probably a Lutheran.[1]

Of course, Weber himself would not admit mere doctrinal orthodoxy as a criterion. His Calvinist was not a strict believer or even practiser of his religion, but a social type, whose character, though originally formed by Calvinist teaching, could easily become detached from it. What we should look for, to confirm his theory, is not merely religious faith, but the moral deposit of faith which can be left behind even when faith has departed. To Weber this moral deposit of Calvinism was 'worldly asceticism': frugality of life, refusal to buy land or titles, disdain for the 'feudal' way of life. Unfortunately, when we look for this moral deposit in our seventeenth-century Calvinist entrepreneurs, we are once again disappointed. In real life, all the great entrepreneurs lived magnificently. Dutch Calvinist merchants might not buy great estates in Holland, where there was

---

[1] Georg Herwarth, Barthélemy's great-grandfather, had headed the Lutheran party at Augsburg in the time of the Smalcaldic War.

so little land to buy, but abroad they let themselves go. Even Louis de Geer bought lands in Sweden 'surpassing in extent the dominions of many small German princes'. He acquired a title of nobility and founded one of the greatest noble houses in Sweden. So did the other Dutch capitalists in Sweden — the Momma brothers, Peter Spiering, Martin Wewitzers, Conrad van Klaenck. Hans de Witte acquired hereditary nobility and vast estates in Bohemia : at the height of his success he owned three baronies, twelve manors (*Höfe*), fifteen landed estates and fifty-nine villages. Barthélemy d'Herwarth showed even less of that puritan asceticism which characterized Weber's ideal type. As his town house, he bought for 180,000 livres the Hôtel d'Épernon, and then, finding this palace of a duke and peer of France inadequate for his splendid tastes, he scandalized Parisian society by demolishing it and rebuilding on a yet more lavish scale. As his suburban villa he bought the maison de Gondi at St-Cloud, where Catherine de Médicis had held her festivals and Henri III had been murdered, and sold it back to the Crown for 250,000 livres. As his country house he bought the château of Bois-le-Vicomte, once the residence of Cardinal Richelieu, of Gaston d'Orléans, and of La Grande Mademoiselle. In such surroundings the Protestant financier entertained royalty and indulged, with his friends, that passion for gambling which was notorious and censured even at the indulgent Court of Louis XIV. Such were the real men whose abstract type was characterized by Weber as 'rational worldly asceticism'.

If the great Calvinist entrepreneurs of the mid-seventeenth century were not united by Calvinist piety, or even by its supposed social expression, what did unite them ? If we look attentively at them we soon find certain obvious facts. First, whether good or bad Calvinists, the majority of them were not natives of the country in which they worked. Neither Holland nor Scotland nor Geneva nor the Palatinate — the four obvious Calvinist societies — produced their own entrepreneurs. The compulsory Calvinist teaching with which the natives of those communities were indoctrinated had no such effect. Almost all the great entrepreneurs were immigrants. Secondly, the majority of these immigrants were Netherlanders : some of them, perhaps, were Calvinists only because they were Netherlanders.

De Geer, the Momma brothers, Spiering in Sweden, the Marcelis family in Denmark, Hoeufft in France, de Witte in Bohemia, were all Netherlanders. The pseudo-Hanseates along the Baltic coast, the newly prospering merchants of the Rhineland cities, were largely Netherlanders. 'We can fairly say', writes the greatest authority on the subject, 'that the old system of the Hanseatic League had been interwoven with a new system, which brought all these cities into peculiar dependence on Dutch entrepreneurs.'[1] Moreover, when we look closer still, we discover that these Netherlanders came generally from a particular class within the Dutch Republic. Even there they were, or their fathers had been, immigrants. Either they were 'Flemings' — that is, immigrants from the southern provinces now under Spanish rule — or they were Liégeois, from the Catholic prince-bishopric of Liège.

The extent to which the new prosperity of Amsterdam, after 1600, was built up by *émigrés* from Antwerp is well known. Amsterdam, in the sixteenth century, was a fishing and shipping port : in the world of international commerce and high finance it had little significance until the reconquest of Antwerp by Alexander Farnese in 1585. The earliest form of marine insurance there dates from 1592, and it had probably been introduced by the more sophisticated southerners — the famous Isaac le Maire of Tournai and Jacob de Velaer of Antwerp — who were among its signatories. There were no bankers in Amsterdam before 1600. The Bank of Amsterdam, founded in 1609, and the Bourse of Amsterdam, founded in 1611, owed their existence to the 'Flemish' immigration and were based on southern, Catholic models. The Dutch West India Company was an almost entirely Flemish company. Peter Lintgens, one of the founders of the Dutch East India Company, had brought his shipping and insurance firm, with its international connections, from Antwerp. The most famous of the great entrepreneurs of Holland in those days — Isaac de Maire, Dirck van Os, Balthasar

[1] Kellenbenz, 'Spanien, die nördlichen Niederlande', etc., p. 308.

Moucheron, Baptist Oyens, Peter Lintgens, Willem Usselincx, Isaac Coymans, Johan van der Veken — were all Flemings. It was they, far more than native Hollanders, who initiated the sudden portent of Dutch prosperity.[1]

If it was Flemings who built up the new prosperity of Holland, equally it was Flemings who, from Holland, formed the *élite* of the Dutch Calvinist entrepreneurs in the rest of Europe. The business life of Hamburg, we have seen, was ruled by Dutchmen ; but these Dutchmen, we soon find, were largely Flemings. If thirty-two of the forty-two largest depositors in the Bank of Hamburg were Dutchmen, at least nineteen of these thirty-two were Flemings. Of the thirty-six families who controlled the Peninsular trade, which was the basis of Hamburg's spectacular fortune in the early seventeenth century, nearly two-thirds came from Antwerp, and the rest from Liège or the industrial Walloon country. In Sweden de Geer, in Bohemia de Witte might count as Dutchmen, but by birth the former was a Liégeois, the latter a Fleming from Antwerp. The most prosperous of the Netherlanders who went to Frankfurt were the Flemings. By 1600 they had a two-thirds majority in its ruling oligarchy : it was they who, in the words of its historian, made the period 1585– 1603 'Frankfurt's second golden age as a Belgian colony', 'the daughter town of Antwerp'.[2] In Emden, trade was largely in the hands of Antwerpers.[3] Wesel was known as 'Little Antwerp'. All along the Rhine it was entrepreneurs from Antwerp and from Liège who, bringing their refugee workmen with them, established first the cloth, then the extractive industries and thus

[1] For this dependence of Amsterdam (and the Dutch Diaspora generally) on the previous expertise of Antwerp, see H. Pirenne, *Histoire de Belgique*, IV, 340 ; Barbour, *Capitalism in Amsterdam*, pp. 15–16, 24 ; Kellenbenz, 'Spanien, die nördlichen Niederlande', pp. 309–10, and *Unternehmekräfte*, pp. 149, 342–3 ; A. E. Sayous, 'Die grossen Händler u. Kapitalisten in Amsterdam', in *Weltwirtschaftliches Archiv*, XLVI and XLVII (1937–8) ; W. J. van Hoboken, 'The Dutch West India Company : the Political Background of its Rise and Decline', in *Britain and the Netherlands*, ed. J. S. Bromley and E. H. Kossmann (1960).

[2] A. Dietz, *Frankfurter Handelgeschichte*, I (1910), 63–69, 305–6 ; II (1921), 1–45 ; G. Witzel, 'Gewerbegeschichtliche Studien zur niederländischen Einwanderung in Deutschland im 16ten Jahrhundert', in *Westdeutsche Zeitschrift*, 1910.

[3] Bernhard Hagedorn, *Ostfrieslands Handel u. Schiffahrt im 16ten Jahrhundert* (Berlin, 1910), I, 124–30.

created, for the Catholic natives, a new prosperity.[1] Even in Calvin's Switzerland it was not Swiss Calvinists who created the new industries : for a whole century after Calvin there is not a single great Swiss entrepreneur. François Grenus, who flourished in the 1640s, was the first — if indeed he was a Swiss native and not a Walloon immigrant.[2] The industry of Switzerland was created almost entirely by immigrants, the most spectacular of them, perhaps, being the converted Jew, Marcus Perez, who offered to make Basel the new economic centre at the cost of his abandoned home-town of Antwerp.[3] In the Calvinist Palatinate it was the same.[4] Even in Scotland, where the Calvinist clergy vigorously opposed any economic enterprise, it was Flemish immigrants who, in 1588, sought to establish that basis of modern industrial capitalism, the cloth industry.[5]

It would be easy to multiply instances. The general pattern is clear. When Weber observed, as evidence for his thesis, that in Hamburg the oldest entrepreneurial family was a Calvinist, not a Lutheran family, or when Slingsby Bethel recorded that it was 'the Reformed', not the Lutherans, who were the active businessmen in the north German cities with which he was familiar, they are merely recording the fact of the Dutch, or rather

[1] W. Sarmenhaus, *Die Festsetzung der niederländischen Religions-Flüchtlingen im 16ten Jahrhundert in Wesel* (Wesel, 1913). Paul Koch, *Der Einfluss des Calvinismus und des Mennonitentums auf der neiderrheinischen Textilindustrie* (Krefeld, 1928).

[2] Baron de Grenus (*Notices biographiques*) describes François Grenus as a native of Morges, in the Pays de Vaud ; but H. Lüthy, *La Banque protestante en France*, I (Paris, 1959), 38, 42, refers to him as an immigrant from Armentières.

[3] On the immigrants into Switzerland, see J. C. Möriköfer, *Geschichte der evangelischen Flüchtlinge in der Schweiz* (Leipzig, 1876), pp. 30–42 ; A. E. Sayous, 'Calvinisme et capitalisme à Genève', in *Annales d'histoire économique et sociale*, 1953 ; Walter Bodmer, *Der Einfluss der Refugianteneinwanderung von 1500–1700 auf die schweizerische Wirtschaft* (Zürich, 1946) ; and the histories of Basel by T. Geering (1886), R. Wackernagel (1907–16) and Paul Burckhardt (1942).

[4] See Eberhard Gothein, *Wirtschaftsgeschichte des Schwarzwaldes* (Strasbourg, 1892), I, 674 ff. ; Richard Frei, *Die Bedeutung der niederländischen Einwanderer für die wirtschaftliche Entwicklung der Stadt Hanau* (Hanau, 1927) ; Paul Koch, *Der Einfluss des Calvinismus*.

[5] For the opposition of the Church of Scotland to economic progress, see W. L. Mathieson, *Politics and Religion : A Study in Scottish History* (Glasgow, 1902), II, 202–3 ; H. G. Graham, *The Social Life of Scotland in the Eighteenth Century* (1906), pp. 159–62. For the introduction of 'Flemyng wobsters' by the burgh of Edinburgh, see *Burgh Records of Edinburgh 1573–89* (Edinburgh, 1882), p. 530.

Flemish, dispersion. And although the men thus dispersed were largely Calvinists, they were not necessarily Calvinists. Their local origins were more constant than their religion. Thus the richest of all the refugees who came to Frankfurt were the so-called Martinists, the Lutherans of Antwerp : a dozen of them, we are told, could buy up all the Calvinists put together. At any time from 1580 the richest man in Frankfurt was probably a Lutheran — but a Lutheran from Antwerp. In Hamburg, too, some of the immigrant Dutch merchants were Lutherans, like the de Meyers and the Matthiesens. In Cologne the two greatest immigrant entrepreneurs, Nicolas de Groote and Georg Kesseler, were not Calvinists but Catholics ; but they came from Antwerp. Even in Calvinist Holland one of the greatest of the Flemish immigrants, Johan van der Veken, the entrepreneur of Rotterdam, was a Catholic — but a Catholic from Antwerp. Similarly, the founders of the new extractive industries were not necessarily Calvinists, but they were generally Liégeois. De Geer's father was a Catholic when he emigrated from Liège. The Biscayan iron industry was organized by that prince of Liégeois industrialists, Jean Curtius. The greatest pioneer of the extractive industry of the Rhineland, Jean Mariotte, was a Catholic — but a Catholic from Liège. Clearly all these men are more united by their Flemish or Liégeois origins than by their religious views.[1]

Once this fact is established, new lines of inquiry soon present themselves. Instead of looking primarily at the religion of the entrepreneurs, we may look at their local origins. And once we do that — once we cease to look only at the Calvinists among them — we soon find that they are not confined to Flanders. Analysing the entrepreneurial class of the new 'capitalist' cities

[1] For Frankfurt, see Dietz, *Frankfurter Handelgeschichte* ; for Cologne, H. Thimme, 'Der Handel Kölns am Ende des 16ten Jahrhundert und die internationale Zusammensetzung der Kölner Kaufmannschaft', in *Westdeutsche Zeitschrift für Geschichte und Kunst*, XXXI (1912) ; for van der Veken, E. Wiersum, 'Johan van der Veken, koopman en banker te Rotterdam, 1583–1616', in *Verslagen der Maatschappij der Nederl. Letterkunde*, 1912. For Curtius, see J. Lejeune, *La Formation du capitalisme moderne dans la Principauté de Liège au 16e siècle* (Paris, 1939) ; for the Mariotte family, J. Yernaux, *La Métallurgie liégeoise et son expansion au 17e siècle* (Liège, 1939).

of the seventeenth century, we find that the whole class is predominantly formed of immigrants, and these immigrants, whatever their religion, come predominantly from four areas. First,
there are the Flemings, by whose Calvinism Weber ultimately
defended his thesis.[1] Secondly, there are the Jews from Lisbon
and Seville, whom Sombart set up as rivals to Weber's Calvinists.[2]
Thirdly, there are the south Germans, mainly from Augsburg.
Fourthly, there are the Italians, mainly from Como, Locarno,
Milan and Lucca. From place to place the proportions vary.
In Hamburg and the Baltic, where they have been systematically
studied by Mr Kellenbenz, the Flemings preponderate, followed
by the Jews. Geography and the old Spanish connection easily
explain this. In France we find a greater number of south
Germans, who came through the branch offices of the great
Augsburg family firms of the sixteenth century. Such were
Barthélemy d'Herwarth, who came through Lyons, and the
Catholic Eberhard Jabach, famous for his magnificent picture
gallery, who came through Cologne.[3] In Switzerland the Italians
predominated : Turrettini, Duni, Balbani, Arnolfini, Burla-
macchi, Calandrini, Minutoli, Diodati, Appiani, Pellizari — these,
not the local disciples of Calvin, were the first makers of modern
Swiss prosperity ; and they continued to make it, without much
help from the bigoted natives, until they were replaced or re-
inforced by a new immigration : the immigration of the French
Huguenots.

[1] Weber afterwards stated that when he had said 'that Calvinism shows the
juxtaposition of intensive piety and capitalism, wherever found', he had meant
'only Diaspora Calvinism' (*Archiv für Sozialwissenschaft u. Sozialpolitik*, xxv, 245 n. 5).
But, in fact, apart from one sentence parenthetically quoted from Gothein, Weber,
in his original work, never referred to Diaspora Calvinism and his arguments are
drawn almost exclusively from English Puritan writers.

[2] Or rather, we should say, the Peninsular *émigrés*, most of whom were Jews ; for
just as the Flemings who emigrated were not all Calvinists, so the *émigrés* from
Lisbon and Seville were not all Jews. The Ximenes family, about whom Mr Kellenbenz has written (*Unternehmekräfte*, pp. 146, 185, 253), were not Marranos : they
were staunch Catholics, who had no religious need to emigrate.

[3] For the south Germans in Lyon, see K. Ver Hees, 'Die oberdeutsche Kaufleute
in Lyon im letzten Viertel des 16ten Jahrhundert', in *Vierteljahrschrift für Sozial- und
Wirtschaftsgeschichte*, 1934. There was also a colony in Marseilles : see A. E. Sayous,
'Le Commerce de Melchior Manlich et Cie d'Augsbourg à Marseilles', in *Revue
historique*, CLXXVI (1935), 389–411.

Antwerp, Liège, Lisbon, Augsburg, Milan, Lucca . . . we only have to recite these names to see what has happened. These are great names in European economic history. On the eve of the Reformation they were the heirs of medieval capitalism, the promising starters of modern capitalism. For large-scale capitalism, before the industrial revolution, depended on long-distance trade and two great industries, cloth and minerals. In the Middle Ages, thanks to the long-distance trade of Italy, the cloth industry had been built up in Italy and its northern depot, Flanders. From the financial accumulation thus created, the capitalists of both Italy and Flanders had been able to mobilize the still more costly, but ultimately still more profitable extractive industry of Europe. By 1500 all the techniques of industrial capitalism were concentrated in a few cities strung along the old Rhineland route from Flanders to Italy. At one end was Antwerp, heir to Bruges and Ghent, commanding the old Flemish cloth industry and financing the extractive industry of Liège ; at the other end were the Italian cities, the commercial and financial cities of Venice and Genoa, the industrial cities of Milan and Florence. To these had recently been added two new centres : Augsburg, whose cloth industry raised the huge financial superstructure of the Fugger and other families and enabled them to rival even Antwerp, concentrating in their hands the extractive industry of central Europe ; and Lisbon, the capital of a new world-wide commercial empire, with possibilities of long-distance trade undreamed of before. These were the centres of European capitalism in 1500. In some way or other, between 1550 and 1620, most of these centres were convulsed, and the secret techniques of capitalism were carried away to other cities, to be applied in new lands.

This is not, of course, the German view. Marx, Weber, Sombart all believed that a new form of capitalism was created in the sixteenth century. Medieval production, they believed, was 'petty production' only. It was not till the Reformation, they believed, that large-scale industrial production was possible. Then Reformation, industrial capitalism, and the economic rise of the Protestant powers synchronized. After that it was easy to see causal connections. But today few scholars believe in this sudden sixteenth-century break-through of industrial capitalism. We know too much about medieval Italian and Flemish capital-ism.[1] The enterprises of Benedetto Zaccaria in Genoa, of Roger de Boinebroke in Ghent, of the great cloth-merchants and bankers in Florence, were as 'rational' in their methods, as 'bureaucratic' in their structure, as any modern capitalism ; [2] and if the founders of these medieval enterprises were sometimes out-rageous characters — 'Jewish adventurer-capitalists' rather than 'worldly ascetics' — why, so (we now find) were the Calvinist de Geers and de Wittes of the seventeenth century. The idea that large-scale industrial capitalism was ideologically impossible before the Reformation is exploded by the simple fact that it existed. Until the invention of the steam engine, its scope may have been limited, but within that scope it probably reached its highest peak in the age of the Fugger. After that there were convulsions which caused the great capitalists to migrate, with their skills and their workmen, to new centres. But there is no reason to suppose that these convulsions, whatever they were, created a new type of man or enabled a new type of capitalism

[1] It is interesting to observe the narrowly German origin of Weber's theory. Its antecedents were German too. It was W. Endemann, in his great work *Studien in der romanisch-kanonistischen Wirtschafts- u. Rechtslehre* (Berlin, 1874–83), I, 371 ff., who wrote that it took the Protestant revolt to free European capitalism from the repressive grip of the Catholic Church, and it was L. Goldschmidt, in his *Universal-geschichte des Handelsrechts* (Stuttgart, 1891), p. 139, who gave currency to the mis-leading statement that, in the Middle Ages, *homo mercator vix aut numquam potest placere Deo*. Endemann's statement was criticized at the time by Sir W. Ashley, *Introduction to Economic History*, II (1893), 377 ff. ; but it still runs its course, as is shown by the extreme statement of the case in Benjamin N. Nelson, *The Idea of Usury* (Princeton, 1949). The fatal dissemination of Goldschmidt's statement, once it had been taken up by Pirenne, is shown in J. Lestocquoy, *Les Villes de Flandre et d'Italie* (Paris, 1952), pp. 195–6. Weber's immediate starting-point — the only factual evidence set out in his work — was a statistical study of Catholic and Protestant education in Baden by Martin Offenbacher. These statis-tics have been questioned by Kurt Samuelsson, *Ekonomi och Religion* (Stockholm, 1957), pp. 146–57. The exclusively German application of Weber's theory is pleasantly remarked by A. Sapori, *Le Marchand italien du moyen âge* (Paris, 1944), pp. xxix–xxx.

[2] For Zaccaria, see R. S. Lopez, *Genova marinara nel dugento : Benedetto Zaccaria, ammiraglio e mercante* (Messina, 1933) ; for Boinebroke, G. Espinas, 'Jehan Boine Broke, bourgeois et drapier douaisien', in *Vierteljahrschrift für Sozial- u. Wirt-schaftsgeschichte*, 1904.

to arise, impossible before. In fact the techniques of capitalism applied in Protestant countries were not new. The century from 1520 to 1620 is singularly barren of new processes. The techniques brought by the Flemings to Holland, Sweden, Denmark, by the Italians to Switzerland and Lyons, were the old techniques of medieval capitalism, as perfected on the eve of the Reformation, and applied to new areas. That is all.

And yet, is it quite all ? In saying this we may have cleared the air ; but we have not solved the problem. We have merely changed it. For Marx, Weber, Sombart, who regarded medieval Europe as non-capitalist, the problem was to discover why capitalism was created in the sixteenth century. For us, who believe that Catholic Europe, at least up to the Reformation, was perfectly able to create a capitalist economy, the question is, why, in the sixteenth century, did so many of the essential agents of such an economy — not only entrepreneurs, but also workers — leave the old centres, predominantly in Catholic lands, and migrate to new centres, predominantly in Protestant lands ? And this is still largely a problem of religion. We may point to many non-religious reasons : the pressure of guild restrictions in the old centres ; the ease with which entrepreneurs and workers (unlike landlords or peasants) can migrate ; the new opportunities which were already presenting themselves in the north. But these reasons, which can explain individual cases, cannot explain the general movement. For, after all, the majority of these men, though they might leave easily, did not leave willingly. They were expelled. And they were expelled for religion. The Italians who fled over the Alps from Milan or Como were largely cloth-merchants and cloth-workers who feared persecution for their religious views. The Italians of Lucca who founded the silk industry of Switzerland were silk-merchants who felt the pressure of the Roman Inquisition not on their looms, but on their 'heretical' views.[1] The Flemings who left the southern Netherlands for the north were either workers from the rural cloth industry fleeing from Alba's Tribunal

---

[1] For the emigration from Lucca, see A. Pascal, 'Da Lucca a Ginevra', in *Rivista Storica Italiana*, 1932–5.

of Blood or Antwerpers to whom Alexander Farnese gave the alternative of Catholicism or exile.[1] All these men, who had worked, or whose ancestors had worked, peacefully in Catholic Flanders and Italy in the past, now found themselves unable to reconcile themselves to Catholicism any longer : economic reasons might point the direction, but religion gave them the push. The question we have to ask is, what had happened to create this new gulf between sixteenth-century Catholicism and the sixteenth-century entrepreneurs and workers : a gulf quite unknown to the medieval Church and the medieval entrepreneurs and workers ?

In face of this question, it is convenient to ask, what was the religious attitude of those actively engaged in economic life in 1500 ? Basically we can define it, for lack of a better word, as 'Erasmianism'. I wish I could find a better word — one more obviously applicable to Italy as well as to northern Europe (for the characteristics were general) — but I cannot. Let me therefore make it clear that by Erasmianism I mean not specifically the doctrines of Erasmus, but those general views to which the early reformers, and Erasmus in particular, gave a clear form. These Erasmians were Christian and Catholic, but they rejected or ignored a great deal of the new external apparatus of official Catholicism : an apparatus which, since it absorbed energy, consumed time, and immobilized property, without having any necessary connection with religion, was equally disliked by educated, by pious, and by active men. So, instead of 'mechanical religion', and of monasticism which had come to represent it, the Erasmians extolled 'primitive Christianity', private devotion, the study of the Bible ; and they believed intensely in the sanctification of lay life. Against the exaggerated pretensions of the clergy, claiming that the clerical or monastic condition was, by itself,

---

[1] Examination of the places of origin of the *émigrés* from Flanders to Frankfurt, Hamburg, etc., shows that the poor immigrants were largely workers from the Walloon clothing and mining towns, while the rich immigrants came predominantly from Antwerp. The massive migration of the cloth-workers of Hondschoote to Leiden is the subject of Mr E. Coornaert's study, *Un Centre industriel d'autrefois : la draperie-sayetterie d'Hondschoote* (Paris, 1930).

holier than the lay condition, the laity exalted the married state as being not a mere concession to base human nature, but a religious state no less holy than clerical celibacy; and they exalted the lay calling as being, if sanctified by inner faith in its daily exercise, no less holy than the clerical office. This belief in the positive religious value of a lay calling was seized upon by Weber as the essence of the 'Protestant ethic', the necessary condition of industrial capitalism. In keeping with his view of a new, revolutionary idea in the sixteenth century, Weber ascribed it, in its verbal form, to Luther and, in its real significance, to Calvin. But in fact, although Weber was no doubt right to see in the idea of 'the calling' an essential ingredient in the creation of capitalism, he was undoubtedly wrong in assuming that this idea was a purely Protestant idea. His philological reasoning is known to be wrong. And, in fact, the idea was a commonplace before Protestantism. It occurs constantly in the works of Erasmus, who regularly extols the real, inner piety of the active layman in his calling above the complacency of the indolent monks who assume a greater holiness because of the costume they wear or the 'mechanical devotions' which they practise.

In all this there is, of course, nothing explicitly heretical. Pressed to extremes, Erasmianism could be subversive of the clerical establishment. Put into practice, it would have diminished the number of the clergy, reduced their influence over the laity, cut down their means of propaganda, blocked the sources of their wealth. But as it was provoked only by the indecent number of the clergy, their indecent power and wealth, so, in normal times, it was unlikely to be pushed to extremes. Nor was it exclusively a doctrine, or rather a mental attitude, of the mercantile classes. It was an attitude which appealed to the educated laity in general. Erasmus had friends and patrons among princes and their officers, even among the clergy, as well as among the mercantile classes. Nevertheless there was a sense in which it was peculiarly the attitude of the *bourgeoisie*. In a time of crisis, Erasmian princes (like Charles V) would remember their 'reason of state': they might (like him) carry their private Erasmianism to the grave, but they would hesitate before attacking the vested interests of the Church, which were so involved with those of the throne — and indeed of the social order. Erasmian officers and lawyers, as a class, would follow their prince. Erasmian clergy, as a class, would go with the Church. Among the educated classes, the urban, mercantile classes — not the great tax-farmers or contractors, economically tied to the Crown or the Church, but the really independent, self-confident entrepreneurs — were most free to follow their philosophy to its logical conclusion, if they were forced to do so.

In the decades of the Reformation they were forced to do so. In those years the abuses of the Church drove its critics into extremity and the Erasmians, wherever they were, found themselves obliged either to surrender at discretion or to admit themselves heretics. If they chose the latter course, they became Calvinists. For Calvin, far more than is generally admitted, was the heir of Erasmus : the heir in a more intolerant age, it is true, the heir who has to fight for his legacy, and whose character is changed by the struggle, but still, in essentials, the heir. If we follow his career, or read his works, we are constantly reminded of Erasmus. Calvin was nurtured on Erasmian teaching. He published his great work in the last city of Erasmus. Some of his writings are almost plagiarisms of Erasmus. Like Erasmus, unlike Luther, Calvin believed in a reformed visible Church : the hierarchy was not to be destroyed but purified, made more efficient, more dynamic. And everywhere the Erasmian *bourgeoisie*, if it did not renounce its Erasmian views altogether, turned to Calvinism as the only form in which it could defend them. The mercantile aristocracy of Venice, preserving inviolate their republican constitution, were able to keep their old character, neither Papist nor Protestant. But their colleagues in Milan, Como, Lucca were not. So the most independent of them slid gradually into Calvinism, or at least, as they slipped over the Alps into Switzerland, accepted (with whatever private reservations) the public leadership of the Calvinists, the only International which could give protection and coherence to a group of urban minorities whose own strength lay not in numbers but in their moral and intellectual quality.

So the change took place. It was not that Calvinism created a new type of man, who in turn created capitalism ; it was rather that the old economic *élite* of Europe were driven into heresy because the attitude of mind which had been theirs for generations, and had been tolerated for generations, was suddenly, and in some places, declared heretical and intolerable. Had the Roman Church and the Spanish State not suddenly resolved to persecute the views of Erasmus and Vives, Ochino and Vermigli, Castellio and Sozzini, the mercantile aristocracies of Antwerp, Milan, Lucca, even Seville [1] would no doubt have continued, like that of Venice, to preserve their orthodoxy, wearing it, as of old, with a slight difference. In fact, this was not so. The abuses of Rome drove the merchant aristocracies into a position which the terrified Court of Rome saw as positively heretical. Justification by faith, this Pauline orthodoxy which consecrated 'interior religion', the religion of the layman without priests — was not this the same doctrine which Luther was using to proclaim a revolt throughout Europe, a revolt from Rome ?

We can see why Rome panicked. But to leave the question thus, as if reaction to a temporary crisis created a major shift in European economy for three centuries, would be unpardonably superficial. For why, we must ask, did the lay princes forward this priestly panic ? And why did the fugitive Calvinist entrepreneurs so easily, and so permanently, leave the economic centres of Europe ? For after all, the era of panic was relatively brief. Catholic princes (as the case of de Witte shows) were prepared to make concessions to economically valuable heretics, and after a generation most of the Calvinist entrepreneurs had lost their doctrinal purity. If de Witte was prepared to serve Wallenstein and have his son baptized as a Catholic, if the merchants of Hamburg were prepared to work for the King of Spain, there is no reason to suppose that they would have absolutely refused to return to their old allegiance in a more tolerant age. Besides,

---

[1] Seville, the only great mercantile city of Spain, was also the last centre of Spanish 'Erasmianism'. This was crushed in 1558–9, with the great purge of the Jeronymite monastery of S. Isidoro, and the flight of eighteen of its monks abroad, mostly to Geneva.

they were not always comfortable in Calvinist countries. Calvinism might have begun as Erasmianism armed for battle ; in its first generation it might have attracted the *élite* of Europe ; but soon, as it widened its base, it changed its character and lowered its standards. By 1600 Calvinism was the religion not only of the educated laity, but also of ambitious noblemen and rural squireens ; it was controlled, often, by fanatical clergy, little better than the monkish inquisitors against whom it had once been a protest. To escape from such company the original intellectual Calvinists turned aside to Arminianism in Holland, to undenominational lay Puritanism in England. Besides, on the Catholic side, a new order had arisen which sought to recapture the *élite* of the laity : the Jesuits whom, in their first generation, the old clerical orders, the Dominican and Franciscan last-ditchers against reform, had rightly seen as dangerous continuators of that hated message, attenuators of clerical apparatus, flatterers of lay piety — in fact, Erasmians.

To pose this question is to go far outside the field of mere doctrine. It is to ask large, hitherto unanswered questions of sociology. It is to ask, not why the ideas of an Erasmus or an Ochino were alarming to the Court of Rome in the days of Luther's revolt, but what was the structure of the Counter-Reformation State, which crushed out that revolt. For always we come back to this : the Calvinist and for that matter the Jewish entrepreneurs of northern Europe were not a new native growth : they were an old growth transplanted. Weber, in seeing the 'spirit of Capitalism' as something new, whose origins must be sought in the sixteenth century, inverted the problem. The novelty lay not in the entrepreneurs themselves, but in the circumstances which drove them to emigrate. And they were driven out not merely by priests, on doctrinal grounds, though these supplied the pretext and the agency of expulsion, but — since the religion of State is a formulation of social ideology — by societies which had hardened against them. In the sixteenth century Italy and Flanders, for centuries the home of commercial and industrial capitalism, so changed their social character that they would no longer tolerate those men who, in the past, had made them the economic heart of Europe. The expulsion of Calvinists from the area of Spanish dominion or patronage — for both Flanders and Italy had passed, by 1550, under Spanish control — is a social fact comparable with the expulsion from Spain, in the same period, of those other socially unassimilable elements, the Moors and the Jews.

In other words, we must look for the explanation of our problem not so much in Protestantism and the expelled entrepreneurs as in Catholicism and the expelling societies. We must ask what was the social change which came over Catholic societies in the sixteenth century. It was a change which occurred predominantly in countries of the Spanish clientele. For instance, it did not occur in France — at least until Louis XIV expelled the Huguenots, with consequences, both to the expelling society and to the rest of Europe, remarkably similar to those of the sixteenth-century expulsions. On the other hand, it was not confined to the Spanish empire, for we find a similar withdrawal, if not positive expulsion, from some other Catholic countries. For instance, there was a gradual exodus from the independent prince-bishopric of Liège.[1] Nor was it exclusively dependent on religion. This is shown in Italy where the Catholic entrepreneurs who had contrived to keep within the bounds of orthodoxy nevertheless believed that the conditions of their prosperity were incompatible not with the doctrines, but with the social forms of the Counter-Reformation. The great instance, of course, is Venice. The Catholic merchant society of Venice fought with surprising solidarity against successive attempts to introduce the social forms of the Counter-Reformation. The resistance of the republic in the early seventeenth century, against the combined pressure of Pope and Spain, is a struggle not between two religions, but between two social forms. When the Republic finally weakened about 1630, the Counter-Reformation moved in and commercial life shrank. The same antithesis can be seen, on a smaller scale, in the republic of Lucca. Cosimo I of Tuscany was restrained from the conquest of Lucca because, having seen the flight of so many of the great silk-merchants under papal pressure, he had

[1] See J. Yernaux, *La Métallurgie liégeoise*, pp. 99–105.

29

no wish to scare away the rest. It was not that they were heretical or that he would willingly have driven them into heresy. The Medici dukes of Tuscany were famous for their encouragement of merchants, whether they were natives, foreigners or even heretics. What Cosimo feared was that, if the republic of Lucca were incorporated in the princely state of Tuscany, the merchants would flee '*come fecero i Pisani*'. Therefore, though he could easily have captured the city, he refrained, because, he said, he could never capture the men who made the wealth of the city.[1]

'The republic' . . . 'the princely state' . . . Already in defining the problem we have suggested the answer. In the remainder of this essay I can still only suggest it, because the subject obviously requires longer treatment than I have space for. But I will try to outline the process as I believe that it happened. If, in doing so, I only reveal the gaps in our knowledge, perhaps that will encourage someone to supply those gaps.

The capitalism of the Middle Ages was the achievement, essentially, of self-governing city-republics : the Flemish and Hanseatic towns in the north, the Italian towns in the Mediterranean, the Rhineland and south German towns between them. In these republics, the merchants who governed them were orthodox, even devout Catholics : the Pope, after all, was the patron of the Italian cities against the Emperor, and the Florentine capitalists, as afterwards the Fugger of Augsburg, were the economic agents of the Pope. But they were Catholics in their own way. Their piety, their charity, was positive, constructive, sometimes even lavish ; but it did not create, directly or indirectly, obstacles to their own mercantile enterprise. They might feed monks with their superfluous profits, but they did not immobilize mercantile wealth in monasticism. They might put a proportion of their sons into the Church, but within reason : they saw to it that the main enterprise of the republic was not impeded by a stampede into the Church.[2] They might subscribe to the building

---

[1] See E. Callegari, *Storia politica d'Italia, preponderanze stranieri* (Milan, 1895), p. 253.

[2] In general, the mercantile cities seem to have prevented the building up of large estates in mortmain by the Church. See, for instance, C. M. Cipolla, 'Comment s'est perdue la propriété ecclésiastique dans l'Italie du Nord entre le XIe et le XVIe siècle?', in *Annales : économies, sociétés, civilisations*, 1947, pp. 317–27.

of churches, and fine churches too, but not on an extravagant scale : there is a difference between the duomo of Florence and the stupendous cathedrals of the north. And this care of the Church was combined with a parallel care of the State. The State, after all, was their instrument : they did not wish it to develop too many organs of its own, or become their master. Nor did they wish either Church or State to become too costly : to impose, through taxation, direct or indirect, an insupportable burden on commerce and manufacture, the nourishment of the city. For the city-republics, or at least those of them that were centres of international commerce, were not solid societies : they were international merchant colonies, and were kept in being by the constant afflux of 'foreign' merchants, drawn to them by favourable circumstances. As such they were extremely sensitive to cost. Even a slight rise in the burden of taxation, a slight fall in the margin of profit, could cause a flight of capital to other more convenient centres — from Siena to Florence, from Ulm to Augsburg. This was a fact which, in episcopal cities like Liège, bishops had to recognize. It was a fact which conditioned the religious outlook of the city aristocracies themselves. In the fifteenth century, when the Church, in its opposition to Conciliar reform, set out to increase its strength by the multiplication of regular clergy and their propagandist and fiscal devices, it was not for nothing that the movement which would culminate in Erasmianism, the positive formulation of opposition to all these processes, found its natural supporters in the educated *bourgeoisie* of the old free cities. They recognized, even at its beginning, the process which, for some of them, would bring prosperity to an end.

Of course there was always an alternative process. A mercantile class could find profit — at least short-term profit — in yielding to the times. In the fifteenth century the cities were being swallowed up by the princes, and the princes, to sustain their new power, were enlisting the support of the rural aristocracy and the Church, and creating around their thrones a new class of 'officers', expensively paid out of indirect public taxes or impositions of trade. Some of the old mercantile families profited by this change. They became court financiers or mono-polists, and because the free-trade area within which they operated was larger than before, they sometimes made spectacular fortunes. But except when whole cities obtained exceptional monopoly positions in the new empires — like Genoa in the Spanish empire — these individual gains of state capitalists were offset by losses among private capitalists, who, since they no longer controlled the State, were powerless to redress it. Naturally, they drew the consequences. If one great merchant saved himself by becom-ing court purveyor or financier to the prince, others brought up their sons to be not merchants but 'officers' of the new Court, or of the expanding Church, thus contributing to the burden which was crushing their class ; and they invested their capital more heavily in land. Those who did not, and felt the added burden of those who did, retreated into critical, Erasmian doc-trines and looked for other mercantile opportunities in freer, less taxed lands.

For already, at the beginning of the sixteenth century, new difficulties were pressing at home, new opportunities were beckoning abroad. In some towns of Flanders, Switzerland, and Germany the craft-guilds had strengthened their power and, to protect their own employment, were impeding technical change. Even without religious pressure, the entrepreneurs of those towns were beginning to seek new bases, and the unprivileged workers willingly followed them. We see this change, uncon-nected with religion, in England, where capital and labour moved from the old towns of the east coast to the 'new towns' farther inland. And the great entrepreneurs were looking still farther afield. The Fugger, having built up their mining organization in the mature economy of the south, were already applying it in the hitherto unexploited mineral wealth of Scandinavia. Even without the Reformation, there were purely economic reasons for a shift.

Then, in the 1520s, came the great revolt : the revolt of Luther. It was not a revolt within the old, mature economy of Europe : it was a revolt of the 'underdeveloped', 'colonial' areas of northern and central Europe, long taxed, frustrated and exploited (as they felt) to sustain the high civilization of the Mediterranean and the Rhine. Like all great social revolts, it used ideas which had been developed in the more advanced societies against which it was directed. The Erasmian criticism of the mercantile republics was adopted by the revolutionaries of the north. But, of course, it was adopted with a great difference. Although the Erasmians might sympathize with part of the Lutheran programme, they could not go the whole way : that would be a betrayal of their civilization. Poised between the new 'bureaucratic' principalities with their hypertrophied organs, the object of their criticism, and the anarchic, revolutionary doctrines of Luther, which ran far ahead of their criticism, the Erasmians suffered a terrible crisis of conscience. But as they were a minority, as the city-republics were no longer an independent force in politics, they had ultimately to choose. Either they must surrender, be absorbed into the world they had criticized, at best be tolerated within it, or they must themselves go forward into revolution. Fortunately in the time of their crisis, they did not have to submit to the anarchic revolution of Luther. In their old homes, in the urban societies of the Netherlands, of the Rhine, of Switzerland, of north Italy, the Erasmian message was being transformed, strengthened, sharpened, made capable of independence and resistance. Between the Catholic princes of the Mediterranean and Burgundy, fighting for the preservation of an old supremacy, and the Lutheran princes of Germany, placing themselves at the head of national revolt, arose that slender dynamic force of the surviving free cities of Europe : the Calvinist International.

With this great struggle we are not here concerned. What concerns us is the structural change which the Catholic countries underwent in the course of it. For in the end the revolt was stayed. If most of northern Europe was lost, and ceased to be an economic colony of the Mediterranean, Catholicism survived in its old home. The dream of the reformers, of carrying revolution to Rome itself, was never realized, and Rome reconquered even the Erasmian Calvinist cities of north Italy and Flanders. But this victory was won at a heavy social cost. Just as the papacy had triumphed over the Conciliar Movement in Europe by multiplying its abuses, its costly apparatus of power and propaganda, and becoming, for the sake of spiritual supremacy, more and more of a secular monarchy, so, in the next century, it triumphed over the Reformation at home by a still further continuation of that process and by a still more intimate alliance with the secular, princely State. The Counter-Reformation, which animated that reconquest, may be seen as a great spiritual revival : a new movement of mysticism, evangelism, charity. But sociologically it represented an enormous strengthening in the 'bureaucratic' structure of society. The reformers had challenged clerical wealth, clerical mortmain and the swollen regular orders which had sustained themselves and enriched the Church by 'mechanical devotions'. At first, in the 1530s, the Church had recognized the justice of the challenge. It had contemplated conciliation, appeasement. But then the mood had hardened. The Counter-Reformation papacy, abandoning all thoughts of conciliation, turned to aggression on every threatened front. Clerical wealth, it declared, must be not diminished but increased ; there must be not fewer but more regular orders, more lavish propaganda, more magnificent buildings, more elaborate devotions. Moreover, since the Church, to defend itself, needed the power of the princes, the princely bureaucracy, in return, was sustained by the clerical bureaucracy. Popery, as wavering Protestant kings were often reminded, was the only real guarantee of monarchy. And indeed, in a sense, it was. Would Charles I so easily have lost his throne if his fragile Court had been buttressed by a rich bureaucratic Church, with numerous offices and tempting perquisites for laymen, and, instead of puritan lecturers, an army of friars evangelizing and preaching obedience among the people ?

Of course, in its early stage, the weight of this enlarged apparatus might be carried. The new mysticism, the spiritual effort of the early Counter-Reformation, could refloat the old hulk which the reformers had vainly sought to lighten. The early Jesuits contrived to breathe into it some of the old Erasmian spirit. They cultivated the laity, modernized the philosophy of

the Church, sought to reassure merchants and other laymen of
the usefulness of their calling.[1] But the enthusiasm evoked by a
heroic effort cannot outlast the generation which has sustained
the effort ; and by the seventeenth century the spirit of the
Counter-Reformation was weary : what remained was the weight
and cost of the new machinery. And if the old princely bureaucracy had tended to squeeze out the mercantile life of urban
societies, how much more was that likely to happen when the
princely bureaucracies had been doubled by the addition, the
inextricable addition, of clerical bureaucracies, no less costly, no
less contemptuous of economic life which was not subservient
to their needs ?

Nor was it merely a question of cost : of the taxes which the
new State imposed on the private capitalist class. The new State
entailed a new society and the new social forms gradually
strengthened themselves by investing in themselves. For any
society which does not apprehend revolution tends to invest in
itself. A capitalist society invests in capitalism, a bureaucratic
society in bureaucracy. The public ethos of society — the order
in which it values the various professions — and the opportunities
for placing its capital both tend in the same direction. In medieval
Flanders or Italy the mercantile profession led to power in the
city oligarchies and to public respect. If a merchant built up a
great fortune, how was he likely to use it ? Whatever spiritual

[1] The economic modernity of the Jesuits has been emphasized by H. M. Robertson, *The Rise of Economic Individualism* (Cambridge, 1935). Mr Robertson tends to
emphasize only the Jesuit teaching and practice in matters of business morality.
This not only involved him in irrelevant religious controversy : it also unnecessarily
narrowed his argument, which I am sure is correct. (Long before it was attacked
as a slander by an Irish Jesuit, it had been put forward as a vindication by an English
Jesuit. See *Usury Explain'd, or conscience quieted in the case of putting out money at
interest*, by Philopenes [John Dormer *alias* Hudleston, S. J.] London, 1695–6.) In
fact, the argument for Calvinism, as put forward by Weber, is that the central,
positive message of Calvinism, the sanctity of secular work — not merely peripheral
teaching on such subjects as usury or business ethics — led indirectly to capitalism.
But this same central message can be found among the Jesuits too. I have not
found a copy of the work, but the title of a book by a Spanish Jesuit — *Los bienes de
honesto trabajo y daños de la ociosidad*, by Pedro de Guzmán (Jérez, 1614) — seems
clear enough. The economic modernity of the early Jesuits is only part of their
general modernity : their determination to recapture from heresy the *élite* of the
laity.

THE EUROPEAN WITCH-CRAZE

and worldly insurance policy he might take out in the form of gifts to the Church or the poor and the purchase of land or annuities for his dependants, his charity would not be at the expense of a future commercial life. A great part of it would be in favour of urban commercial institutions. He would keep the bulk of his fortune in commerce, and if he would show his orthodoxy by putting some of his family into the Church, he would put those on whom its worldly fortune would depend into business. Thus the wealth and manpower of society would be directed into commerce and industry and the Church would be the consecration of a business community. But in seventeenth-century Flanders and Italy it would be different. Even if a man had made a great fortune in commerce or industry, when he came to invest it for the future of his family he would look to the society around him and draw the appropriate conclusions. That society, he would observe, was no longer a mercantile urban society : it was a courtly, bureaucratic society, and its values and its opportunities were quite different. For his spiritual salvation, and for his dependants, he would still take out an insurance policy. He would still give his tithe to the Church, buy land or *rentes* for his widow. But for those of his sons on whom the worldly hopes of the family rested he would use his capital accumulation to buy offices in the administration of Church or State. Under the pashalik of the prince, officers would never starve : merchants might. Thus the wealth and power of society would be directed into office and the Church would be the consecration not of a mercantile but of an official society.

Thus the Counter-Reformation State gradually created, even in the old mercantile cities which it conquered, a new kind of society : a society, moreover, which then strengthened itself by its own social momentum. In Venice, because it was not absorbed by or converted into a princely State, in Amsterdam, because it continued the republican society which had been suppressed in Antwerp, the old character was preserved. The merchant of Amsterdam invested his fortune and placed his sons in continuing business, partly because it was honourable, partly because it was profitable — unlike a prince, a self-governing city-state could be trusted not to adopt laws or a policy ruinous to business — partly because there were fewer alternatives. In Milan and Antwerp the reverse happened. There independent capitalism wilted. The only great profits in business were the profits of state capitalism. But as even state capitalism generally begins with private capitalism, the great state capitalists of the princely states are often found to have made their first fortunes abroad. And even the state capitalists, if they plant their families and invest their fortunes within the State, tend to invest their profits in office and land, not commerce. The Genoese pluto-cracy, tolerated as a self-governing urban enclave in order to be the state financiers of the Spanish empire, and investing their profits in offices, titles and land within that empire, are typical of this history. So is Hans de Witte, an immigrant into Bohemia who became the state capitalist of the Emperor and invested in office, titles and land in Bohemia. As for the native capitalists, absorbed by conquest into the Counter-Reformation States, they turned necessarily the same way. If we take any great Counter-Reformation city in 1630 and compare it with its own condition in 1530, the pattern of change is similar. Outwardly the difference may not be obvious. The number of rich men may not have perceptibly diminished. There may be as many fine town houses, as many carriages, as much — perhaps even more — evidence of private spending. There is still a prosperous, conspicuous *haute bourgeoisie*. But when we look behind this front we find that the source of wealth is different. The spending in 1530 had been predominantly by an *élite* of merchants and manufacturers. In 1630 it is predominantly by an *élite* of 'officers'.[1]

The Counter-Reformation State was generalized in Europe, above all, by the power of Spain. It is one of the great accidents, perhaps misfortunes, of history that it was the Castilian monarchy, that archaic 'feudal' society accidentally raised to world power by American silver, which stood out, in the sixteenth century, as the champion of the Catholic Church, and thus fastened

[1] This is shown, for Belgium, by Pirenne ; for Como by B. Caizzi : *Il Comasco sotto il dominio spagnolo* (Como, 1955). Cf. E. Verga, *Storia della vita milanese* (1931), pp. 272–8.

something of its own character upon both Church and State wherever their combined patronage prevailed. The Roman Catholic religion, as medieval history had shown, was perfectly compatible with capitalist expansion. The growth of princely States in the advanced capitalist societies undoubtedly, in itself, marked an economic regression, whether those States were patronized by Spain or not. Rome, with its swollen clerical bureaucracy, would have been an unmercantile city at any time. But the Spanish patronage, by its own character and by the necessities of State, imposed the pattern in a yet more extreme form. Moreover, it was fatally successful. The wealth and military support of Spain enabled the princely States under its protection to work : to seem economically viable even if they were not ; and this illusion lasted long enough for the new system to become permanent. In 1610 the patronage of Spain was the natural sustenance of every princely Court which felt itself no longer secure : even a Protestant Court, like that of James I, was its pensionary. Conversely, every mercantile society, even if it were Catholic, like Venice, regarded Spain as its enemy. By 1640 Spanish patronage could be of little help to anyone ; but by then the societies of Counter-Reformation Europe had been fixed : fixed in economic decline.[1]

A general tendency is sometimes illustrated by its exceptions. I have suggested a general pattern of change in Counter-Reformation States. First, there is the reanimation not only of

[1] This general antithesis between two alternative systems — the 'bureaucratic' system of the princes which may encourage state capitalism, but squeezes out free enterprise, and the mercantile system of the free cities, which is not incompatible with a more flexible type of monarchy — may be illustrated also in Chinese history. In China the bureaucratic society which had been strengthened by the earlier dynasties was loosened in the ninth century A.D. with the massive secularization of monastic property. Thereafter, under the Sung Dynasty, came a great efflorescence of science and technology. 'Wherever one follows up any specific piece of scientific or technological history in Chinese literature', says Dr Joseph Needham, in his *Science and Civilisation in China*, 1 (Cambridge, 1954), 134, 'it is always at the Sung Dynasty that one finds the major focal point.' But with the Ming dynasty, the old bureaucratic structure was restored and the great Chinese inventions — including the three which, according to Francis Bacon, 'have changed the whole face and state of things throughout the world', viz. printing, gunpowder and the compass — were followed up not in China but in Europe. The force of this parallel has been impressed upon me by the studies of the late Mr Étienne Balasz.

Catholic dogma but also of the whole structure of the Church : a wave of mysticism reinvigorates the old, decadent machinery, which the reformers have attacked. New religious orders are founded. New forms of charity, new devotions, new methods of propaganda bring new resources to the Church and increase its possessions in mortmain. This reinvigoration of the Church is a reinvigoration also of the State which accepts it and which, by definition, is a princely State ; for urban republics are opposed to such large subtractions from economic life. But when a generation has passed and this spirit has evaporated, the burden of this great increase is both felt and resented. The newly established society, feeling itself vulnerable and threatened, becomes intolerant and turns against the uncomfortable, unassimilated elements in its midst. The obstinate survivors of the old reforming party are expelled, and the State settles down to enjoy its security, which it celebrates by pullulation of offices in the happily united Church-State. Such is the general rule which I have posited. It can easily be illustrated in Italy, Spain, Flanders, Bavaria, Austria. The apparent exception is France. But once we look below the surface we soon find that this exception is more apparent than real. For obvious reasons, the Counter-Reformation came late to France ; but when it came the consequences were the same. It is only the timing that is different.

As the great power opposed to Spain, France found itself opposed to the Counter-Reformation, which, in its first century, had been so openly associated with Spanish power. Consequently, in France, the social repression of the Counter-Reformation was long unfelt. Henri IV might outdo many other Catholic princes in gestures of papalism (for he had a past to bury), but the apparatus of the Counter-Reformation State was not adopted in his time. The France of Richelieu contained Huguenots and Jansenists ; it received the fugitives of the Roman and Spanish Inquisitions ; it published the works suppressed by the Roman censorship ; and it benefited by the vast sales of Church lands carried out in the Wars of Religion. But this happy state did not last long. Even in the time of Richelieu, the pro-Spanish party of the *dévots*, defeated in politics, was gaining ground in

society. It was then that the new Catholic mysticism flowed in
from Spanish Flanders and led to the foundation of new religious
orders ; then that the structure of the French Church was at last
reformed. In the early years of Louis XIV the two opposite
tendencies were fully revealed. Colbert, the heir to Richelieu's
economic policy, preached a mercantilist doctrine of consecrated
work, containment of Church lands, reduction of venal offices in
the State, diminution of monks and nuns. But the monarchy
which Louis XIV set out to establish was not of that kind, and
he preferred to base it on the Spanish model, consecrated by
the Counter-Reformation Church. So, with the death of Colbert,
offices were multiplied as never before, regular clergy were increased, and as the burden and the repression became apparent,
the old remedy was applied. In 1685 the Huguenots were
expelled. A new Dispersion, comparable with the dispersion of
the Flemings and the north Italians, fertilized the economy of
Protestant Europe. And just as the Habsburgs, in the Thirty
Years War, had to seek their state capitalists among the private
capitalists whom they had previously expelled from their
dominions as heretics, so the Bourbons, in the eighteenth century, had to finance their wars by applying to the Swiss financiers
who, in fact, were not Swiss at all but French Huguenots whom
earlier Bourbon kings had expelled from France.[1]

Such was the effect on society of the fatal union of Counter-
Reformation Church and princely State. What of its effect on
the Church ? In the Middle Ages the Church, which had been
the organ of a feudal, rural society, adapted itself to the growth
of commercial and industrial capitalism. This had entailed some

---

[1] See Lüthy, *La Banque protestante en France*, 1. In general it is interesting to
note the criteria of urban success adopted by the social propagandist of the Counter-
Reformation, Giovanni Botero. In his treatise on the Greatness of Cities, he
assumes, as the cause of wealth, the residence of princes and noblemen, the presence
of government offices and law courts and — very parenthetically — state-controlled
industry ; but the cities in which free capitalists assembled and formed merchant
oligarchies receive short shrift. Taking Geneva and Frankenburg as types, he
describes them as the asylums of rebels and heretics 'unworthy to be commemorated
by us as cities'. And yet these and such cities were the true heirs of the medieval
communes, with their cosmopolitan merchant colonies, composed, in the first
instance, of 'foreign' refugees (*Cause della Grandezza delle Città*, 1588, II, i).

difficult adjustments, for neither the merchant employers nor the industrial workers — that is, primarily, the weavers and the miners — had been content with the doctrines elaborated for a society of landlords and peasants. The entrepreneurs had disliked external 'works', had rejected the ban on usury. But the Church met them half-way and all was well. The industrial workers, brought together by their conditions of work, listened to radical preachers urging mystical faith, community of life and 'primitive Christianity'. The Church was alarmed and sometimes declared them heretics. It drove out of its communion the followers of Arnold of Brescia, the Poor Men of Lyons, the Waldenses, the Lollards, the Taborites. But others it met half-way. The Beghards in Bruges, the Umiliati in Milan, the Brethren of the Common Life in the north continued within the fold of an expanded orthodoxy.[1] Thus the medieval Church, by its relative elasticity, by its toleration and accommodation — however limited — of new tendencies, remained the universal Church not only geographically, as the Church of all western Europe, but socially, as the Church of all classes. But after the Reformation this changed. In its years of panic, the bloated, rigid Church of the inquisitors and the friars saw the Erasmianism of the entrepreneur as a form of German Lutheranism: *Erasmus posuit ova, Lutherus eduxit pullos*; and it saw the 'primitive Christianity' of weavers and miners as a form of German Anabaptism. So it drove both out of the fold. In the 1550s the popes of the Counter-Reformation drove the Italian Erasmists over the Alps and closed down the Order of the Umiliati (much changed from their former poverty) in Rome. In the late sixteenth and seventeenth centuries the Catholic Church was not only, in politics, the Church of the princely system, and, in society, the Church of a 'feudal', official system: it was also exclusively tied to these systems. Its old elasticity had gone, intellectually and spiritually as well as politically. While the Protestant Churches (or some of them) contained within them a wide range of ideas and attitudes — liberal Calvinism for their merchants and entrepreneurs, Anabaptism and Mennonism for their industrial workers — the

[1] For the Umiliati, see L. Zanoni, *Gli Umiliati* (Milan, 1911).

Catholic Church no longer had anything similar. Without heresy, without variety, it was the Church of one form of State and one form of society only. It was not without reason that the theorists of the Counter-Reformation States, like Botero, harped on the essential unity of Church and State. The Catholic Church was the Church of their State. Equally it was not for nothing that Paolo Sarpi, the theorist of the one genuine mercantile republic which sought to remain within the Catholic Church, constantly and trenchantly insisted on the separation of Church and State. The Catholic Church was no longer the Church of his State : if it was to survive in Venice without destroying Venetian society, it must be kept rigorously distinct. Nor was it for nothing that the most famous work of Paolo Sarpi, the greatest of Catholic historians, a Servite friar of unimpeachable doctrinal orthodoxy, remained unpublished in any Catholic country until the eighteenth century.[1]

Of course, this was not the end of the story. By the eighteenth century the economic and intellectual failure of the Counter-Reformation States was obvious, and the statesmen and thinkers of those States began to draw the consequences. Society, they agreed, must be loosened. Its 'feudal' structure must be lightened. The Church must both itself share in this lightening and cease to consecrate the present heaviness. So the Spanish

[1] The same general point which I have made about economic enterprise — that it was the Counter-Reformation State which extruded it from society, not Calvinist doctrine which created it, or Catholic doctrine which stifled it, in individuals — can be made also in respect of another phenomenon closely related to economic enterprise : scientific advance. Both Weber and his followers argued that Calvinist doctrine led, as Catholic or non-Calvinist doctrine did not, to the empirical study of Nature ; and this theory has become an orthodoxy in America and elsewhere (cf. the influential works of Robert K. Merton, 'Puritanism, Pietism and Science', in *Sociological Review*, xxviii, 1936, and 'Science, Technology and Society, in seventeenth-century England', *Osiris*, iv (1938), and R. F. Jones, *Ancients and Moderns* (St Louis, 1936) ; R. Hooykaas, 'Science and Reformation', in *Cahiers d'histoire moderne*, iii, 1956–7, pp. 109–39). But it seems to me that such conclusions can only be reached either by concentrating all study on Calvinist ideas and Dutch or Huguenot scientists, while ignoring the contemporary development of similar ideas in other Churches (e.g. among the Catholic Platonists and the Jesuits) and their no less successful application by Catholic, Lutheran and Anglican scientists like Galileo, Kepler and Harvey, or by 'saving the phenomena' with the aid of elaborate explanations, comparable with Ptolemaic epicycles, such as the suggestion that Bacon was 'really' a Puritan (Hooykaas), or may have derived his ideas from

reformers of the eighteenth century preached a Catholic reform indistinguishable from the old Erasmianism which had been so ferociously extinguished in the Spain of Charles V and Philip II. In France and Italy the new Jansenists preached a very similar message. Their recommendations were not entirely without effect. Statistics are hard to come by, but it seems that in both France and Spain the weight of the Church, measured in the number of regular clergy, having increased throughout the seventeenth century, diminished again in the eighteenth. But it did not diminish fast enough. So the reformers called for political action. The call was heard. First, reforming princes intervened. Throughout Catholic Europe the Jesuits were expelled. Febronianism was the new Erasmianism of State. Joseph II, like Henry VIII, defied the Pope and dissolved the monasteries. Then came the revolution and after it, the reaction : a reaction in which the hope of reform seemed, for a time, to be finally lost.

However, it was not lost. A generation later the attack was renewed. When it was renewed, its character had changed. South of the Alps, it was openly anti-clerical. But in France, the home of Calvin, which had once had a strong Protestant party, the battle was fought, once again, in familiar form. In the reign of Louis-Philippe, and even more in the reign of Napoleon III, the economy of France was revolutionized by Protestant entrepreneurs. But once again it was not because they were Calvinists,

'his very Puritan mother' (Christopher Hill, 'Protestantism and the Rise of Capitalism', in *Essays . . . in Honour of R. H. Tawney*, Cambridge, 1961, p. 31). If these relevant facts are fairly included in the study, it seems to me that the exclusive causal connection between Calvinism and science necessarily dissolves. What remains is the irreducible fact that whereas Pico and Ficino died in the aura of Catholic sanctity, and Copernicus' work was dedicated to and accepted by the Pope, the Jesuits found it necessary to limit their scientific studies, and Bruno, Campanella and Galileo were all condemned south of the Alps. In other words, ideas which were perfectly entertainable in Catholic societies before the Counter-Reformation, and by individual Catholics thereafter (Galileo protested that 'no saint could have shown more reverence for the Church, or greater zeal'), were repudiated by Counter-Reformation society. For it was not the theology of the Pope, it was Counter-Reformation reason of State and the social pressure of the religious orders which forced the condemnation of Galileo, just as they had forced the condemnation of Erasmus, whom Pope Paul III would have made a cardinal (cf. my article, 'Galiléo et l'Église romaine : un procès toujours plaidé', in *Annales : économies, sociétés, civilisations*, 1960, pp. 1229–34).

43

and therefore animated by the 'capitalist spirit', that these men were able to achieve the *Wirtschaftswunder* of the Second Empire and the Third Republic. They were not the authentic French Protestants, the true believers who, since 1685, had preserved the Calvinist faith in the 'Churches of the Desert' in Languedoc. If we examine closely the great Protestant entrepreneurs of nineteenth-century France we find that, once again, they are nearly all immigrants. They are either Calvinists from Switzerland — the descendants of those earlier refugees, Italians of the 1550s or Frenchmen of 1685 — or Lutherans from Alsace : Alsace which, as an imperial fief, had been outside the reach of the Edict of Nantes, and so also of its Revocation. In either case the pattern is the same. In the sixteenth and seventeenth centuries the under-developed countries which had revolted from Rome offered opportunities to the entrepreneurs of the old industrial centres, Flanders, Italy and south Germany ; in the nineteenth century the underdeveloped Catholic countries offered opportunities to the heirs of those entrepreneurs to return. In the first period the hardening of the Counter-Reformation State had driven those men out ; in the nineteenth the loosening of that State made it easy for them to return.

For in the nineteenth century the Counter-Reformation State at last dissolved. The ideas of the Enlightenment, the necessity of progress, the painful contrast with Protestant societies all contributed to the process. But in the long run perhaps another force was equally powerful. In the seventeenth century the Roman Catholic Church had suffered a general spiritual and intellectual contraction. After the effort of the Counter-Reformation, there had followed a long period of narrow bigotry. The humanism of the early Jesuits had been a flash in the pan : by 1620 they had settled down to be the mere sophists of the Counter-Reformation State. Even in the eighteenth century the union of Church and State was not denied : the Febronian princes sought to reform both, not to disunite them. But in the nineteenth century an effort was at last made to detach the Catholic Church from the Catholic princely State. Naturally enough, the attempt was made in France, the Catholic monarchy which was the last to admit and the first to disavow the fatal union. Naturally enough, it was most strongly resisted in Rome, the Church-State *par excellence*, driven into new postures of rigidity by the last struggle for the Temporal Power. But in the end it prevailed. That the countries of the Counter-Reformation could, in the end, catch up, economically, with those of the Reformation without a new revolt from Rome was due in part to the new elasticity which Catholicism acquired in the nineteenth century: to its painful severance from the *ancien régime*. The European Common Market of today, that creation of the Christian Democrats of Italy, Germany and France, owes something to Hugues de Lamennais.

2 The General Crisis of the Seventeenth Century

The middle of the seventeenth century was a period of revolutions in Europe. These revolutions differed from place to place, and if studied separately, seem to rise out of particular, local causes ; but if we look at them together they have so many common features that they appear almost as a general revolution. There is the Puritan Revolution in England which fills the twenty years between 1640 and 1660, but whose crisis was between 1648 and 1653. In those years of its crisis there was also the series of revolts known as the Frondes in France, and in 1650 there was a *coup d'état* or palace revolution, which created a new form of government in the United Provinces of the Netherlands. Contemporary with the troubles of England were those of the Spanish empire. In 1640 there was the revolt of Catalonia, which failed, and the revolt of Portugal, which succeeded ; in 1641 there was nearly a revolt of Andalusia too ; in 1647 there was the revolt of Naples, the revolt of Masaniello. To contemporary observers it seemed that society itself was in crisis, and that this crisis was general in Europe. 'These days are days of shaking . . .' declared an English preacher in 1643, 'and this shaking is universal : the Palatinate, Bohemia, Germania, Catalonia, Portugal, Ireland, England.' [1] The various countries of Europe seemed merely the separate theatres upon which the same great tragedy was being simultaneously, though in different languages and with local variations, played out.

[1] Jeremiah Whittaker, Εἰρηνοποιός, *Christ the Settlement of Unsettled Times*, a fast sermon before the House of Commons, 25 Jan. 1642/3. Cf. H. G., B.L.C., *England's Present Distractions parallel'd with those of Spaine and other foreign countries* (1642). Many other instances could be given.

1. Louis de Geer
at the age of 62

2. Philippe Duplessis-Mornay,
founder of the Protestant
Academy at Saumur

3. The Apocalypse of the seventeenth century

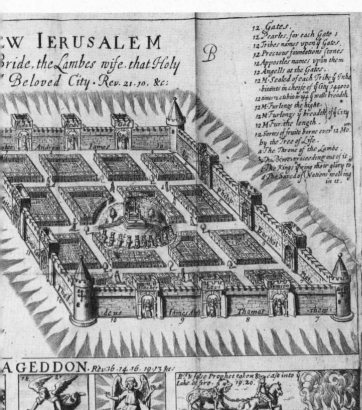

:w IERUSALEM

Bride, the Lambes wife, that Holy
Beloved City. Rev. 21. 10. &c:

B

Judah ... God
... Andrew James Ja ...
... Philip
... Barthol ...

Thad ...
deus   James Ap.   Thomas   ... thew
10   9   8   7

12 Gates .
12 Pearles. for each Gate 1
12 Tribes names upon y Gates
12 Preciou foundations stones
12 Apostles names vpon them
12 Angells at the Gates .
12 M. Sealed of each Tribe y Inha-
  bitants in cheife of y City 144000
12 times 12 cubits or 144 y wall breadth
12 M. Furlongs the hight .
12 M. Furlongs y breadth of y City
12 M. Fur. the length .
12 Sortes of fruite borne ever y 12 Mo.
  by the Tree of Lyfe
a The Throne of the Lambe
b The River proceeding out of it
c The Kings bring their glory to it
d The Saued of Nations walking
  in it .

:AGEDDON. Rev. 16. 14. 16. 19. 13 &c:

The Angel in y sun calling y fowles to
eate the flesh of Kings Cap. horses &c. 19. 18.

B. & false Prophet taken & cast into y
Lake of fire. 19. 20.

THE IUDICATURE Rev. 20. 4. 18. 6.
The Dragon taken & cast into the Botomless pitt.
Rev. 20. 1. 2. 3.

as there any other City wth in Johns time had the Rule over the Kings of the Earth but
2d. cap. 3

4. Jean Bodin

What was the general cause or character of this crisis ? Contemporaries, if they looked beyond mere surface parallels, tended to find deep spiritual reasons. That there was a crisis they felt sure. For a generation they had felt it coming. Ever since 1618 at least there had been talk of the dissolution of society, or of the world ; and the undefined sense of gloom of which we are constantly aware in those years was justified sometimes by new interpretations of Scripture, sometimes by new phenomena in the skies. With the discovery of new stars, and particularly with the new comet of 1618, science seemed to support the prophets of disaster. So also did history. It was at this time that cyclical theories of history became fashionable and the decline and fall of nations was predicted, not only from Scripture and the stars, but also from the passage of time and the organic processes of decay. Kingdoms, declared a Puritan preacher in 1643, after touching lightly on the corroborative influence of the comet of 1618, last for a maximum period of 500 or 600 years, 'and it is known to all of you how long we have been since the Conquest'.[1] From our rationalist heights we might suppose that the new discoveries of science would tend to discredit the apocalyptic vaticinations of Scripture ; but in fact this was not so. It is an interesting but undeniable fact that the most advanced scientists of the early sixteenth century included also the most learned and literal students of biblical mathematics ; and in their hands science and religion converged to pinpoint, between 1640 and 1660, the dissolution of society, the end of the world.[2]

This intellectual background is significant because it shows that the crisis of the mid-seventeenth century did not come by surprise, out of sudden accidents : it was deep-seated and anticipated, if only vaguely anticipated, even before the accidents

[1] William Greenhill, 'Αξίνη πρὸς τὴν 'Ρίζαν, a sermon preached before Parliament, 26 April 1643. Similar views were common in Spain. See Sancho de Moncada, *Restauración Política de España* (Madrid, 1619), Discurso 1. Moncada also touches on the comet.

[2] It is enough to refer to J. H. Alsted, the scholar and educationalist of Herborn, who was also 'the standard-bearer of millenaries in our age' ; to his Bohemian pupil, J. A. Comenius ; and to the Scottish mathematician Napier of Merchistoun, who invented logarithms in order to speed up his calculations of the number of the Beast.

which launched it. No doubt accidents made revolution longer or deeper here, shorter or more superficial there. No doubt, too, the universality of revolution owed something to mere contagion : the fashion of revolution spreads. But even contagion implies receptivity : a healthy or inoculated body does not catch even a prevailing disease. Therefore, though we may observe accidents and fashions, we still have to ask a deeper question. We must ask, what was the general condition of western European society which made it, in the mid-seventeenth century, so universally vulnerable — intellectually as well as physically — to the sudden new epidemic of revolution ?

Of course there are some obvious answers. Most obvious of all is the Thirty Years War, which began in 1618, the year of the comet, and was still raging in the 1640s, the years of revolution. The Thirty Years War, in the countries affected by it, undoubtedly prepared the ground for revolution. The burden of war-taxation, or military oppression, or military defeat, precipitated the revolts in Catalonia, Portugal, Naples. The dislocation of trade, which may have been caused by the Thirty Years War, led to unemployment and violence in many manufacturing or commercial countries. The destructive passage or billeting of soldiers led to regular peasant mutinies in Germany and France. One need only look at M. Roupnel's study of Burgundy in those years, or at the reports sent to the chancellor Séguier describing the constant risings of the French peasants under the stress of war-taxation, or at the grim etchings of Callot, to realize that the Thirty Years War was a formidable factor in the making of that discontent which was sometimes mobilized in revolution.[1]

And yet it is not a sufficient explanation. After all, the European wars of 1618–59 were not new phenomena. They were a resumption of the European wars of the sixteenth century, the wars of Charles V against François I and Henri II, of Phillip II against Elizabeth and Henri of Navarre and the Prince of Orange.

[1] See G. Roupnel, *La Ville et la campagne au XVIIe siècle dans le pays dijonnais* (Paris, 1955) ; Séguier's documents are printed, in French, in the appendix to B. F. Porshnev, *Narodnie Vosstaniya vo Frantsii pered Frondoi, 1623–48* (Moscow, 1948).

Those sixteenth-century wars had ended with the century, in 1598, in 1604, in 1609 : in 1618 and 1621 and 1635 they had been resumed, consciously resumed. Philip IV looked back constantly to the example of Philip II, 'mi abuelo y mi señor' ; Prince Maurice and Prince Frederick Henry to William of Orange, their father ; Oliver Cromwell to 'Queen Elizabeth of glorious memory'. Richelieu and Mazarin sought to reverse the verdict of Câteau-Cambrésis in 1559. And yet, in the sixteenth centuries these wars had led to no such revolutions. Moreover, the seventeenth-century revolutions were sometimes independent of the war. The greatest of those revolutions was in England, which was safely — some said ignominiously—neutral. In the country which suffered most from the war, Germany, there was no revolution.

I have said that the sixteenth-century wars had led to no such revolutions. Of course there had been revolutions in the sixteenth century : famous, spectacular revolutions : the religious revolutions of Reformation and Counter-Reformation. But we cannot say that those revolutions had been caused by those wars. Moreover, those revolutions, however spectacular, had in fact been far less profound than the revolutions of the next century. They had led to no such decisive breach in historical continuity. Beneath the customary wars of Habsburg and Valois, beneath the dramatic changes of the Reformation and Counter-Reformation, the sixteenth century goes on, a continuous, unitary century, and society is much the same at the end of it as at the beginning. Philip II succeeds to Charles V, Granvelle to Granvelle, Queen Elizabeth to Henry VIII, Cecil to Cecil ; even in France Henri IV takes up, after a period of disturbance, the mantle of Henri II. Aristocratic, monarchical society is unbroken : it is even confirmed. Speaking generally, we can say that for all the violence of its religious convulsions, the sixteenth century succeeded in absorbing its strains, its thinkers in swallowing their doubts, and at the end of it, kings and philosophers alike felt satisfied with the best of possible worlds.[1]

---

[1] This point — the growing social insensitivity of the sixteenth-century thinkers as monarchical, aristocratic society becomes more self-assured — is made by Fritz Caspari, *Humanism and the Social Order in Tudor England* (Chicago, 1954), pp. 198–204.

How different from this is the seventeenth century! For the seventeenth century did not absorb its revolutions. It is not continuous. It is broken in the middle, irreparably broken, and at the end of it, after the revolutions, men can hardly recognize the beginning. Intellectually, politically, morally, we are in a new age, a new climate. It is as if a series of rainstorms has ended in one final thunderstorm which has cleared the air and changed, permanently, the temperature of Europe. From the end of the fifteenth century until the middle of the seventeenth century we have one climate, the climate of the Renaissance; then, in the middle of the seventeenth century, we have the years of change, the years of revolution; and thereafter, for another century and a half, we have another, very different climate, the climate of the Enlightenment.

Thus I do not believe that the seventeenth-century revolutions can be explained merely by the background of war, which had also been the background of the previous, unrevolutionary century. If we are to find an explanation, we must look elsewhere. We must look past the background, into the structure of society. For all revolutions, even though they may be occasioned by external causes, and expressed in intellectual form, are made real and formidable by defects of social structure. A firm, elastic, working structure — like that of England in the nineteenth century — is proof against revolution however epidemic abroad. On the other hand a weak or over-rigid social structure, though it may last long in isolation, will collapse quickly if infected. The universality of revolution in the seventeenth century suggests that the European monarchies, which had been strong enough to absorb so many strains in the previous century, had by now developed serious structural weaknesses: weaknesses which the renewal of general war did not cause, but merely exposed and accentuated.

What were the general, structural weaknesses of the western monarchies? Contemporaries who looked at the revolutions of the seventeenth century saw them as political revolutions: as struggles between the two traditional organs of the ancient 'mixed monarchy' — the Crown and the Estates. Certainly this was the form they took. In Spain, the Crown, having reduced the Cortes of Castile to insignificance, provoked the Catalan revolution by challenging the Cortes of the kingdom of Aragon. In France, after the meeting of the Estates-General in 1614, Richelieu contrived to discontinue them, and they never met again till 1789 ; the Parlement of Paris struck back in the Fronde, but only to be defeated by Mazarin and reduced to the insignificance which was afterwards so bluntly rubbed in to it by Louis XIV. In Germany the Emperor challenged and reduced the Electoral College, even though the electors, as individual princes, reduced their own diets to insignificance. In England the Parliament challenged and defeated the king. At the same time the kings of Denmark and Sweden, struggling with or within their diets, ended by establishing personal monarchies, while the king of Poland, unable to imitate them, became the puppet of his. Altogether, we may say, the universal casualty of the seventeenth century was that Aristotelean concept, so admired in 1600, so utterly extinct in 1700, 'mixed monarchy'. The position was described summarily by the English political philosopher James Harrington, who, in 1656, diagnosed the general crisis which had produced such violent results in his own country of Oceana. 'What', he asked, 'is become of the Princes of Germany ? Blown up. Where are the Estates or the power of the people in France ? Blown up. Where is that of the people of Aragon and the rest of the Spanish kingdoms ? Blown up. Where is that of the Austrian princes in Switz ? Blown up. . . . Nor shall any man show a reason that will be holding in prudence why the people of Oceana have blown up their king, but that their kings did not first blow up them.'

Now there can be no doubt that politically Harrington was right. The struggle was a struggle for power, for survival, between crowns and estates. But when we have said this, have we really answered our questions ? If revolution was to break out otherwise than in hopeless rural *jacqueries*, it could be only through the protest of estates, parliaments, cortes, diets ; and if it was to be crushed, it could be only through the victory of royal power over such institutions. But to describe the form of a revolution is not to explain its cause, and today we are reluctant to accept constitutional struggles as self-contained or self-explanatory. We look for the forces or interests behind the constitutional claims of either side. What forces, what interests were represented by the revolutionary parties in seventeenth-century Europe — the parties which, though they may not have controlled them (for everyone would agree that there were other forces too), nevertheless gave ultimate social power and significance to the revolts of cortes and diets, estates and parliaments ?

Now to this question one answer has already been given and widely accepted. It is the Marxist answer. According to the Marxists, and to some other historians who, though not Marxists, accept their argument, the crisis of the seventeenth century was at bottom a crisis of production, and the motive force behind at least some of the revolutions was the force of the producing *bourgeoisie*, hampered in their economic activity by the obsolete, wasteful, restrictive, but jealously defended productive system of 'feudal' society. According to this view, the crisis of production was general in Europe, but it was only in England that the forces of 'capitalism', thanks to their greater development and their representation in Parliament, were able to triumph. Consequently, while other countries made no immediate advance towards modern capitalism, in England the old structure was shattered and a new form of economic organization was established. Within that organization modern, industrial capitalism could achieve its astonishing results : it was no longer capitalist enterprise 'adapted to a generally feudal framework' : it was capitalist enterprise, from its newly won island base, 'transforming the world'.

This Marxist thesis has been advanced by many able writers, but, in spite of their arguments, I do not believe that it has been proved or even that any solid evidence has been adduced to sustain it. It is, of course, easy to show that there were economic changes in the seventeenth century, and that, at least in England, industrial capitalism was more developed in 1700 than in 1600 ; but to do this is not the same as to show either that the economic changes precipitated the revolutions in Europe, or that English capitalism was directly forwarded by the Puritan 'victory' of

1640–60. These are hypotheses, which may of course be true ; but it is equally possible that they are untrue : that problems of production were irrelevant to the seventeenth-century revolutions generally, and that in England capitalist development was independent of the Puritan Revolution, in the sense that it would or could have occurred without that revolution, perhaps even was retarded or interrupted by it. If it is to be shown that the English Puritan Revolution was a successful '*bourgeois* revolution', it is not enough to produce evidence that English capitalism was more advanced in 1700 than in 1600. It must be shown either that the men who made the revolution aimed at such a result, or that those who wished for such a result forwarded the revolution, or that such a result would not have been attained without the revolution. Without such evidence, the thesis remains a mere hypothesis.

Now in fact no advocate of the Marxist theory seems to me to have established any of these necessary links in the argument. Mr Maurice Dobb, whose *Studies in the Development of Capitalism* may be described as the classic textbook of Marxist history, consistently assumes that the English Puritan Revolution was the crucial 'break-through' of modern capitalism. It bears, he says, 'all the marks of the classic *bourgeois* revolution' : before it, capitalism is cramped and frustrated, never progressing beyond a certain stage, a parasite confined to the interstices of 'feudal' society ; in it, the 'decisive period' of capitalism reaches its 'apex' ; after it, the bonds are broken and the parasite becomes the master. Similarly, Mr E. J. Hobsbawm, in his two articles on 'The Crisis of the Seventeenth Century',[1] consistently maintains the same thesis. 'Had the English Revolution failed', he writes, 'as so many other European revolutions in the seventeenth century failed, it is entirely possible that economic development might have been long retarded.' The results of the Puritan 'victory' were 'portentous' : nothing less than the transformation of the world. But it is to be observed that although Mr Dobb assumes this position throughout his book, he nowhere

[1] In *Past and Present*, no. 5 (May 1954) and no. 6 (Nov. 1954) ; reprinted in *Crisis in Europe 1560–1660*, ed. Trevor Aston (1965).

gives any evidence to prove it. As soon as he reaches the 'decisive period' of capitalism, he suddenly becomes vague. 'The lines of this development', we learn, 'are far from clearly drawn'; 'the details of this process are far from clear and there is little evidence that bears directly upon it'. In fact, not a single piece of documented evidence is produced for what is throughout assumed to be the crucial event in the whole history of European capitalism. And Mr Hobsbawm is even more summary. He dwells at length upon the economy of Europe at the time of the revolutions. He assumes the 'portentous' importance of the Puritan Revolution in changing the economy. But of the actual connection between the two he says not a word.[1]

Altogether, it seems to me that the Marxist identification of the seventeenth-century revolutions with '*bourgeois* capitalist' revolutions, successful in England, unsuccessful elsewhere, is a mere *a priori* hypothesis. The Marxists see, as we all see, that, at some time between the discovery of America and the Industrial Revolution, the basis was laid for a new 'capitalist' form of society. Believing, as a matter of doctrine, that such a change cannot be achieved peacefully but requires a violent break-through of a new class, a '*bourgeois* revolution', they look for such a revolution. Moreover, seeing that the country which led in this process was England, they look for such a revolution in England. And when they find, exactly half-way between these terminal dates, the

[1] As far as I can see, Mr Dobb's only arguments of such a connection are the statements (1) that agricultural capitalists supported the Parliament while old-fashioned 'feudal' landlords supported the Crown; (2) that 'those sections of the bourgeoisie that had any roots in industry . . . were wholehearted supporters of the parliamentary cause'; and (3) that the industrial towns, particularly the clothing towns, were radical. None of these statements seems to me sufficient. (1) is incorrect: the only evidence given consists in undocumented statements that Oliver Cromwell was an improving agriculturalist (which is untrue: in fact having — in his own words — 'wasted his estate', he had declined from a landlord to a tenant farmer), and that 'Ireton his chief lieutenant was both a country gentleman and a clothier' (for which I know of no evidence at all). In fact some of the most obvious 'improving landlords', like the Earl of Newcastle and the Marquis of Worcester, were royalists. (2) is unsubstantiated and, I believe, incorrect; wherever the industrial *bourgeoisie* has been studied — as in Yorkshire and Wiltshire — it has been found to be divided in its loyalty. (3) is correct, but inconclusive; the radicalism of workers in a depressed industry may well spring from depression, not from 'capitalist' interest.

violent Puritan Revolution in England, they cry εὕρηκα ! Thereupon the other European revolutions fall easily into place as abortive *bourgeois* revolutions. The hypothesis, once stated, is illustrated by other hypotheses. It has yet to be proved by evidence. And it may be that it rests on entirely false premises. It may be that social changes do not necessarily require violent revolution : that capitalism developed in England (as industrial democracy has done) peacefully, and that the violent Puritan Revolution was no more crucial to its history than, say, the fifteenth-century Hussite and Taborite revolutions in Bohemia, to which it bears such obvious resemblances.

If the crisis of the seventeenth century, then, though general in western Europe, is not a merely constitutional crisis, nor a crisis of economic production, what kind of a crisis was it ? In this essay I shall suggest that, in so far as it was a general crisis — i.e. ignoring inessential variations from place to place — it was something both wider and vaguer than this : in fact, that it was a crisis in the relations between society and the State. In order to explain this, I shall try to set it against a longer background of time than is sometimes supposed necessary. For general social crises are seldom explicable in terms of mere decades. We would not now seek to explain the communist revolution in Russia against a background merely of the twelve years since 1905, nor the great French Revolution against the background merely of the reign of Louis XVI. For such a purpose we would think it necessary to examine the whole *ancien régime* which came to an end here in 1917, there in 1789. Similarly, if we are to seek an explanation of the general European crisis of the 1640s, we must not confine ourselves to the preceding decade, ascribing all the responsibility (though we must undoubtedly ascribe some) to Archbishop Laud in England or the Count-Duke of Olivares in Spain. We must look, here too, at the whole *ancien régime* which preceded the crisis : the whole form of State and society which we have seen continually expanding, absorbing all shocks, growing more self-assured throughout the sixteenth century, and which, in the mid-seventeenth century, comes to an end : what for convenience we may call the State and society of the European Renaissance.

The Renaissance — how loose and vague is the term ! Defining it and dating it has become a major industry among scholars, at international congresses and in learned papers. But let us not be deterred by this. All general terms — '*ancien régime*', 'capitalism', 'the Middle Ages' — are loose and vague ; but they are nevertheless serviceable if we use them only generally. And in general terms we know well enough what we mean by the European Renaissance. It is the sudden expansion of our civilization, the excited discovery of world upon world, adventure upon adventure : the progressive enlargement of sensitivity and show which reached its greatest extension in the sixteenth century and which, in the seventeenth century, is no more. Expansion, extension — these are its essential characteristics. For the sixteenth century is not an age of structural change. In technology, in thought, in government, it is the same. In technology, at least after 1520, there are few significant changes. The expansion of Europe creates greater markets, greater opportunities, but the machinery of production remains basically constant. Similarly, in culture, the great representatives of the European Renaissance are universal, but unsystematic. Leonardo, Montaigne, Cervantes, Shakespeare, take life for granted : they adventure, observe, describe, perhaps mock ; but they do not analyse, criticize, question. And in government it is the same too. The political structures of Europe are not changed in the sixteenth century : they are stretched to grasp and hold new empires, sometimes vast new empires, vaster than they can contain for long without internal change. Nevertheless, as yet, there is no such internal change. It is not till the seventeenth century that the structure of government is adjusted to cope with the territorial expansion of the sixteenth, in Spain, in France, in Britain.[1] Until then, the Renaissance State expands continuously without bursting its old envelope. That envelope is the medieval, aristocratic monarchy, the rule of the Christian prince.

It is a fascinating spectacle, the rise of the princes in sixteenth-century Europe. One after another they spring up, first in Italy

[1] See my essay, 'The Union of Britain in the Seventeenth Century', below, pp. 445–67.

and Burgundy, then all over Europe. Their dynasties may be old, and yet their character is new : they are more exotic, more highly coloured than their predecessors. They are versatile, cultivated men, sometimes bizarre, even outrageous : they bewilder us by their lavish tastes, their incredible energy, their ruthlessness and *panache*. Even when they are introverted, bigoted, melancholic, it is on a heroic scale : we think of Charles V solemnly conducting his own funeral at Yuste or Philip II methodically condemning millions of future lives to the treadmill of ceaseless prayer for his own soul. Undoubtedly, in the sixteenth century, the princes are everything. They are tyrants over past and future ; they change religion and divine truth by their nod, even in their teens ; they are priests and popes, they call themselves gods, as well as kings. And yet we should remember, if we are to understand the crisis at the end of their rule, that their power did not rise up out of nothing. Its extraordinary expansion in the early sixteenth century was not *in vacuo*. Europe had to make room for it. The princes rose at the expense of someone or something, and they brought in their train the means of securing their sudden, usurped new power. In fact, they rose at the expense of the older organs of European civilization, the cities ; and they brought with them, as the means of conquest, a new political instrument, 'the Renaissance Court'.

Not much has been written about the eclipse of the European cities on the eve of the Renaissance ; but it is an important phenomenon.[1] For how can we think of the Middle Ages without thinking of the cities, and yet who thinks of them after 1500 ? In the Middle Ages the free communes of Flanders and Italy had been the founders of Europe's trade and wealth, the centres of its arts and crafts, the financiers of its popes and kings. The German cities had been the means of colonizing and civilizing the barbarous north, the pagan east of Europe. These cities, moreover, had had their own way of life and had imposed upon Europe some of their own methods of government and standards of value. In its earliest form, the Renaissance itself had been a

[1] M. Fernand Braudel has touched on it in his great work *La Méditerranée et le monde méditerranéen à l'époque de Philippe II* (Paris, 1949), pp. 285–91.

city phenomenon : it had begun in the cities of Italy, Flanders and south Germany before it was taken over, and changed, by princes and popes. And this early Renaissance had the character of the cities within which it was still contained. Like them it was responsible, orderly, self-controlled. For however great their wealth, however splendid their town halls and hospitals, their churches and squares, there is always, in the cities, a trace of calculation and self-restraint. It is the virtue of civic self-government, however oligarchically controlled : a spirit very different from the outrageous, spendthrift, irresponsible exhibitionism of the princes which was to come.

For between the fifteenth and the sixteenth centuries the princely suitors came, and one after another the cities succumbed. The rich cities of Flanders gave in to the magnificent dukes of Burgundy, the rich cities of Lombardy and Tuscany to the magnificent princes of Italy. The Baltic cities of the Hanse were absorbed by the kings of Poland or Denmark or ruined themselves by vain resistance. Barcelona yielded to the King of Aragon, Marseilles to the King of France. Even those apparent virgins, Genoa and Augsburg, were really 'kept cities', attached by golden strings to the King of Spain and the Emperor. The Doge of Venice himself became a prince, ruling over lesser cities in the *terra ferma*. Only a few, like Geneva, remained obstinate spinsters ; and that sour, crabbed city missed the gaiety of the Renaissance. Even the exceptions prove the rule. Accidental princely weakness, or indirect princely patronage, lies behind the new prosperity of Frankfurt, Ragusa, Hamburg, Danzig.

For as a rule surrender was the price of continued prosperity : how else could the cities survive, once the princes had discovered the secret of State ? By subduing the Church, extending their jurisdiction, mobilizing the countryside, the princes had created a new apparatus of power, 'the Renaissance State', with which they could tax the wealth of the cities, patronize and extend their trade, take over and develop their art and architecture. If the cities hope to thrive now, it must be by new methods. It must not be through independence : those days are past. It must be through monopoly, as the sole grantees of princely trade in these

expanding dominions ; as Lisbon and Seville throve on the
grants of the kings of Portugal and Spain. Or they might thrive
as centres of extravagant princely consumption, as royal capitals.
For in some of the old cities the victorious princes would establish
their new courts : courts which sucked up the wealth of the
whole country and rained it down on the city of their residence.
Essentially the sixteenth century is an age not of cities but of
courts : of capital cities made splendid less by trade than by
government. It was not as industrial or commercial cities, but
as courts, that Brussels, Paris, Rome, Madrid, Naples, Prague
achieve their splendour in the sixteenth century. And the bril-
liance of these courts is not the discreet, complacent self-
advertisement of great merchants out of their calculated profits :
it is the carefree magnificence of kings and courtiers, who do not
need to count because they do not have to earn.

Of course the cities wriggled at first. Ghent resisted its Burgundian dukes. The old cities of Spain struck back against their
foreign king. Florence sought to throw out the Medici. Genoa
and Augsburg surrendered only after doubt and strife. But in
the end each in turn was overpowered, subdued, and then — if
lucky — rewarded with the golden shower which fell not from
trade, or at least not directly from trade, but from the Court.
And with the cities the old city culture was transformed too.
Erasmus, preaching peace and civic justice and denouncing the
heedless wars and wasteful magnificence of princes, is a true
figure of the first, the city Renaissance, cultivated, pious, rational ;
but he is swept up in the princely embrace and made a mascot
of royal courts, until he flees to die in a free city on the Rhine.
Sir Thomas More, whose Utopia was a league of virtuous, independent cities, is captured and broken by the splendid, cannibal
Court of Henry VIII. Soon after 1500 the age of independent
city culture is over. So is the age of careful accountancy. We
are in the age of the Field of Cloth-of-Gold, of heroic conquests
and impossible visions and successive state bankruptcies : the
age of Columbus and Cortés, of Leonardo da Vinci and St
Francis Xavier, each, in his way, like Marlowe's hero, still climb-
ing after knowledge infinite, or, like Don Quixote, pursuing

unattainable mirages, heedless of mortal limitations. It is the age, also, whose fashionable handbooks were no longer civic or clerical, but were called *The Courtier*, *The Governour*, *The Prince*, *The Institution of a Christian Prince*, *The Mirror* (or *the Horologe*) *of Princes*.

How was this miracle possible ? When we look back at that age, with its incredible audacities, its contemptuous magnificence in speculation and spending, we are amazed that it lasted so long. Why did not European civilization burst in the sixteenth century ? And yet not only did it not burst, it continued to expand, absorbing all the time the most fearful strains. The Turks in the east wrenched away the outposts of Europe ; Christendom was split asunder by religious revolution and constant war ; and yet at the end of the century the kings were more spendthrift, their courts more magnificent than ever. The Court of Spain, once so simple, had been changed to a Burgundian pattern ; the Court of England, once so provincial, had become, under Queen Elizabeth, the most elaborate in Europe ; and the princes of Italy and Germany, with palaces and libraries, picture-galleries and *Wunderkammer*, philosophers, fools and astrologers, strove to hold their own. As the century wore on, social conscience dwindled, for social change seemed impossibly remote. Was ever an architect more effortlessly aristocratic than Palladio, or a poet than Shakespeare, or a painter than Rubens ?

How indeed was it possible ? One answer is obvious. The sixteenth century was an age of economic expansion. It was the century when, for the first time, Europe was living on Asia, Africa and America. But there was also another reason. The reason why this expansion was always under the princes, not at their expense, why the princes were always carried upwards, not thrown aside by it, was that the princes had allies who secured their power and kept them firmly in place. For the princes could never have built up their power alone. Whatever weaknesses in society gave them their opportunity, they owed their permanence to the machinery of government which they had created or improved, and to the vested interests which that machinery fostered. This machinery, the means and result of princely triumph, is the Renaissance State, and it is to this that we must now turn : for it was the Renaissance State which, in so much of Europe, first broke or corroded the old power of the cities and then, in its turn, in the seventeenth century, faced its own crisis and dissolved.

We often speak of the Renaissance State. How can we define it ? When we come down to facts, we find that it is, at bottom, a great and expanding bureaucracy, a huge system of administrative centralization, staffed by an ever-growing multitude of 'courtiers' or 'officers'. The 'officers' are familiar enough to us as a social type. We think of the great Tudor ministers in England, Cardinal Wolsey, Thomas Cromwell, the two Cecils ; or of the *letrados* of Spain, Cardinal Ximénez, the two Granvelles, Francisco de los Cobos, António Pérez ; and we see their common character : they are formidable administrators, Machiavellian diplomats, cultivated patrons of art and letters, magnificent builders of palaces and colleges, greedy collectors of statues and pictures, books and bindings. For of course these men, as royal servants, imitated their masters, in lavishness as in other matters. But what is significant about the sixteenth century is not merely the magnificence of these great 'officers', it is the number — the ever-growing number — of lesser officers who also, on their lesser scale, accepted the standards and copied the tastes of their masters. For all through the century the number of officers was growing. Princes needed them, more and more, to staff their councils and courts, their new special or permanent tribunals which were the means of governing new territories and centralizing the government of old. It was for this reason that the Renaissance princes and their great ministers founded all those schools and colleges. For it was not merely to produce scholars, or to advance learning or science, that old colleges were reorganized or new founded by Cardinal Ximénez or Cardinal Wolsey, by Henry VIII of England or John III of Portugal, or François I of France. The new learning, it is notorious, grew up outside the colleges and universities, not in them. The function of the new foundations was to satisfy the royal demand for

officers — officers to man the new royal bureaucracies — and, at
the same time, the public demand for office : office which was
the means to wealth and power and the gratification of lavish,
competitive tastes.

Thus the power of the Renaissance princes was not princely
power only : it was also the power of thousands of 'officers'
who also, like their masters, had extravagant tastes and, somehow, the means of gratifying them. And how in fact were they
gratified ? Did the princes themselves pay their officers enough
to sustain such a life ? Certainly not. Had that been so, ruin
would have come quicker : Cobos and Granvelle alone would
have brought Charles V to bankruptcy long before 1556, and
Henry VIII would have had to dissolve the monasteries fifteen
years earlier to sustain the economic burden of Cardinal Wolsey.
The fact is, only a fraction of the cost of the royal bureaucracy
fell directly on the Crown : three-quarters of it fell, directly or
indirectly, on the country.

Yes, three-quarters : at least three-quarters. For throughout
Europe, at this time, the salaries paid to officers of State were
small, customary payments whose real value dwindled in times
of inflation ; the bulk of an officer's gains came from private
opportunities to which public office merely opened the door.
'For the profits of these two great offices, the Chancellor and the
Treasurer', wrote an English bishop, 'certainly they were very
small if you look to the ancient fees and allowances ; for princes
heretofore did tie themselves to give but little, that so their
officers and servants might more depend upon them for their
rewards.'[1] What Bishop Goodman said of Jacobean England
was true of every European country. Instances could be multiplied indefinitely.[2] Every officer, at every Court, in every

[1] Godfrey Goodman, *The Court of King James I* (1839 ed.), I, 279.
[2] On this subject generally see Federico Chabod's essay 'Y a-t-il un état de la
Renaissance ?' in *Actes du colloque sur la renaissance, Sorbonne, 1956* (Paris, 1958), and
also, for Milanese instances, his 'Stipendi nominali e busta paga effettiva dei
funzionari nell' amministrazione milanese alla fine del cinquecento', in *Miscellanea in
onore di Roberto Cessi II* (Rome, 1958) and 'Usi e abusi nell' amministrazione dello
stato di Milano a mezzo il 1500', in *Studi storici in onore di Gioacchino Volpe* (Florence,
n.d.). For Naples, see G. Coniglio, *Il Regno di Napoli al tempo di Carlo V* (Naples,
1951), pp. 11–12, 246, etc. For France see R. Doucet, *Les Institutions de la France*

country, lived by the same system. He was paid a trivial 'fee' or salary and, for the rest, made what he could in the field which his office had opened to him. Some of these profits were regarded as perfectly legitimate, for no man could be expected to live on his 'fee' alone : it was taken for granted that he would charge a reasonable sum for audiences, favours, signatures, that he would exploit his office to make good bargains, that he would invest public money, while in his hands, on his own account. But of course there were other profits which were generally regarded as 'corruption' and therefore improper. Unfortunately the line dividing propriety from impropriety was conventional only : it was therefore invisible, uncertain, floating. It differed from person to person, from place to place. It also differed from time to time. As the sixteenth century passed on, as the cost of living rose, as the pressure of competition sharpened and royal discipline slackened, there was a general decline of standards. The public casuists became more indulgent, the private conscience more elastic, and men began to forget about that conventional, invisible line between 'legitimate profits' and 'corruption'.

Let us consider a few instances which illustrate the system. In England, the Master of the Wards had a 'fee' of £133 p.a., but even Lord Burghley, a conscientious administrator, made 'infinite gains' — at least £2000 p.a. — out of its private opportunities, quite apart from its non-financial advantages. His son did far better. The Lord Treasurer's fee was £365 p.a., but in 1635 even Archbishop Laud, a notable stickler for administrative honesty, reckoned that that great officer had 'honest advantages' for enriching himself to the tune of over £7000 p.a. The archbishop made this calculation because he had been shocked by the much larger sums which recent lord treasurers had been making at the expense of king and subject alike. In 1600 the

---

au XVIe siècle (Paris, 1948), pp. 403 ff. ; cf. Menna Prestwich, 'The Making of Absolute Monarchy, 1559–1683', in *France : Government and Society*, ed. J. M. Wallace-Hadrill and J. McManners (1957). I have given some English instances in *The Gentry, 1540–1640 (Economic History Review*, supp. no. 1, 1953). See also J. E. Neale, 'The Elizabethan Political Scene', in *Proceedings of the British Academy*, XXIV (1948); K. W. Swart, *The Sale of Offices in the Seventeenth Century* (The Hague, 1949).

Lord Chancellor's fee was £500 p.a., but in fact the office was known to be 'better worth than £3000 p.a.'. To Lord Chancellor Ellesmere this did not seem enough, and, like many great men, he sighed that he could not make ends meet. He was thought conscientious : perhaps (like Burghley) he was also hypocritical. At all events, his successors had no such difficulty.

> How have the Lord Chancellors lived since [exclaimed Bishop Goodman], how have they flowed with money, and what great purchases have they made, and what profits and advantages have they had by laying their fingers on purchases ! For if my Lord desired the land, no man should dare to buy it out of his hands, and he must have it at his own price ; for any bribery or corruption, it is hard to prove it : men do not call others to be witnesses at such actions.[1]

All writers of the early seventeenth century agree that the casual profits of office had grown enormously ; and these casual profits were multiplied at the expense of the consumer, the country.

Thus each old office granted, each new office created, meant a new burden on the subject. Royal parsimony made little difference. Our Queen Elizabeth, we all know, was judged very parsimonious : far too parsimonious by her own officers. After her death, her parsimony became one of her great retrospective virtues : how favourably it compared with the giddy extravagance of James I, the fiscal exactions of Charles I ! But she was not praised for her parsimony in her own time. For what in fact did it mean ? 'We have not many precedents of her liberality', says a contemporary, 'nor of any large donatives to particular men. . . . Her rewards consisted chiefly in grants of leases of offices, places of judicature ; but for ready money, and in any great sums, she was very sparing.'[2] In other words, she gave to her courtiers not cash but the right to exploit their fellow subjects : to Sir Walter Ralegh the right to despoil the

---

[1] See, for the Master of the Wards, J. Hurstfield, 'Lord Burghley as Master of the Court of Wards', in *Transactions of the Royal Historical Society*, 5th ser., xxxi (1949) ; for the Lord Treasurer, P. Heylin, *Cyprianus Anglicus* (1668), p. 285 ; for the Lord Chancellor, Goodman, *The Court of King James I*, I, 279 ; *Manningham's Diary* (Camden Society, 1868), p. 19.

[2] Sir R. Naunton, *Fragmenta Regalia*, ed. A. Arber (1870), p. 18.

bishops of Bath and Wells and Salisbury and to interpose his pocket between the producer and consumer of tin ; to the Earl of Essex the right to lease the monopoly of sweet wines to merchants who would recoup themselves by raising the cost to the consumer. Thanks to these invisible *douceurs* she contrived, at the same time, to keep her taxes low and her officers sweet.

Whether they kept taxes low or not, all European sovereigns did likewise. They had no alternative. They had not the ready money, and so, if they were to gratify their servants, reward their favourites, service their loans, they had to raise it at a discount or pay excessively in kind. They leased Crown lands at a quarter (or less) of their true value in order that 'officers' or 'courtiers' could live, as lessees, on the difference. They granted monopolies which brought in to the Crown less than a quarter of what they cost the subject. They collected irrational old taxes, or even irrational new taxes, by imposing, fourfold, irrational burdens on the tax-payers. The King of France obliged his peasants to buy even more salt than they needed, in order to raise his yield from the *gabelle*. We all know what a burden wardship and purveyance became in the reigns of Queen Elizabeth and King James. Both visibly cost the subject four times what they brought to the Crown. Invisibly — that is, beyond that invisible line — they cost far more.[1]

Nor was it only the Crown which acted thus. The practice was universal. Great men rewarded their clients in exactly the

[1] For the cost of monopolies, see W. R. Scott, *The Constitution and Finance of . . . Joint-Stock Companies to 1720*, I (1911). The cost of wardship appears clearly from Mr Joel Hurstfield's studies. He concludes that 'the unofficial profits from fiscal feudalism taken as a whole, were at least three times as high as the official ones' : 'The Profits of Fiscal Feudalism, 1541–1602', in *Economic History Review*, 2nd ser., VIII (1955–6), 58. Of purveyance, Bacon wrote, 'There is no pound profit which redoundeth to Your Majesty in this course but induceth and begetteth £3 damage upon your subjects, besides the discontentment' (*Works*, ed. J. Spedding *et al.* (1857–74), III, 185). The truth of this statement is clearly demonstrated in Miss Allegra Woodworth's excellent study, *Purveyance in the Reign of Queen Elizabeth* (Philadelphia, 1945). For Crown lands, Bacon told King James that, properly administered, they 'will yield four for one' (*Works*, IV, 328) : others put the proportion far higher, sometimes twenty to one. Cf. E. Kerridge, 'The Movement of Rent', in *Economic History Review*, 2nd ser., VI (1953–4), 31–32. The Earl of Bedford similarly, in 1641, calculated that in some places the proportion was twenty to one (Woburn Abbey, Duke of Bedford's manuscripts).

same way. It was thus that those great empires of personal patronage were built up which at times threatened to disrupt the whole system of monarchy. In France, it was through his 'clients' — that is, 'le grand nombre d'officiers que son crédit avoit introduit dans les principales charges du royaume' — that the Duke of Guise was able to make royal government impossible, to control the Estates-General of France, and nearly place his own dynasty on the throne of the Valois. It was to prevent the recurrence of such a portent that Henri IV afterwards, by the institution of the *Paulette*, made offices hereditary, subject to an annual payment to the Crown. This did not cure the social fact, but it cured the aristocratic abuse of it.[1] In Elizabethan England the Earl of Leicester similarly built up a great system of patronage, 'Leicester's Commonwealth', which rivalled Lord Burghley's *regnum Cecilianum*. Queen Elizabeth managed to control Leicester, but not his stepson, the heir to his ambitions, the Earl of Essex. Essex, for a moment, looked like the Guise of England. Like Guise, he had to be removed, surgically. Later the Duke of Buckingham would build up, by royal permission, a similar empire of patronage. He would be removed surgically too.

The Church, in this respect, was similar to the State : it was, after all, by now a department of State, and it must be seen, sociologically, as an element in the bureaucratic structure. Originally an attempt had been made to separate it from that structure. The Reformation movement, Catholic as well as Protestant, was in many respects a revolt against the papal 'Court' —using the word 'Court', as I always do, in the widest sense— that is, not merely a national revolt against a foreign Church, but a social revolt against the indecent, costly and infinitely multiplied personnel, mainly of the regular orders, which had overgrown the working episcopal and parish structure. We only have to read the history of the Council of Trent to see this : the exclusion of the Protestants from that assembly merely shows that, socially, Catholic demands were identical. Protestant

[1] See Cardinal de Richelieu, *Testament politique*, ed. Louis André, 7th ed. (Paris, 1947), pp. 233–4, 241–2.

societies, by revolution, disembarrassed themselves of much of the papal Court. But even Protestant princes, as princes, preferred to take over, rather than to destroy the bureaucracy of the Church. Catholic princes went further : they accepted both the existing clerical structure and the positive increase which was entailed upon it by the Counter-Reformation. For although, in one sense, the Counter-Reformation may have been a movement of moral and spiritual reform, structurally it was an aggravation of the bureaucracy. However, the princes found that it paid them to accept this aggravation, for in return for their allegiance it was placed under their control, and became at once an extended field of patronage and a social palliative. The Catholic princes had vast clerical patronage for laymen as well as clergy : the Church absorbed the potential critics : and the new or strengthened religious orders, by evangelization, reconciled society to the burden which they imposed upon it. Thus the Catholic princes of the Counter-Reformation were generally able to stifle the forces of change to which Protestant princes found themselves more nakedly exposed, and it became a truism, and perhaps a truth, that popery was the sole internal preservative of monarchy. But even in Protestant monarchies, the bureaucratic pressure of the Church was felt and resented. The Church, it was said, was burdened with absentee clergy, tithe-eating laity, a swollen number of ecclesiastical officers, and parasitic lessees who lived happily on 'beneficial leases' of Church lands. For Church lands, like Crown lands, were regularly leased at absurd under-rents. It was not only the State : the whole of society was top-heavy.

Moreover, and increasingly as the seventeenth century succeeded to the sixteenth, this multiplication of ever more costly offices outran the needs of State. Originally the need had created the officers ; now the officers created the need. All bureaucracies tend to expand. By the process known to us as Parkinson's Law, office-holders tend to create yet more offices beneath them in order to swell their own importance or provide for their friends and kinsmen. But whereas today such inflation is curbed by the needs of the Treasury, in the sixteenth century the needs of the

Treasury positively encouraged it. For offices, in the sixteenth century, were not granted freely : they were sold, and — at least in the beginning — the purchase-price went to the Crown. If the Crown could sell more and more offices at higher and higher prices, leaving the officers to be paid by the country, this was an indirect, if also a cumbrous and exasperating, way of taxing the country. Consequently, princes were easily tempted to create new offices, and to profit by the competition which forced up the price. As for the purchaser, having paid a high price, he naturally sought to raise his profits still higher, in order to recoup himself, with a decent margin, for his outlay : a decent margin with which an ambitious man might hope, in the end, to build a house like Hatfield or Knole, entertain royalty to feasts costing thousands, retain and reward an army of clients, plant exotic gardens and collect *objets d'art* and pictures.

So 'the Renaissance State' consisted, at bottom, of an ever-expanding bureaucracy which, though at first a working bureaucracy, had by the end of the sixteenth century become a parasitic bureaucracy ; and this ever-expanding bureaucracy was sustained on an equally expanding margin of 'waste' : waste which lay between the taxes imposed on the subject and the revenue collected by the Crown. Since the Crown could not afford an absolute loss of revenue, it is clear that this expansion of the waste had to be at the expense of society. It is equally clear that it could be borne only if society itself were expanding in wealth and numbers. Fortunately, in the sixteenth century, the European economy was expanding. The trade of Asia, the bullion of Africa and America, was driving the European machine. This expansion may have been uneven ; there may have been strains and casualties ; but they were the strains of growth, which could be absorbed, individual casualties which could be overlooked. Occasional state bankruptcies clear off old debts : they do not necessarily affect new prosperity. War increases consumption : it does not necessarily consume the sources of wealth. A booming economy can carry many anomalies, many abuses. It could even carry — provided it went on booming — the incredibly wasteful, ornamental, parasitic Renaissance court and Churches.

Provided it went on booming . . . But how long would it boom? Already, by 1590, the cracks are beginning to appear. The strains of the last years of Philip II's wars release everywhere a growing volume of complaint: complaint which is not directed against constitutional faults — against the despotism of kings or the claims of estates — but against this or that aspect or consequence of the growth and cost of a parasitic bureaucracy. For of course, although war has not created the problem, war aggravates it: the more the costs of government are raised, the more the government resorts to those now traditional financial expedients—creation and sale of new offices; sale or long lease, at under-values, of Crown or Church lands; creation of monopolies; raising of 'feudal' taxes: expedients which, on the one hand, multiply the already overgrown bureaucracy and thus the cost to the country, and, on the other hand, further impoverish the Crown.

But if the strains are already obvious in the 1590s, they are, as yet, not fatal: for peace comes first. A few opportune deaths — Philip II in 1598, Queen Elizabeth in 1603 — hasten the process, and throughout Europe war after war is wound up. And then, with peace, what relief! The overstrained system is suddenly relaxed, and an era of pleasure and renewed extravagance follows. Was there ever an era of such lavishness as the time between the end of Philip II's wars and the outbreak of the Thirty Years War, the time when the world was ruled, or at least enjoyed, by Philip III and the Duke of Lerma in Spain, James I and the Duke of Buckingham in England, 'The Archdukes' in Flanders, Henri IV and Marie de Médicis in France? It is a world of giddy expenditure, splendid building, gigantic feasts and lavish, evanescent shows. Rubens, when he came to the Duke of Buckingham's England, marvelled at such unexpected magnificence 'in a place so remote from Italian elegance'. No nation in the world, said a contemporary Englishman, spent as much as we did in building. We built houses, said another, thinking of Hatfield and Audley End, 'like Nebuchadnezzar's'. All 'the old good rules of economy', said a third, had gone packing. But the Spanish ambassador, reporting to his king these costly Jacobean festivals, would only say that no doubt they would seem very impressive 'to anyone who had not seen the grandeur and state with which we do such things in Spain' — as well he might, in the days when the Duke of Lerma, the courtier of the almost bankrupt King of Spain, went forth to meet his future queen with 34,000 ducats' worth of jewels on his person, and another 72,000 ducats' worth carried behind him.[1]

Such is the character of the Renaissance courts in their last Indian summer after the close of the sixteenth century. And even this, of course, is only the conspicuous, still sunlit tip of the iceberg whose sides are hidden from us by intervening oblivion and whose greater base was always, even at the time, submerged. How, we may ask, could it go on ? Even in the 1590s, even a far less expensive, more efficient bureaucracy had been saved only by peace : how could this much more outrageous system survive if the long prosperity of the sixteenth century, or the saving peace of the seventeenth, should fail ?

In fact, in the 1620s they both failed at once. In 1618 a political crisis in Prague had set the European powers in motion, and by 1621 the wars of Philip II had been resumed, bringing in their train new taxes, new offices, new exactions. Meanwhile the European economy, already strained to the limit by the habits of peacetime boom, was suddenly struck by a great depression, the universal 'decay of trade' of 1620. Moreover, in those twenty years, a new attitude of mind had been created : created by disgust at that gilded merry-go-round which cost society so much more than society was willing to bear. It was an attitude of hatred : hatred of 'the Court' and its courtiers, hatred of princely follies and bureaucratic corruption, hatred of the Renaissance itself : in short, Puritanism.

In England we naturally think of our own form of Puritanism : extreme Protestantism, the continuation, to unbearable lengths, of the half-completed sixteenth-century Reformation. But let us

---

[1] *Correspondencia oficial de D. Diego Sarmiento de Acuña, conde de Gondomar*, ed. A. Ballesteros y Beretta (*Documentos inéditos para la historia de España*), III (Madrid, 1944), 232. P. Mantuano, *Casamientos de España y Francia* (Madrid, 1618), pp. 124–5, quoted in Agustín Gonzales de Amezúa, *Lope de Vega en sus cartas* (Madrid, 1935), I, 70–71.

not be deceived by mere local forms. This reaction against the Renaissance courts and their whole culture and morality was not confined to any one country or religion. Like the thesis, the antithesis also is general. In England there is an Anglican Puritanism, a 'Puritanism of the Right'. What greater enemy had English Puritanism, as we know it, than Archbishop Laud, the all-powerful prelate who drove it to America till it returned to destroy him? And yet he too illustrates this same reaction. Did English Puritans denounce 'the unloveliness of lovelocks', gay clothes, the drinking of toasts? The archbishop forbade long hair in Oxford, reformed clerical dress, waged war on ale-houses. In Roman Catholic countries it was the same. Did the English Puritans first denounce, then close the London theatres? In Spain — even the Spain of Lope de Vega — *pragmática* after *pragmática* denounced stage plays. In France the Jansenist Pascal disliked them hardly less. In Bavaria there was a Catholic prudery, and a police enforcement of it, as disagreeable as the worst form of English Puritanism. There was the same war against luxury too. In 1624 Philip IV of Spain cut down his household, published sumptuary laws, and banished the ruff — that symbol of sartorial magnificence — from Spain by decree, from Europe by example. In France Cardinal Richelieu was doing likewise. It was a sudden war, almost a crusade, against the old Renaissance extravagance. In Flanders Rubens would find himself surviving his old Court patrons and would turn to country landscapes. Literature reflects the same change. Of Castiglione's famous manual, *The Courtier*, at least sixty editions or translations were published between 1528 and 1619; after the latter date, for a whole century, none.

In the 1620s Puritanism — this general mood of Puritanism — triumphs in Europe. Those years, we may say, mark the end of the Renaissance. The playtime is over. The sense of social responsibility, which had held its place within the Renaissance courts of the sixteenth century — we think of the paternalism of the Tudors, the 'collectivism' of Philip II — had been driven out in the early seventeenth century, and now it had returned, and with a vengeance. War and depression had made the change

71

emphatic, even startling. We look at the world in one year, and
there we see Lerma and Buckingham and Marie des Médicis.
We look again, and they have all gone. Lerma has fallen and
saved himself by becoming a Roman cardinal; Buckingham is
assassinated; Marie de Médicis has fled abroad. In their stead
we find grimmer, greater, more resolute figures : the Count-Duke
of Olivares, whose swollen, glowering face almost bursts from
Velázquez's canvases; Strafford and Laud, that relentless pair,
the prophets of Thorough in Church and State; Cardinal
Richelieu, the iron-willed invalid who ruled and remade France.
In literature too it is the same. The fashion has changed. After
Shakespeare, Cervantes, Montaigne, those universal spirits, with
their scepticism, their acceptance of the world as it is, we are
suddenly in a new age : an age here of ideological revolt, Milton's
'jubilee and resurrection of Church and State', there of conservative pessimism, cynicism and disillusion, of John Donne and Sir
Thomas Browne, of Quevedo and the Spanish Baroque : for the
baroque age, as Mr Gerald Brenan says, '— one cannot say it too
often — was a tight, contracted age, turned in on itself and lacking
self-confidence and faith in the future'.[1]

Such was the mood of general, non-doctrinal, moral Puritanism
which, in the 1620s, launched its attack — here from within, there
from without — on the Renaissance courts. There are differences
of incidence, of course, differences of personality from place to
place, and these differences could be crucial — who can say what
would have happened if Archbishop Laud had really been, as Sir
Thomas Roe thought, 'the Richelieu of England' ? There were
also differences in society itself. But if we look closely we see
that the burden on society is the same even if the shoulders which
creak under it are different. For instance, in England the cost of
the Court fell most heavily on the gentry : they were the tax-
paying class : wardships, purveyance and all the indirect taxes
which were multiplied by the early Stuarts fell heaviest on them.
On the other hand in France the *noblesse* was exempt from taxation, and the *taille* and *gabelle*, which were multiplied by the early
Bourbons, fell heaviest on the peasants. No doubt English land-

[1] Gerald Brenan, *The Literature of the Spanish People* (Cambridge, 1951), p. 272.

lords could pass some of their burdens on to their tenants. No doubt impoverishment of French peasants diminished the rents of their landlords. But the difference is still significant. It was a commonplace in England, where 'the asinine peasants of France', with their 'wooden shoes and canvas breeches', were regularly contrasted with our own, more prosperous yeomen. It is illustrated by the ultimate result : in England, when revolution came, it was a great revolution, controlled by the gentry ; in France, there were, every year for the same twenty years, revolts — little but serious revolts — of the peasants. Nevertheless, if the rebels were different, the general grievance against which they rebelled — the character and cost of the State — was the same.

For wherever we look, this is the burden of all complaints. From 1620 to 1640 this is the cry of the country, the problem of the courts. We can hear the cry from the back benches of the English parliaments in the 1620s. We can see the problem in Bacon's great essays, written between 1620 and 1625, on 'Sedition and Troubles' and 'The True Greatness of Kingdoms'. We hear the cry in Spain in the protests of the Cortes, see the problem in the pamphlets of the *arbitristas* : Sancho de Moncada's *Restauración Política de España* ; in Fernández Navarrete's *Conservación de monarquías* with its wonderful analysis of the social ills of Spain, and in Olivares's long memorandum to Philip IV, outlining his new programme for the country,[1] all written in the critical years 1619–21. We see it in France, above all, in the *Testament politique* of Richelieu, written in 1629 and the early 1630s, the period when governments everywhere were facing these problems, or trying to face them, before it was too late. And these demands, these problems, are not constitutional, they are not concerned with monarchy or republic, Crown or Parliament. Nor are they economic : they are not concerned with methods of production. Essentially they are demands for emancipation from the burden of centralization ; for reduction of fees ; reduction of useless, expensive offices, including — even in Spain — clerical offices ; abolition of the sale of offices ('for whosoever doth

[1] Published in A. Valladares de Sotomayor, *Semanario erudito*, xi (Madrid, 1788). I owe this reference to Mr J. H. Elliott.

farm or buy offices doth bind himself to be an extortioner', and 'they which buy dear must sell dear') ; abolition of heredity of offices ; abolition of those wasteful, indirect taxes which yield so little to the Crown but on whose superabundant 'waste' the ever-expanding fringe of the Court is fed.

Thus the tension between Court and country grew, and the 'revolutionary situation' of the 1620s and 1630s developed. But revolutionary situations do not necessarily lead to revolutions — nor (we may add) are violent revolutions necessary in order to create new forms of production or society. Society is an organic body, far tougher, far more resilient, than its morbid anatomists often suppose. The frontiers between opposing classes are always confused by a complex tissue of interests. Office-holders and *bourgeoisie*, consumers and producers, tax-gatherers and tax-payers are not neatly distinguishable classes. On the contrary, men who think of themselves as 'country' at one moment often discover that they are 'Court' at another, and such discoveries may lead to unpredictable apostasy. For this reason, social tensions seldom if ever lead to a clean split : rather they lead to an untidy inward crumbling whose stages are determined not by the original social tensions but by intervening political events and political errors. Therefore, if we are to carry this study further, from revolutionary situation to revolution, we must take account of these intervening events and errors : events and errors which, by definition, must vary from place to place, and whose variation will explain, in part, the difference between the revolutions in those different places.

Perhaps we can see the problem best if we consider the means of avoiding revolution. If the Renaissance courts were to survive, it was clear that at least one of two things must be done. On the one hand the parasitic bureaucracies must be cut down ; on the other hand the working bureaucracy must be related to the economic capacity of the country. The first programme was one of administrative, the second of economic reform. The first was easy enough to define — any country gentleman could put it in two words — but difficult to carry out : it meant the reduction of a parasitic, but living and powerful class ; and although this can be done without revolution, as it was done in nineteenth-century England — one only has to read the *Extraordinary Black Book* of 1831 to see the huge parasitic fringe which had grown again around the eighteenth-century Court — it is at best a delicate and difficult operation. The second was far more difficult to define : it meant the discovery, or rediscovery, of an economic system. Nevertheless, such a definition was not beyond the wit of seventeenth-century thinkers, and in fact several thinkers did point out, clearly enough, the kind of economic system which was required.

What was that system ? It was not a 'capitalist' system — or at least, if it was capitalist, there was nothing new about it. It did not entail revolution or a change in method of production or in the class structure. Nor was it advocated by revolutionary thinkers : in general, those who advocated it were conservative men who wished for little or no political change. And in fact the economic programme which they advocated, though applied to modern conditions, looked back for its example. For what they advocated was simply the application to the new, centralized monarchies of the old, well-tried policy of the medieval communes which those monarchies had eclipsed : mercantilism.

For what had been the policy of the medieval cities ? It had been a policy of national economy — within the limits of the city-state. The city had seen itself at once as a political and as an economic unit. Its legislation had been based on its trading requirements. It had controlled the price of food and labour, limited imports in the interest of its own manufactures, encouraged the essential methods of trade — fishing and shipbuilding, freedom from internal tolls — invested its profits not in conspicuous waste or pursuit of glory, or wars merely of plunder, but in the rational conquest of markets and the needs of national economy : in technical education, municipal betterment, poor relief. In short, the city had recognized that its life must be related to its means of livelihood. In the sixteenth-century eclipse of the cities, in their transformation into overgrown, overpopulated capitals, centres merely of exchange and consumption, much of this old civic wisdom had been forgotten. Now, in the seven-teenth-century eclipse of the spendthrift Renaissance Courts, it was being remembered. The economists wished to go farther : to reapply it.

Of course, they would reapply it in changed circumstances, to different national forms. The princes, it was agreed, had done their work : it could not be reversed. The new nation-states had come to stay. But, said the reformers, having come, let them now apply to their different conditions the old good rules of the cities. Let them not merely pare down the parasitic fringe that had grown around them, but also relate their power, in a positive sense, to economic aims. Let them favour a gospel of work instead of aristocratic, or pseudo-aristocratic *hidalguía*. Let them protect industry, guarantee food-supplies, remove internal tolls, develop productive wealth. Let them rationalize finance and bring down the apparatus of Church and State to a juster proportion. To reverse the Parkinson's Law of bureaucracy, let them reduce the hatcheries which turned out the superfluous bureaucrats : grammar schools in England, colleges in France, monasteries and theological seminaries in Spain. Instead, let them build up local elementary education : skilled workers at the base of society now seemed more important than those unemploy-able university graduates, hungry for office, whom the new Renaissance foundations were turning out. 'Of grammar-schools', declared that great intellectual, Sir Francis Bacon, 'there are too many' : many a good ploughboy was spoiled to make a bad scholar ; and he and his followers advocated a change in the type of education or the diversion of funds to elementary schools. Of colleges, declared the founder of the French Aca-demy, Cardinal Richelieu, there are too many : the commerce of letters, if unchecked, would banish absolutely that of merchandise 'which crowns states with riches' and ruin agriculture 'the true nursing-mother of peoples'. Of monasteries, declared the Catholic Council of Castile in 1619, there are too many, and it prayed that the Pope be asked to authorize their reduction, for although the monastic state is no doubt, for the individual, the most perfect, 'for the public it is very damaging and prejudicial'.

Monasteries, protested the Cortes of Castile, have outgrown the needs of religion : they now contain persons 'rather fleeing from necessity to the delights of indolence than moved by devotion'. So, in country after country, the protest was raised. It was the backswing of the great educational impulse of the Renaissance and Reformation, the great religious impulse of the Counter-Reformation.[1]

To cut down the oppressive, costly sinecures of Church and State, and to revert, *mutatis mutandis*, to the old mercantilist policy of the cities, based on the economic interest of society — such were the two essential methods of avoiding revolution in the seventeenth century. How far were either of them adopted in the states of western Europe ? The answer, I think, is instructive. If we look at those states in turn, we may see, in the extent to which either or both of these policies were adopted or rejected, some partial explanation of the different forms which the general crisis took in each of them.

In Spain neither policy was adopted. It was not for lack of warning. The Cortes of Castile, the Council of State, the *arbitristas*, individual statesmen continually pressed both for reduction of officers and clergy and for a mercantilist policy. In 1619 Philip III was urged to abolish, as a burden to society, the hundred *receptores* newly created six years earlier, even though that should mean repaying the price at which they had bought their offices. In the same year the greatest of Spanish ambassadors, Gondomar, whose letters show him to have been a consistent mercantilist, wrote that Church and Commonwealth were both endangered by the multiplication of clergy 'since the shepherds now outnumber the sheep' ; and he added that the same was true in the State, where 'ministers of justice, *escribanos*, *comisarios* and *alguaziles*' were multiplying fast, but there was no increase of 'ploughmen, ships or trade'.[2] Two years later, under

---

[1] For Bacon's proposal see his *Works*, ed. Spedding, IV, 249 ff. ; for Richelieu, his *Testament politique*, ed. Louis André, pp. 204-5 ; for Spain the *Consulta del Consejo Supremo de Castilla*, published in P. Fernández Navarrete, *Conservación de monarquías* (Madrid, 1947, Biblioteca de Autores Españoles, XXV), p. 450 ; *Actas de las Cortes de Castilla*, XXII, 434, etc.

[2] *Correspondencia oficial de* . . . II (Madrid, 1943), 140. Cf. the other letters of Gondomar printed in Pascual Gayangos, *Cinco cartas político-literarias de D. Diego Sarmiento, conde de Gondomar* (Madrid : Sociedad de Bibliófilos, IV, 1869).

the pressure of economic crisis and the renewal of war, it seemed that something would at last be done. The reign of Philip IV began with the famous *capítulos de reformación*. The number of royal officers was fixed by law. Next year the king declared that since an excessive number of offices is pernicious in the State ('most of them being sold, and the officers having to make up the price they have paid'), and since a great number of *escribanos* is prejudicial to society ('and the number at present is excessive, and grows daily') the number of *alguaciles, procuradores*, and *escribanos* in Castile must be reduced to one-third, and recruitment must be discouraged by various means.[1] For a moment, it seemed that the problem was to be faced. The leaders of the war-party themselves, implicitly, recognized the cause of Spain's weakness. The purpose of *las Pazes* — the successive treaties of peace in 1598, 1604, 1609 — they said, had been to repair the strength of Spain ; but in fact peace had strengthened the mercantilist Dutch and only weakened bureaucratic Spain.[2] Now war was necessary to redress the balance ; but even to make war the structure of society must be reformed ; the bureaucratic state had failed alike as a system of peace and as a system of war.

So spoke the reformers of the 1620s. But their voice was soon stifled, for there was no social or institutional force behind them to make their protest effective. The Castilian middle class was weak and penetrated by office-holders ; the power of the old Cortes towns had been suppressed in their last rising against the Burgundian State a century before ; and the Cortes of Castile was now an aristocratic body which hardly sought to do more than demur. Besides, war, which exposed the economic weakness of the bureaucratic system, equally prevented any reform of that system. A few reforms were attempted, or at least enacted on paper ;[3] but the mood soon changed. The need for immedi-

---

[1] Archivo Histórico Español, *Colección de documentos inéditos para la historia de España y de sus Indias*, v (Madrid, 1932), 28, 281, etc.

[2] A. Rodriguez Villa, *Ambrósio Spínola, primer marqués de los Balbases* (Madrid, 1904), pp. 342–8, 382 ff. ; J. Carrera Pujal, *Historia de la economía española* (Barcelona, 1943), i, 485 ff. ; Pascual de Gayangos, *Cinco cartas politico-literarias*.

[3] For a summary of these reforms see H. Bérindoague, *Le Mercantilisme en Espagne* (Bordeaux, 1929), pp. 85–104.

ate funds caused the government to exploit the existing machinery, not to reform it for the sake of future efficiency. So all the projects of the reformers were soon forgotten, and in 1646 the Cortes of Castile would draw attention to their failure. In spite of all those protests and those efforts, offices had not diminished during the war : they had multiplied. Instead of one president and three councillors of the Treasury, there were now three presidents and eleven councillors ; instead of three *contadores* and a *fiscal*, there were now fourteen *contadores* ; instead of four councillors at war there were now more than forty ; and all these, salaried or unsalaried (for their salaries, their 'fees', were anyway trifles), had entertainment, expenses, lodgings, privileges and perquisites at the expense of the subject.[1] The weight of this burden might have been redistributed a little within the country, but it had certainly not been reduced.[2] Nor had the Spanish economy been enabled to bear it. For meanwhile the national wealth of Spain had not increased : it had diminished. The voices of the mercantilists were stifled. The trade of Spain was taken over almost entirely by foreigners. The vitality of the country was crushed beneath the dead weight of an unreformed *ancien régime*. It was not till the next century that a new generation of *arbitristas* — philosophers inspired by English and French examples — would again have the strength and spirit to urge on a new dynasty the same reforms which had clearly but vainly been demanded in the days of Philip III and Philip IV.[3]

Very different was the position in the emancipated northern Netherlands. For the northern Netherlands was the first European country to reject the Renaissance Court, and the Court they

[1] *Consulta* of the Cortes of Castile, 18 Aug. 1646, printed in Alonso Núñez de Castro, *Libro historico-politico, solo Madrid es Corte*, 2nd ed. (Madrid, 1669), pp. 84 ff. This whole book, first published in 1658, illustrates the process I am describing.

[2] For the factual (though not legal) redistribution of fiscal burdens in Spain under Philip IV, see A. Domínguez Ortiz, 'La desigualidad contributiva en Castilla en el siglo XVIII', in *Anuario de historia del derecho español*, 1952.

[3] For these *arbitristas* of the eighteenth century, see Jean Sarrailh, *L'Espagne éclairée* (Paris, 1954) : which does not, however, bring out the extent to which Ward, Jovellanos, Campomanes, etc., were repeating the programme of the early seventeenth-century Spanish mercantilists — e.g. of Sancho de Moncada, whose work (originally dedicated to Philip III in 1619) was reprinted, dedicated to Ferdinand VI, in 1746.

rejected was their own Court, the greatest, most lavish Court of all, the Burgundian Court which, with the abdication of Charles V, had moved and made itself so fatally permanent in Spain. The revolt of the Netherlands in the sixteenth century was not, of course, a direct revolt of society against the Court. That is not how revolutions break out. But in the course of the long struggle the Court itself, in those provinces which freed themselves, was a casualty. There the whole apparatus of the Burgundian Court simply dissolved under the stress of war. So did the Burgundian Church, that huge, corrupt department of State which Philip II unskilfully sought to reform and whose abuses the great patrons of revolt, in the beginning, were seeking to preserve. Whatever the causes or motives of the revolution, the United Provinces emerged from it incidentally disembarrassed of that top-heavy system whose pressure, a generation later, would create a revolutionary situation in other countries. Consequently, in those provinces, there was no such revolutionary situation. The new Court of the Princes of Orange might develop some of the characteristics of the old Court of the dukes of Burgundy, but only some : and as it started lean, it could better afford a little additional fat. There were crises no doubt in seventeenth-century Holland — the crises of 1618, of 1650, of 1672 : but they were political crises, comparable with our crisis not of 1640 but of 1688 ; and they were surgically solved for the same reason : the social problem was no longer acute : the top-heavy apparatus of the State had been purged : society beneath was sound.

Moreover, if accident rather than design had rid the United Provinces of the Renaissance State, policy had also achieved there the other, economic reform of which I have written. It was not that there was a *bourgeois* or 'capitalist' revolution in Holland.[1] Dutch industry was relatively insignificant. But the new rulers

---

[1] That the economy of the United Provinces was not a new, revolutionary form of capitalism, but a return to the system of the medieval Italian cities, is argued by Mr Jelle C. Riemersma in his article 'Calvinism and Capitalism in Holland, 1550–1650', in *Explorations in Entrepreneurial History*, I (1), 8, and is admitted even by Marxists like Mr Dobb and Mr Hobsbawm. Mr Hobsbawm indeed goes so far as to call the Dutch economy 'a feudal business economy' (*Past and Present*, no. 6, 1954).

of Holland, seeking the means of guarding their hard-won freedom, set out to imitate the fortune and the methods of those older mercantile communities which had preserved their independence through centuries by rationally combining commercial wealth and maritime power. By adopting the techniques of Italy, welcoming the *émigré* experts of Antwerp, and following the old good rules of Venetian policy, Amsterdam became, in the seventeenth century, the new Venice of the north. The economic originality of seventeenth-century Holland consisted in showing that, even after the victory and reign of the Renaissance princes, whom they alone had driven out, the mercantilism of the cities was not dead : it could be revived.

Midway between completely unreformed Spain and completely reformed Holland lies what is perhaps the most interesting of all examples, Bourbon France. For France, in the seventeenth century, was certainly not immune from the general crisis, and in the Frondes it had a revolution, if a relatively small revolution. The result was, as in Spain, a victory for the monarchy. Triumphant over its critics and adversaries, the monarchy of the *ancien régime* survived in France, and survived for another century and a half. On the other hand the French monarchy of Louis XIV was not like the Spanish monarchy of Philip IV and Charles V. It was not economically parasitic. Industry, commerce, science flourished and grew in France, in spite of the 'failure' of the '*bourgeois* revolution', no less than in England, in spite of its 'success', To all appearances, in 1670, in the age of Colbert, absolutism and the *ancien régime* were perfectly compatible with commercial and industrial growth and power.

And indeed, why not ? For what had hindered such growth in the past, what had caused the crisis in society, was not the form of government, but its abuses ; and though these abuses might be removed by revolution, or might fall as incidental casualties of a revolution, their removal did not necessarily require revolution. There was always the way of reform. It is not necessary to burn down the house in order to have roast pig. And although France (like Holland) had had a fire in the sixteenth century, in which some of its burden of waste matter had been incidentally consumed, it did also, in the years thereafter, achieve some measure of reform. The fire, indeed, had prepared the ground. The French civil wars of the sixteenth century, if they had done much harm, had also done some good. They had burnt up the over-grown patronage of the great nobles and reduced the patronage of the Court to the patronage of the king. Henri IV, like the Prince of Orange, like Charles II of England after him, found himself at his accession disembarrassed of much ancient para-sitism: he could therefore afford to indulge a little new. And on this basis, this *tabula partim rasa*, he was able to achieve certain administrative changes. The *Paulette*, the law of 1604 which systematized the sale of offices, did at least regulate the abuses which it has often, and wrongly, been accused of creating. Sully, by his *économies royales*, did keep down the waste around the throne. And Richelieu, in the 1630s not only meditated a complete mer-cantilist policy for France: he also, even in the midst of war, succeeded — as Laud and Olivares, whether in peace or war, did not — in regulating that most expensive, most uncontrollable of all departments, the royal household.[1] Thanks to these changes, the *ancien régime* in France was repaired and strengthened. The changes may not have been radical, but they were enough — at least for the time being.

Of course the French solution was not permanent. The advan-tage of the French government, in the early seventeenth century, was simply that it had shed some of its burdens: it was less encumbered than the Spanish by the inheritance of the past. In the course of time the old weight would soon be resumed: the later reign of Louis XIV would be notorious for its plethora of offices and benefices, multiplied deliberately in order to be sold. And even in the earlier years, the pressure of war had the same effect. Again and again, as in Spain, there were demands that the venality of office be reformed or abolished; again and again the government considered such reform; but in the end, on each occasion, the French monarchy, like the Spanish, faced with the

[1] For Richelieu's mercantilism see H. Hauser, *La Pensée et l'action économique du cardinal de Richelieu* (Paris, 1944). For his reform of the royal household, see M. Roland Mousnier's article in vol. 1 of *Histoire de France*, ed. M. Reinhard (Paris, 1955).

demands of war, postponed its projects and instead of reforming, positively strengthened the system.[1] Richelieu at first, like Olivares in Spain, sought to combine war and reform, but in the end (again like Olivares) sacrificed reform to war. Marillac would have sacrificed war to reform.[2] By the end of the seventeenth century, Louis XIV would be financing his wars by massive creations of useless offices. But at the beginning of the century the position was different. Richelieu and Mazarin no doubt had other advantages in their successful struggle to maintain the French *ancien régime* in the era of the Huguenot revolt and the Frondes. They had an army absolutely under royal control; they had taxes whose increase fell not on gentry, assembled and vocal in Parliament, but on scattered, inarticulate peasants; and they had their own political genius. But they had also an apparatus of state which had already undergone some salutary reform: a State which, in the mind of Richelieu and in the hands of his disciple Colbert, could become a mercantilist State, rationally organized for both profit and power.

Finally there is England. In England the Crown had not the same political power as in France or Spain, and the taxes fell on the gentry, powerful in their counties and in Parliament. In England therefore, it was doubly important that the problem be faced and solved. How far was it in fact faced? To answer this question let us look in turn at the two sides of the problem, administrative and economic.

In the sixteenth century the apparatus of the English State had neither suffered nor benefited from any such destructive accident as had befallen Holland or France. The Renaissance Court of the Tudors, whose parsimony under Elizabeth had been so unreal and whose magnificence and ceremony had so impressed foreign visitors, survived intact into the new century, when its cost and show were magnified beyond all measure by King James and his favourites. Already in 1604, Francis Bacon warned the new king of the danger. The Court, he said, was like a nettle: its root,

---

[1] See Roland Mousnier, *La Vénalité des offices sous Henri IV et Louis XIV* (Rouen, n.d.), *passim*.

[2] See Georges Pagès, 'Autour du Grand Orage', in *Revue historique*, 1937.

the Crown itself, was 'without venom or malignity', but it sustained leaves 'venomous and stinging where they touch'.[1] Two years later, King James' greatest minister, Robert Cecil, Earl of Salisbury, apprehended revolution against the same burden of the Court; and in 1608, on becoming Lord Treasurer, he applied all his energies to a large and imaginative solution of the whole problem. He sought to rationalize the farming of taxes and the leasing of Crown lands, to reform the royal household, liberate agriculture from feudal restrictions and abolish archaic dues in exchange for other forms of income whose full yield, or something like it, instead of a mere fraction, would come to the Crown. In 1610 Salisbury staked his political career on this great programme of reorganization. But he failed to carry it through. The 'courtiers', the 'officers' who lived on the 'waste', mobilized opposition, and the king, listening to them, and thinking 'not what he got but what he might get' out of the old, wasteful, irritant sources of revenue, refused to surrender them. Within two years of his failure, Salisbury died, out of favour with the king, completely unlamented, even insulted by the whole Court which he had sought to reform and, by reform, to save.[2]

After Salisbury, other reformers occasionally took up the cause. The most brilliant was Francis Bacon. He had been an enemy of Salisbury, but once Salisbury was dead he sang the same tune. He diagnosed the evil — no man, perhaps, diagnosed it so completely in all its forms and ultimate consequences — but he could do nothing to cure it except by royal permission, which was refused, and he was overthrown. After his fall, in the years of the great depression, even the Court took alarm, and a new

[1] Francis Bacon, *Works*, ed. Spedding, III, 183.
[2] Public justice has never been done to Salisbury's programme of reform in 1608–12, although the 'Great Contract', which was only part of it, is well known. The evidence of it is scattered among the official papers of the time. Of contemporaries, only Sir Walter Cope and Sir William Sanderson, both of whom had been employed in it, sought to make it known and understood, but neither Cope's *Apology for the Late Lord Treasurer* (which was given to the king in manuscript) nor Sanderson's *Aulicus Coquinariae* was published at the time. Lord Ellesmere, Bishop Goodman and Sir Henry Wotton also appreciated it, but also did not publish their appreciation. See L. Pearsall Smith, *Life and Letters of Sir Henry Wotton* (1907), II, 487–9; Goodman, *The Court of King James I*, I, 36–42; and Ellesmere's paper entitled *Il dì loda la sera* in Huntington Library, Ellesmere MS. 1203.

reformer seemed to have obtained that permission. This was Lionel Cranfield, Earl of Middlesex, who set out to carry through some at least of Salisbury's proposals. But permission, if granted, was soon, and conspicuously withdrawn. Cranfield, like Bacon, was ruined by Court faction, led from above by the royal favourite, the Duke of Buckingham, the universal manager and profiteer of all those marketable offices, benefices, sinecures, monopolies, patents, perquisites and titles which together constituted the nourishment of the Court. Thus when Buckingham was murdered and Strafford and Laud, the 'Puritans of the right', came to power, they inherited from him an utterly unreformed Court.[1]

Did they do anything to reform it? Ostensibly they did. 'The face of the court', as Mrs Hutchinson wrote, 'was changed.' King Charles was outwardly frugal compared with his father: but such frugality, as we have seen in the case of Queen Elizabeth, was relatively insignificant. Laud and Strafford waged war on the corruption of the Court, whenever they perceived it; but they left the basic system untouched. Whenever we study that system we find that, in their time, its cost had not been reduced: it had grown. The greatest of Court feasts in Buckingham's days had been his own entertainment of the king in 1626, which had cost £4000; the Earl of Newcastle, in 1634, went up to £15,000. An office which was sold for £5000 in 1624 fetched £15,000 in 1640. Wardships, which had brought in £25,000 to the Crown when Salisbury had sought to abolish them in 1610, were made to yield £95,000 in 1640. And the proportion that ran to waste was no smaller. For every £100 which reached the Crown, at least £400 was taken from the subject. As Clarendon says, 'The envy and reproach came to the King, the profit to other men.'

---

[1] Bacon's projects are scattered through his writings, which Spedding collected. One only has to compare his various proposals for reform of the Court, the law, education, the Church, the Crown estates, etc., with the demands of the radical party in the 1640s, to see the truth of Gardiner's statement (in *Dictionary of National Biography*, s.v. Bacon) that his programme, if carried out, might have prevented the revolution. For Cranfield's work, see R. H. Tawney, *Business and Politics under James I* (1958), Menna Prestwich, *Cranfield* (Oxford, 1966).

Thus in 1640 the English Court, like the Spanish, was still unreformed. But what of the English economy ? Here the parallel no longer holds. For in England there was not that absolute divorce between Crown and *arbitristas* that was so obvious in Spain. The early Stuart governments did not ignore matters of trade. They listened to the City of London. By their financial methods, whether deliberately or not, they encouraged the formation of capital, its investment in industry. There were limits, of course, to what they did. They did not satisfy the systematic mercantilist theorists. They paid less attention to the base of society than to its summit. Nevertheless, in many respects, they favoured or at least allowed a mercantilist policy. They sought to naturalize industrial processes ; they sought to protect supplies of essential raw-materials ; they sought to monopolize the herring-fisheries ; they protected navigation ; they preferred peace abroad and looked to their moat. The years of their rule saw the growth of English capitalism, sponsored by them, on a scale unknown before. Unfortunately such growth entailed dislocation, claimed victims ; and when political crisis increased the dislocation and multiplied the victims, the stiff and weakened structure of government could no longer contain the mutinous forces which it had provoked.

For in 1640 the leaders of the Long Parliament did not seek — they did not need to seek — to reverse the economic policy of the Crown. They sought one thing only : to repair the administration. The Earl of Bedford as Lord Treasurer, John Pym as Chancellor of the Exchequer, intended to resume the frustrated work of Salisbury : to abolish monopolies, wardships, prerogative taxes, cut down the 'waste', and establish the Stuart Court on a more rational, less costly basis. Having done this, they would have continued the mercantilist policy of the Crown, perhaps extending it by redistribution of resources, and rationalization of labour, at the base of society. They would have done for the English monarchy what Colbert would do for the French. All they required was that the English monarchy, like the French, would allow them to do it.

For, of course, monarchy itself was no obstacle. It is absurd to say that such a policy was impossible without revolution. It was no more impossible in 1641 than it had been in the days of Salisbury and Cranfield. We cannot assume that merely human obstacles — the irresponsibility of a Buckingham or a Charles I, the reckless obscurantism of a Strafford — are inherent historical necessities. But in fact these human obstacles did intervene. Had James I or Charles I had the intelligence of Queen Elizabeth or the docility of Louis XIII, the English *ancien régime* might have adapted itself to the new circumstances as peacefully in the seventeenth century as it would in the nineteenth. It was because they had neither, because their Court was never reformed, because they defended it, in its old form, to the last, because it remained, administratively and economically as well as aesthetically, 'the last Renaissance Court in Europe', that it ran into ultimate disaster : that the rational reformers were swept aside, that more radical men came forward and mobilized yet more radical passions than even they could control, and that in the end, amid the sacking of palaces, the shivering of statues and stained-glass windows, the screech of saws in ruined organ-lofts, this last of the great Renaissance Courts was mopped up, the royal aesthete was murdered, his splendid pictures were knocked down and sold, even the soaring gothic cathedrals were offered up for scrap.

So, in the 1640s, in war and revolution, the most obstinate and yet, given the political structure of England, the frailest of the Renaissance monarchies went down. It did not go down before a new '*bourgeois* revolution'. It did not even go down before an old 'mercantilist revolution'. Its enemies were not the '*bourgeoisie*' — that *bourgeoisie* who, as a Puritan preacher complained, 'for a little trading and profit' would have had Christ, the Puritan soldiers, crucified and 'this great Barabbas at Windsor', the king, set free.[1] Nor were they the mercantilists. The ablest politicians among the Puritan rebels did indeed, once the republic was set up, adopt an aggressive mercantilist policy ; but in this they simply resumed the old policy of the Crown and, on that account, were promptly attacked and overthrown by the same enemies,

[1] The preacher was Hugh Peter, as quoted in *State Trials*, v (1), 129–30.

who accused them of betraying the revolution.[1] No, the triumphant enemies of the English Court were simply 'the country' : that indeterminate, unpolitical, but highly sensitive miscellany of men who had mutinied not against the monarchy (they had long clung to monarchist beliefs), nor against economic archaism (it was they who were the archaists), but against the vast, oppressive, ever-extending apparatus of parasitic bureaucracy which had grown up around the throne and above the economy of England. These men were not politicians or economists, and when the Court had foundered under their blows, they soon found that they could neither govern nor prosper. In the end they abdicated. The old dynasty was restored, its new mercantilist policy resumed. But the restoration was not complete. The old abuses, which had already dissolved in war and revolution, were not restored, and, having gone, were easily legislated out of existence. In 1661 Salisbury's 'Great Contract', Bedford's excise, were at last achieved. The old prerogative courts — whose offence had been not so much their policy as their existence — were not revived. Charles II began his reign free at last from the inherited lumber of the Renaissance Court.

Such, as it seems to me, was 'the general crisis of the seventeenth century'. It was a crisis not of the constitution nor of the system of production, but of the State, or rather, of the relation of the State to society. Different countries found their way out of that crisis in different ways. In Spain the *ancien régime* survived : but it survived only as a disastrous, immobile burden on an impoverished country. Elsewhere, in Holland, France and England, the crisis marked the end of an era : the jettison of a top-heavy superstructure, the return to responsible, mercantilist policy. For by the seventeenth century the Renaissance Courts had grown so great, had consumed so much in 'waste', and had sent their

---

[1] Those who regard the whole revolution as a *bourgeois* revolution on the strength of the mercantile policy of the Rump between 1651 and 1653 might well reflect (a) that this policy, of peace with Spain, navigation acts, and rivalry with Holland over fishery and trade, had been the policy of Charles I in the 1630s, and (b) that it was repudiated, emphatically and effectively, by those who had brought the revolution to a 'successful' issue — the Puritan army — and only revived at the Restoration of the monarchy.

multiplying suckers so deep into the body of society, that they could flourish only for a limited time, and in a time, too, of expanding general prosperity. When that prosperity failed, the monstrous parasite was bound to falter. In this sense, the depression of the 1620s is perhaps no less important, as a historical turning-point, than the depression of 1929 : though itself only a temporary economic failure, it marked a lasting political change.

At all events, the princely Courts recognized it as their crisis. Some of them sought to reform themselves, to take physic and reduce their bulk. Their doctors pointed the way : it was then that the old city-states, and particularly Venice, though now in decadence, became the admired model, first of Holland, then of England. And yet, asked the patient, was such reform possible, or even safe ? Could a monarchy really be adapted to a pattern which so far had been dangerously republican ? Is any political operation more difficult than the self-reduction of an established, powerful, privileged bureaucracy ? In fact, the change was nowhere achieved without something of revolution. If it was limited in France, and Holland, that was partly because some of the combustible rubbish had already, in a previous revolution, been consumed. It was also because there had been some partial reform. In England there had been no such previous revolution, no such partial reform. There was also, under the early Stuarts, a fatal lack of political skill : instead of the genius of Richelieu, the suppleness of Mazarin, there was the irresponsibility of Buckingham, the violence of Strafford, the undeviating universal pedantry of Laud. In England, therefore, the storm of the mid-century, which blew throughout Europe, struck the most brittle, most overgrown, most rigid Court of all and brought it violently down.

3 The European Witch-craze of the Sixteenth and Seventeenth Centuries

I

The European witch-craze of the sixteenth and seventeenth centuries is a perplexing phenomenon : a standing warning to those who would simplify the stages of human progress. Ever since the eighteenth century we have tended to see European history, from the Renaissance onwards, as the history of progress, and that progress has seemed to be constant. There may have been local variations, local obstacles, occasional setbacks, but the general pattern is one of persistent advance. The light continually, if irregularly, gains at the expense of darkness. Renaissance, Reformation, Scientific Revolution mark the stages of our emancipation from medieval restraints. This is natural enough. When we look back through history we naturally see first those men, those ideas, that point forward to us. But when we look deeper, how much more complex the pattern seems ! Neither the Renaissance nor the Reformation nor the Scientific Revolution are, in our terms, purely or necessarily progressive. Each has a Janus-face. Each is compounded both of light and of darkness. The Renaissance was a revival not only of pagan letters but of pagan mystery-religion. The Reformation was a return not only to the unforgettable century of the Apostles but also to the unedifying centuries of the Hebrew kings. The Scientific Revolution was shot through with Pythagorean mysticism and cosmological fantasy. And beneath the surface of an ever more sophisticated society what dark passions and inflammable credulities do we find, sometimes accidentally released, sometimes deliberately mobilized ! The belief in witches is one such force. In the sixteenth and seventeenth centuries it was not, as the

prophets of progress might suppose, a lingering ancient superstition, only waiting to dissolve. It was a new explosive force,
constantly and fearfully expanding with the passage of time. In
those years of apparent illumination there was at least one-quarter
of the sky in which darkness was positively gaining at the expense
of light.

Yes, gaining. Whatever allowance we may make for the mere
multiplication of the evidence after the discovery of printing,
there can be no doubt that the witch-craze grew, and grew terribly,
after the Renaissance. Credulity in high places increased, its
engines of expression were made more terrible, more victims
were sacrificed to it. The years 1550–1600 were worse than the
years 1500–1550, and the years 1600–1650 were worse still. Nor
was the craze entirely separable from the intellectual and spiritual
life of those years. It was forwarded by the cultivated popes of
the Renaissance, by the great Protestant reformers, by the saints
of the Counter-Reformation, by the scholars, lawyers and churchmen of the age of Scaliger and Lipsius, Bacon and Grotius,
Bérulle and Pascal. If those two centuries were an age of light,
we have to admit that, in one respect at least, the Dark Age was
more civilized.

For in the Dark Age there was at least no witch-craze. There
were witch-beliefs, of course — a scattered folk-lore of peasant
superstitions : the casting of spells, the making of storms, con-
verse with spirits, sympathetic magic. Such beliefs are universal,
in time and place, and in this essay I am not concerned with them.
I am concerned with the organized, systematic 'demonology'
which the medieval Church constructed out of those beliefs and
which, in the sixteenth and seventeenth centuries, acquired a
terrible momentum of its own. And when we make this necessary distinction between the organized witch-craze and the
miscellaneous witch-beliefs out of which it was constructed, we
have to admit that the Church of the Dark Age did its best to
disperse these relics of paganism which the Church of the Middle
Ages would afterwards exploit. Of course it was not entirely
successful. Some of the pagan myths, like pagan gods and pagan
rites, had crept into the Christian synthesis at an early date and

had found lodgment in its outer crannies. St Augustine in particular, with his baroque mind and African credulity, did much to
preserve them : they form an incidental bizarre decoration of the
huge doctrinal construction which his authority launched into
western Christendom. But in general, the Church, as the civilizer
of nations, disdained these old wives' tales. They were the frag-
mentary rubbish of paganism which the light of the Gospel had
dispelled.

So, in the eighth century, we find St Boniface, the English
apostle of Germany, declaring roundly that to believe in witches
and werewolves is unchristian.[1] In the same century Charlemagne decreed the death penalty for anyone who, in newly converted Saxony, burnt supposed witches. Such burning, he said,
was 'a pagan custom'.[2] In the next century St Agobard,[3] Bishop
of Lyon, repudiated the belief that witches could make bad
weather, and another unknown Church dignitary declared that
night-flying and metamorphosis were hallucinations and that
whoever believed in them 'is beyond doubt an infidel and a
pagan'. This statement was accepted into the canon law and
became known as the *canon Episcopi* or *capitulum Episcopi*.[4] It
remained the official doctrine of the Church. In the eleventh
century the laws of King Coloman of Hungary declined to notice
witches 'since they do not exist',[5] and the twelfth-century John
of Salisbury dismissed the idea of a witches' sabbat as a fabulous
dream.[6] In the succeeding centuries, when the craze was being
built up, all this salutary doctrine would have to be reversed.
The laws of Charlemagne and Coloman would be forgotten ; to
deny the reality of night-flying and metamorphosis would be
officially declared heretical ; the witches' sabbat would become

[1] Sermon xv, cited in *Materials toward a History of Witchcraft collected by H. C. Lea*,
arranged and edited by Arthur C. Howland, with an introduction by George
Lincoln Burr (New York, 1957), pp. 178–82 ; hereafter cited as Lea, *Materials*.
(See also below, p. 99.)
[2] *Capitulatio de Partibus Saxoniae*, cap. 6. This decree, issued at Paderborn in
A.D. 785, is printed in Wilhelm Boudriot, *Die alt-germanische Religion* (*Untersuchungen
zur allgemeinen Religionsgeschichte*, ed. Carl Clemen, Heft 2, Bonn, 1928, p. 53).
[3] In his *Liber contra insulsam vulgi opinionem de grandine et tonitruis*, written c. A.D. 820.
[4] Lea, *Materials*, pp. 178–82.
[5] Ibid., p. 1252.   [6] Ibid., p. 172.

an objective fact, disbelieved only (as a doctor of the Sorbonne would write in 1609 [1]) by those of unsound mind ; and the ingenuity of churchmen and lawyers would be taxed to explain away that inconvenient text of canon law, the *canon Episcopi*.

By the end of the Middle Ages this reversal would be complete. By 1490, after two centuries of research, the new, positive doctrine of witchcraft would be established in its final form. From then on it would be simply a question of applying this doctrine : of seeking, finding and destroying the witches whose organization has been defined.

The monks of the late Middle Ages sowed : the lawyers of the sixteenth century reaped ; and what a harvest of witches they gathered in ! All Christendom, it seems, is at the mercy of these horrifying creatures. Countries in which they had previously been unknown are now suddenly found to be swarming with them, and the closer we look, the more of them we find. All contemporary observers agree that they are multiplying at an incredible rate. They have acquired powers hitherto unknown, a complex international organization and social habits of indecent sophistication. Some of the most powerful minds of the time turn from the human sciences to explore this newly discovered continent, this America of the spiritual world. And the details which they discover, and which are continually being confirmed by teams of parallel researchers — field researchers in torture-chamber or confessional, academic researchers in library or cloister — leave the facts more certainly established and the prospect more alarming than ever.

Consider the situation as shown at any time in the half-century from 1580 to 1630 : that half-century which corresponds with the mature life of Bacon and brings together Montaigne and Descartes. The merest glance at any report by the acknowledged experts of the time reveals an alarming state of affairs. By their own confession, thousands of old women — and not only old women — had made secret pacts with the Devil, who had now emerged as a great spiritual potentate, the Prince of Darkness,

---

[1] *Joannis Filesaci Theologi Parisiensis Opera Varia*, 2nd ed. (Paris, 1614), pp. 703 ff., 'de Idololatria Magica Dissertatio', Dedication.

bent on recovering his lost empire. Every night these ill-advised
ladies were anointing themselves with 'devil's grease', made out
of the fat of murdered infants, and, thus lubricated, were slipping
through cracks and keyholes and up chimneys, mounting on
broomsticks or spindles or airborne goats, and flying off on a
long and inexpressibly wearisome aerial journey to a diabolical
rendezvous, the witches' sabbat. In every country there were
hundreds of such sabbats, more numerous and more crowded
than race-meetings or fairs. There were no less than 800 known
meeting-places in Lorraine alone. Some countries had national,
some international centres. Such were the Blocksberg or Brocken
in the Harz Mountains of Germany, the 'delicate large meadow'
called Blåkulla in Sweden and the great resort of La Hendaye
in south-west France where no less than 12,000 witches would
assemble for the gathering known as the *Aquelarre*. The meetings
too were remarkably frequent. At first the interrogators in
Lorraine thought that they occurred only once a week, on
Thursday; but, as always, the more the evidence was pressed,
the worse the conclusions that it yielded. Sabbats were found
to take place on Monday, Wednesday, Friday and Sunday, and
soon Tuesday was found to be booked as a by-day. It was all
very alarming and proved the need of ever greater vigilance by
the spiritual police.

And what happened when the witch had reached the sabbat?
The unedifying details, alas, were only too well authenticated.
First, she was surprised to observe nearly all her friends and
neighbours, whom she had not previously suspected to be
witches. With them there were scores of demons, their paramours, to whom they had bound themselves by the infernal pact;
and above all, dominating them all, was the imperious master of
ceremonies, the god of their worship, the Devil himself, who
appeared sometimes as a big, black, bearded man, more often as
a stinking goat, occasionally as a great toad. Those present
recognized their master. They all joined to worship the Devil
and danced around him to the sound of macabre music made
with curious instruments — horses' skulls, oak-logs, human
bones, etc. Then they kissed him in homage, under the tail if

he were a goat, on the lips if he were a toad. After which, at the
word of command from him, they threw themselves into promiscuous sexual orgies or settled down to a feast of such viands
as tempted their national imagination. In Germany these were
sliced turnips, parodies of the Host; in Savoy, roast or boiled
children; in Spain, exhumed corpses, preferably of kinsfolk; in
Alsace, fricassées of bats; in England, more sensibly, roast beef
and beer. But these nice distinctions of diet made little difference:
the food, all agreed, was cold and quite tasteless, and one necessary ingredient, salt, for some arcane demonological reason, was
never admitted.

Such was the witches' sabbat, the collective orgy and com-
munal religious worship of the new diabolical religion. In the
intervals between these acts of public devotion, the old ladies had,
of course, good works to do in the home. They occupied themselves by suckling familiar spirits in the form of weasels, moles,
bats, toads or other convenient creatures; by compassing the
death of their neighbours or their neighbours' pigs; by raising
tempests, causing blights or procuring impotence in bridegrooms;
and as a pledge of their servitude they were constantly having
sexual intercourse with the Devil, who appeared (since even he
abhors unnatural vice [1]) to she-witches as an *incubus*, to he-witches
as a *succubus*.

What Gibbon called 'the chaste severity of the Fathers' was
much exercised by this last subject, and no detail escaped their
learned scrutiny. As a lover, they established, the Devil was of
'freezing coldness' to the touch; his embrace gave no pleasure —
on the contrary, only pain; and certain items were lacking in his
equipment. But there was no frigidity in the technical sense:
his attentions were of formidable, even oppressive solidity. That
he could generate on witches was agreed by some doctors (how
else, asked the Catholic theologians, could the birth of Luther
be explained?); but some denied this, and others insisted that
only certain worm-like creatures, known in Germany as *Elben*,
could issue from such unions. Moreover, there was considerable

---

[1] Except, apparently, in Alsace. See R. Reuss, *L'Alsace au 17ᵉ siècle* (Paris, 1898),
II, 106. Elsewhere 'the nobleness of his nature' repudiates it.

doubt whether the Devil's generative power was his own, as a Franciscan specialist maintained ('under correction from our Holy Mother Church'), or whether he, being neuter, operated with borrowed matter. A nice point of theology was here involved and much interested erudition was expended on it in cloistered solitudes. Some important theologians conjectured that the Devil equipped himself by squeezing the organs of the dead. This view was adopted (among others) by our King James.[1] Other experts advanced other theories, more profound than decent. But on the whole, Holy Mother Church followed the magisterial ruling of the Angelic Doctor, St Thomas Aquinas, who, after St Augustine, must be regarded as the second founder of demonological science. According to him, the Devil could discharge as *incubus* only what he had previously absorbed as *succubus*. He therefore nimbly alternated between these postures . . . There are times when the intellectual fantasies of the clergy seem more bizarre than the psychopathic delusions of the madhouse out of which they have, too often, been excogitated.

Such were the human witches, the fifth column of Satan on earth, his front-line agents in the struggle for control of the spiritual world. All through the sixteenth century, and for much of the seventeenth, men believed in the reality of this struggle. Laymen might not accept all the esoteric details supplied by the experts, but they accepted the general truth of the theory, and because they accepted its general truth, they were unable to argue against its more learned interpreters. So the experts effectively commanded the field. For two centuries the clergy preached against witches and the lawyers sentenced them. Year after year inflammatory books and sermons warned the Christian public of the danger, urged the Christian magistrate to greater vigilance, greater persecution. Confessors and judges were supplied with manuals incorporating all the latest information, village hatreds were exploited in order to ensure exposure, torture was used to extract and expand confessions, and lenient judges were denounced as enemies of the people of God, drowsy guardians of the beleaguered citadel. Perhaps these 'patrons of witches'

[1] James VI, *Demonologie, in form of a Dialogue* . . . (Edinburgh, 1597), pp. 66 ff.

were witches themselves. In the hour of danger, when it almost seemed that Satan was about to take over the world, his agents were found to be everywhere, even in judges' seats, in university chairs and on royal thrones.

But did this campaign against the witches in fact reduce their number? Not at all. The more fiercely they were persecuted, the more numerous they seemed to become. By the beginning of the seventeenth century the witch-doctors have become hysterical. Their manuals have become encyclopaedic in bulk, lunatic in pedantry. They demand, and sometimes achieve, wholesale purges. By 1630 the slaughter has broken all previous records. It has become a holocaust in which lawyers, judges, clergy themselves join old women at the stake. That at least, if nothing else, must have enforced an agonizing reappraisal.

And indeed, it was in the wake of the greatest of all purges — perhaps in revulsion after it — that the solidity of the witch-hunters began to give way. In the middle of the seventeenth century — in the 1650s — scepticism, unavailing hitherto, begins at last to break through. Imperceptibly, the whole basis of the craze begins to dissolve, in Catholic and Protestant countries alike. By the 1680s the battle is effectively won, at least in the west. The old habits of mind may linger on; there will be pockets of resistance here and there, recurrence of persecution now and then, but somehow the vital force behind it is spent. Though the argument may go on, the witch-trials and witch-burnings have become once again mere sporadic episodes, as they had been before the Renaissance. The rubbish of the human mind which for two centuries, by some process of intellectual alchemy and social pressure, had become fused together in a coherent, explosive system, has disintegrated. It is rubbish again.

How are we to explain this extraordinary episode in European history? In the eighteenth century, when the men of the Enlightenment looked back on this folly of 'the last age', they saw it merely as evidence of the 'superstition' from which they had recently been emancipated, and the nineteenth-century historians, who approached it in a more detached, scientific spirit, interpreted their more abundant material in the same general

97

terms. To the German Wilhelm Gottlieb Soldan,[1] the first historian of the craze, the witch-cult was a legacy of Greco-Roman antiquity, naturally developed, artificially preserved. To him, as to the Englishman W. E. H. Lecky, its gradual conquest was one aspect of the rise of 'rationalism' in Europe.[2] To the American Andrew Dickson White it was a campaign in 'the warfare of science with theology'.[3] But none of these scholars sought to explain why the centuries of Renaissance and Reformation were so much less 'rational', less 'scientific' than the Dark and early Middle Ages. Even the profoundest of nineteenth-century historians of witchcraft, Joseph Hansen, the liberal, free-thinking archivist of Cologne, hardly faced this problem. In two important works [4] he collected a mass of documentary material and presented a lucid narrative of 'the rise of the great witch-craze'; but as he aimed only to document its origins, he concluded his work once he had brought it to the early sixteenth century, when 'the system of the new witch-craze had achieved its final form'.[5] The fact that, in this final form, the craze was to last for two centuries, and those the centuries of Renaissance, Reformation and experimental science, did indeed perplex him. He suggested that the explanation lay in the survival of 'the medieval spirit'. This answer, says the modern historian of magic, is 'unconvincing'.[6] But is his own explanation any more convincing? The witch-craze, says Lynn Thorndike (echoing Michelet [7]), grew

---

[1] W. G. Soldan, *Geschichte der Hexenprozesse* (Stuttgart, 1843). Soldan's pioneering work has been twice reprinted, each time with substantial additions and revisions: first by his own son-in-law Heinrich Heppe in 1879; secondly, under the double name of Soldan-Heppe, by Max Bauer in 1911. The differences between the first and the last edition are so great that in this essay I shall always distinguish them, citing the original work as Soldan and the later edition as Soldan-Heppe.

[2] W. E. H. Lecky, *History of the Rise and Influence of the Spirit of Rationalism in Europe* (1865). My references to this work will be to the edition of 1900.

[3] A. D. White, *A History of the Warfare of Science with Theology, in Christendom* (New York, 1897).

[4] Joseph Hansen, *Quellen und Untersuchungen zur Geschichte des Hexenwahns und der Hexenverfolgung im Mittelalter* (Bonn, 1901); *Zauberwahn, Inquisition und Hexenprozess im Mittelalter* (Munich, 1900); hereafter cited as *Quellen* and *Zauberwahn* respectively.

[5] Hansen, *Zauberwahn*, p. 473.

[6] Lynn Thorndike, in *Cambridge Medieval History*, VIII, § xxii, 686–7.

[7] Jules Michelet, *La Sorcière* (Paris, 1862). My references are to the edition Garnier-Flammarion, 1966.

naturally out of the misery of the fourteenth century, that century of the Black Death and the Hundred Years War. These disasters no doubt helped; but they do not explain. As Hansen had already observed, the craze gathered force before either of them had begun, and it continued, in its 'final form', for two centuries after both were over: two centuries not of misery, but of European recovery and expansion.

While Hansen was writing about the witch-craze in Germany, another great historian was thinking about it in America. In his youth H. C. Lea had begun a work on 'man's assumed control over spiritual forces' in which he hoped to deal with the whole question of witchcraft in the world; but illness interrupted it, and he afterwards deviated into what he described as the 'by-path' of 'a simpler and less brain-fatiguing amusement'. In other words, he wrote his two monumental works on the medieval and the Spanish Inquisition.[1] But the Inquisition cannot be divorced from the subject of witchcraft and in both works Lea found himself brought up against it. In his history of the medieval Inquisition, he showed the gradual merging of sorcery and heresy, and in his Spanish studies he showed that in Spain, 'thanks to the good sense of the Inquisition', the witch-craze 'was much less dreadful than in the rest of Europe'. It was not till he was eighty-one that Lea returned to his original subject. He collected, annotated and arranged a vast mass of material covering the whole history of witchcraft in Christendom; but when he died, the book itself was unwritten. His material, however, has been edited and published,[2] and his interpretation is clear from his notes, as also from his earlier works.

Lea is one of the greatest of liberal historians. It is inconceivable that his work on the Inquisition, as an objective narrative of fact, will ever be replaced. Its solidity has withstood all partisan criticism. His 'History of Witchcraft', had it been written, would no doubt have stood as firm. Nevertheless, as interpreters of social history, even the greatest of the

[1] H. C. Lea, *The History of the Inquisition in the Middle Ages* (London and New York, 1888); *The History of the Inquisition in Spain* (New York, 1906).

[2] See above, p. 92, n. 1.

nineteenth-century liberal historians now seem to date. Their philosophy was formed in the happy years before 1914, when men could look back on the continuous progress, since the seventeenth century, of 'reason', toleration, humanity, and see the constant improvement of society as the effect of the constant progress of liberal ideas. Against such a background it was natural to see the witch-craze of the past, like the persecution of Moors and Jews, or the use of torture, or the censorship of books, as a residue of mere obscurantism which growing enlightenment had gradually dispelled, and which would now never return.

Unfortunately, we have seen them return. With the advantage of after-knowledge, we look back and we see that even while the liberal historians were writing, their olympian philosophy was being threatened from beneath. It was in the 1890s that the intellectual foundations of a new witch-craze were being laid. It was then that *The Protocols of the Elders of Zion* were forged in France and the grotesque mythology of anti-semitism was used to inspire the pogroms of eastern Europe. To the liberals of the time this new form of superstition was beneath contempt. At most, it was a lingering survival of past superstition. We who have seen its vast and hideous consequences cannot accept so comforting an explanation. Faced by the recrudescence, even in civilized societies, of barbarous fantasies in no way less bizarre and far more murderous than the witch-craze, we have been forced to think again, and thinking, to devalue the power of mere thought. Even intellectual history, we now admit, is relative and cannot be dissociated from the wider, social context with which it is in constant interaction.

This being so, we are prepared to admit, as our ancestors were not, that mental structures differ with social structures, that the 'superstition' of one age may be the 'rationalism' of another, and that the explanation of intellectual change may have to be sought outside purely intellectual history. We cannot see the long persistence and even aggravation of the witch-craze merely as a necessary effect of clerical domination, or its dissolution as the logical consequence of release from religious fundamentalism. Therefore we may be forgiven for looking at this whole episode, whose basic facts, thanks to the work of our predecessors, are not in dispute, with eyes different from theirs. They saw, through all the centuries, a continuous dialogue between superstition, whose form constantly varied, and reason, which was always the same. We agree with one of the most perceptive and philosophical of modern French historians, that the mind of one age is not necessarily subject to the same rules as the mind of another, that 'dans sa structure profonde, la mentalité des hommes les plus éclairés de la fin du XVIᵉ siècle, du début du XVIIᵉ siècle, ait différé, et radicalement, de la mentalité des hommes les plus éclairés de notre temps'.[1]

II

When Hansen wrote that the system of the new witch-craze had achieved its final form by the 1480s, he was referring to the two documents of that decade from which the centralized European witch-craze, as distinct from spasmodic local outbursts, can be dated. The first of these is the papal bull *Summis Desiderantes Affectibus*, issued by Pope Innocent VIII in December 1484, deploring the spread of witchcraft in Germany and authorizing his beloved sons, the Dominican inquisitors Heinrich Institor (Krämer) and Jakob Sprenger, to extirpate it. The second is the earliest great printed encyclopaedia of demonology, the *Malleus Maleficarum*, 'the Hammer of Witches', published by these same two inquisitors two years later, in 1486. The relationship between these two documents is perfectly clear : they are complementary one to the other. The papal bull had been solicited by the inquisitors, who wished for support in their attempt to launch the witch-craze in the Rhineland. Having obtained it, they printed it in their book, as if the book had been written in response to the bull. The book thus advertised to all Europe both the new epidemic of witchcraft and the authority which had been given to them to suppress it.

The importance of the papal bull of 1484 is incontestable.

[1] L. Fèbvre, 'Sorcellerie : sottise ou révolution mentale', in *Annales : économies, sociétés, civilisation*, 1948, p. 14.

Apologists for the papacy have protested that it made no change : it was merely a routine document which authorized the Dominicans to go on doing what they were already doing and told other authorities — bishops and secular powers — not to obstruct their work.[1] No doubt it did this ; but it also did something else, which was new. What the Dominicans had been doing hitherto was local. They had been persecuting and burning witches locally. From now on a general mandate was given, or implied. And the *Malleus*, which is inseparable from the bull, gave force and substance to that mandate. First, by its content, by gathering together all the curiosities and credulities of Alpine peasants and their confessors, it built up a solid basis for the new mythology. Secondly, by its universal circulation, it carried this mythology, as a truth recognized by the Church, over all Christendom. Finally, the *Malleus* explicitly called on other authorities, lay and secular, not merely not to obstruct, but positively to assist the inquisitors in their task of exterminating witches. From now on, the persecution, which had been sporadic, was — at least in theory — made general, and secular authorities were encouraged to use the methods and mythology of the Inquisition. Rome had spoken.

Why did Rome speak ? Why did Innocent VIII, that worldly humanist, the patron of Mantegna and Pinturicchio, Perugino and Filippino Lippi, yield to these fanatical Dominican friars ? The answer, obviously, is not to be sought in his personality. It is to be sought rather in circumstances : in the historical situation out of which the witch-beliefs had arisen and in the war which the Dominican inquisitors had long been waging against them. This question brings us at once to a particular area, the area in which these beliefs had always been endemic and in which, for two centuries, they had already been persecuted : the mountain areas of Catholic Europe, the Alps and the Pyrenees.

The mountain origin of the witch-craze is by now well established. So are the circumstances in which it was formulated, and in which the Dominicans came to be its great adversaries. These circumstances bring us back to the very foundation of the order,

---

[1] This is the argument of Ludwig Pastor, *History of the Popes*, v, 2nd English ed. (1901), 347.

in the struggle between the Catholic Church and the heretics of the twelfth century, the Albigensians of Languedoc and the Vaudois of the Alps. It was to combat these heretics that the Inquisition and the Dominican order had been founded, and it was in the course of that 'crusade' that the inquisitors had discovered, beneath the forms of one heresy, the rudiments (as they thought) of another. From an early date, therefore, they had pressed the Pope to grant them jurisdiction over withcraft as well as over recognized theological heresy. To the Dominicans the two forms of error were inseparable : one continued the other, and the pursuit must not cease when the formal error had disappeared underground. They could still recognize it by its smell. So, although the form might seem to change, the old names persisted. By the fifteenth century we hear little of Vaudois or Cathari as theological terms : those errors had been burnt out, at least for a time. But in the Alps, in the Lyonnais and in Flanders witches are known as *Waudenses* and their gatherings as a *Valdesia* or *Vauderye*, and in the Pyrenees we find them described as *Gazarii* or 'Cathars'.[1]

When the Dominicans pressed for inquisitorial power over witchcraft, the papacy had at first resisted. The old canons of the Church, and particularly the *canon Episcopi*, denied the reality of witches and forbade their persecution. Therefore, in 1257, Pope Alexander IV had refused these demands unless manifest heresy, not merely witchcraft, could be proved. But little by little, under constant pressure, the papacy had yielded. The great surrender had been made by the French popes of Avignon, and particularly by the two popes from southern France, John XXII and his successor Benedict XII, who had already, as bishops in Languedoc, waged war on nonconformity in the old Albigensian and Vaudois areas. John XXII, who declared heretical the Franciscan doctrine of the poverty of Christ (so dangerously akin to the old Vaudois ideas), also, by his constitution *Super illius specula* of 1326, authorized the full use of inquisitorial procedure against witches, of whom he lived in personal terror. For the

[1] For instances of the use of the term *Vauderye*, see especially Hansen, *Quellen*, pp. 408–15 ; *Zauberwahn*, pp. 409–18. For *Gazarii*, see *Quellen*, pp. 118, 232.

next century and a half — until the Witch Bull of Innocent VIII,
and indeed afterwards — the main effort of the inquisitors (although there were some spectacular 'political' witchcraft trials
in France, Burgundy and England) had been directed against the
witches of the Alps and the Pyrenees.

At first the campaign was most vigorous in the Pyrenees. From
the papacy of John XXII onwards, witch-trials were held all over
the old Albigensian territory ; but soon they spread to the Alps
also. The sitting of the Council of the Church in Basel in 1435–
1437 gave a great opportunity to the local witch-hunters, and it
was in those years that a zealous inquisitor, John Nider, wrote
what has been called 'the first popular essay on witches'.[1] It
was called *Formicarius*, 'the Ant-heap', and was based principally
on confessions of Swiss witches collected by a Swiss magistrate,
Peter of Berne. The *Formicarius* may be regarded as a little
Malleus, and it had a similar effect in a more restricted field.
Papal instructions were sent out to the witch-inquisitors to
redouble their zeal, and in 1440, the Pope took the opportunity
to denounce his rival, ' that eldest son of Satan, Amadeus, Duke
of Savoy', as having given himself over to the witches 'or
Vaudois' who abound in his land.[2] In the next hundred years
some famous inquisitors were busy in the Alpine valleys — Bernard
of Como, Jerome Visconti, Bartolomeo Spina. In 1485, according
to the *Malleus*, the inquisitor of Como burnt forty-one witches,
all of whom confessed to sexual intercourse with *incubi*, and yet
even so the practice was increasing. This was the point of time
at which the Witch Bull and the *Malleus* were published.

Meanwhile the Pyrenean inquisitors, after a temporary lull, had
resumed their activities. In 1450 they too produced a little
Malleus. This was a tract by Jean Vineti, Dominican inquisitor
of Carcassonne : the first work, it seems, to declare that witchcraft was a new heresy, unconnected with the old rural beliefs
which the Church of the past had tolerated. This separation of
the new witchcraft from the old was a point of great technical

---

[1] G. L. Burr, 'The Literature of Witchcraft', in *George Lincoln Burr: his Life
and Selections from his Writings* (Ithaca, N.Y., 1943), p. 166. This volume will hereafter be cited as Burr, *Life*.   [2] Hansen, *Quellen*, p. 18.

importance. Indeed, we can say that it gave the witch-craze its charter : for it enabled the inquisitors to get round the greatest obstacle in the way of witch-persecution : the *canon Episcopi*.[1] About the same time witch-beliefs were found to have spread to the Spanish slopes of the Pyrenees and the King of Castile was invited to take action against them.[2]

Thus by the time that the authors of the *Malleus* obtained the blessing of Pope Innocent VIII, the craze had already been in operation for nearly two centuries in the mountain areas, the old homes of heresy and centres of inquisitorial persecution. The two authors of the *Malleus*, the solicitors of the bull, were themselves natives of the Alpine regions, and all their examples and cases are drawn from upper Germany. The most active of the pair was Krämer, who was inquisitor in the Tyrol ; he afterwards became inquisitor in Bohemia and Moravia, where he acted vigorously against the 'Waldenses' of Bohemia as well as against witches.[3]

The Alps and the Pyrenees, the original cradle of the witch-craze, would long remain its base. Individual witches, of course, might be found anywhere, and in certain circumstances might infect whole areas : for the old unorganized superstitions of the countryside were always there, always ready to be inflamed. Isolated rural societies anywhere — in the dreary flats of the Landes in France, or of Essex in England, or in the sandy plain of north Germany — would always be subject to witch-beliefs. Psychopathic disturbances, which could easily be rationalized as witchcraft, are independent of geography. Individual inquisitors, too, would discover or create beliefs in any area in which they happened to operate : Krämer and Sprenger would have plenty of counterparts among the Protestant clergy — and among the laity too, like Matthew Hopkins, the famous 'witch-finder general' of the English civil war. But these are secondary developments, individual extensions. As a continuing social

[1] For Vineti's *Tractatus contra Daemonum Invocatores*, see Lea, *Materials*, p. 272.

[2] Julio Caro Baroja, *Las brujas y su mundo*, Madrid, 1961 (English trans. N. Glendinning, *The World of the Witches*, 1964, pp. 103, 143–5).

[3] For the history of the *Malleus* and its authors, see Hansen, *Quellen*, pp. 360–407, *Zauberwahn*, pp. 473 ff.

phenomenon, involving not merely individuals but whole societies, the witch-craze would always be associated particularly with the highlands. The great European witch-hunts would centre upon the Alps and their foothills, the Jura and the Vosges, and upon the Pyrenees and their extensions in France and Spain. Switzerland, Franche-Comté, Savoy, Alsace, Lorraine, the Valtelline, the Tyrol, Bavaria and the north Italian bishoprics of Milan, Brescia and Bergamo ; Béarn, Navarre and Catalonia : these would be the primary centres. Here the new heresy had been discovered, hence it would be generalized. From the fantasies of mountain peasants, the Dominicans elaborated their systematic demonology and enabled or compelled Renaissance popes to denounce a new heresy in Europe. The heads of the old Albigensian and Vaudois heresy were sprouting again.

This prevalence of witchcraft, and of illusions that can be interpreted as witchcraft, in mountainous areas doubtless has a physical explanation. Rural poverty, as Michelet observed, naturally drives men to invoke the spirits of revenge.[1] The thin air of the mountains breeds hallucinations, and the exaggerated phenomena of nature — the electric storms, the avalanches, the cracking and calving of the mountain ice — easily lead men to believe in demonic activity.[2] But these explanations, by themselves, are not enough. Rural poverty, after all, was a commonplace of all centuries. So, no doubt, were some of the beliefs that it engenders. The superstitions of the mountain are but exaggerations of the superstitions of the plain. Why then, we ask, did the Dominicans wage such war on them ? Why did they insist on seeing them as something different from the superstitions which, in the plain, the Church had so long tolerated or ignored ? What was the underlying, permanent difference which the Dominicans rationalized as successive layers of 'heresy' ?

Sometimes, no doubt, it was a difference of race. The Basques, for instance, were racially distinct from the latinized Germans — Franks and the Visigoths — around them. But difference of race,

[1] 'D'où date la sorcière ? Je dis sans hésiter, des temps du désespoir', Jules Michelet, *La Sorcière*. Introduction.
[2] Cf. Hansen, *Zauberwahn*, pp. 400–2 ; Lea, *Materials*, p. 245.

though it may sharpen other differences, is not in itself decisive. It is only when it corresponds with difference of social organiza- tion that conflict or incompatibility arises ; and then it is the social difference which decides. In the Middle Ages the men of the mountains differed from the men of the plains in social organization, and therefore they also differed in those customs and patterns of belief which grow out of social organization and, in the course of centuries, consecrate it. Theirs, we may almost say, were different civilizations.

Medieval civilization, 'feudal' civilization, was a civilization of the plains, or at least of the cultivated lands which could sustain the manor and its organization. In the poor mountain areas, pastoral and individualist, this 'feudalism' had never fully estab- lished itself. Sometimes Christianity itself had hardly penetrated thither, or at least it had not been maintained there in comparable form. Missionaries might have carried the Gospel into the hills, but a settled Church had not institutionalized it, and in those closed societies a lightly rooted orthodoxy was easily turned to heresy or even infidelity. M. Fernand Braudel, in his incomparable work on the Mediterranean, has commented, briefly but brilliantly, on this fact. He has pointed to isolated mountain societies long untouched, or only superficially touched, by the religion of state and easily — if as superficially — converted to the heresy of new evangelists or the religion of a sudden conqueror. The conver- sion of the mountains to Christianity — or, for that matter, to Islam — (he writes) was far from complete in the sixteenth cen- tury ; and he refers to the Berbers of the Atlas mountains, and the highland Kurds in Asia, so slowly won for Mohammed, 'while the highlands of Spain will preserve the religion of the Prophet in Christian Spain and the wild Alps of Lubéron protect the lingering faith of the Vaudois'.[1]

The mountains, then, are the home not only of sorcery and witchcraft, but also of primitive religious forms and resistance to new orthodoxies. Again and again they have to be won back to sound religion ; for missionaries come and go and the established

---

[1] Fernand Braudel, *La Méditerranée et le monde méditerranéen à l'époque de Philippe II* (Paris, 1949), pp. 12–15.

Church does not easily take root in such poor soil. We see this in England, where the north and west, 'the dark corners of the realm', would have to be re-evangelized by Puritan missionaries a century after the Reformation, and in Scotland, where the Highlands would relapse into 'paganism' and would need to be recovered by a new Puritan movement in the eighteenth century. What would happen in Britain after the Reformation had happened in Europe before it. The Dominicans were the evangelists of the 'dark corners' of Europe where the Catholic Church was not permanently established. As such they carried the gospel of 'feudal' Christian Europe into the unfeudal, half-Christian societies of the mountains, and inevitably, in that different world, found that their success was transitory : that ancient habits of thought reasserted themselves, that social incompatibility clothed itself in religious heresy, and that when formal heresy had been silenced or burnt out, the same fundamental incompatibility took, or seemed to take, another form. The old rural superstition, which had seemed harmless enough in the interstices of known society, assumed a more dangerous character when it was discovered, in strange, exaggerated form, among the barely subdued 'heretics' of the highlands. Thanks to that social gulf, that social unassimilability, witchcraft became heresy.

Once we see the persecution of heresy as social intolerance, the intellectual difference between one heresy and another becomes less significant. Innocent VIII was the persecutor of Bohemian Hussites and Alpine 'Vaudois' as well as of witches, just as John XXII had persecuted Fraticelli as well as witches. Social persecution is indivisible, or at least does not stop at mere intellectual frontiers. But if we wish to see this point more strikingly illustrated, it is useful to turn from one form of Inquisition to another. Only four years before the worldly, humanist Pope, Innocent VIII, yielded to the German Dominicans and launched his bull against the witches of Germany, his predecessor, the even more worldly humanist Pope Sixtus IV, had yielded to the Spanish Dominicans and approved the new Inquisition in Spain. It is difficult entirely to separate these two gestures, so close in time, so similar in consequence, so distinct in place and circumstance ; and in fact, by looking at them together, we may be able to shed some light upon them both.

For the Spanish Inquisition, like the medieval Inquisition, was ostensibly set up to deal with formal heresy, and therefore neither the Jews nor the Moors of Spain, at the time of its creation, were subject to it. Heresy is a crime of Christians : the Jews and Moors were then 'unbelievers'. But gradually both Jews and Moors were brought under the control of this organ of social conformity, just as witches had been brought under the control of the medieval Inquisition. The witches had been brought under this control by the device of an extended definition of heresy ; the Jews and Moors were brought under that of the Spanish inquisitors by the device of compulsory conversion to Christianity. In both cases the engine of persecution was set up before its future victims were legally subject to it. In both cases, once legally subject to it, the original pretext of their subjection was forgotten. Both witches and converted Jews were first subjected to the Inquisition as heretics ; but before long both were being burnt without reference to ideas, the former as witches, the latter as Jews.

Moreover, in both cases the persecutors were the same. It was the Dominicans who, from the start, had persecuted the witches in the Alps and the Pyrenees. It was the Dominicans also who, with some help from the Franciscans, had been the great persecutors of the Jews. This too had been, at first, a sporadic persecution. It had broken out in Germany during the Black Death, when the Jews were accused of poisoning the wells and were burnt in hundreds by angry crowds and petty magistrates. It had broken out in Italy, where the stern Franciscan St Bernardino of Siena had inflamed the mobs against the usurious crucifiers of Christ. From 1391 pogroms had been constant in Spain where the Catalan demagogue, the Franciscan St Vicente Ferrer, had rivalled the exploits of St Bernardino in Italy. The establishment of the Inquisition in Spain was a triumph of the Spanish Dominicans, the expulsion of the unconverted Jews (which left the rest of them subject to the Inquisition) a triumph for the Franciscan Cardinal Ximénez. Both these campaigns can be seen as part of a general evangelical crusade by the friars. That crusade would culminate, in the reign of Innocent VIII's successor, Alexander VI, with the attack on the 'pagan' papacy itself by the Dominican friar Savonarola.

The similarity between the persecution of Jews and the persecution of witches, which reached their climax in different places at the same time, suggests yet again that the pressure behind both was social. The witch and the Jew both represent social nonconformity. At first both are persecuted sporadically, without much reason given ; for the witch is not condemned by the old law of the Church, and the Jew, as an unbeliever, is outside it. Then legal grounds are devised to prosecute both : the former by a redefinition of terms, the latter by enforced baptism, is made liable to a charge of heresy. Finally, when that charge is no longer convenient, it is no longer used. The witch, as we shall see, is persecuted simply for 'being a witch', the Jew for 'being a Jew', for reasons not of belief but of blood, for defect of *limpieza de sangre*. Thus the reasons vary but the persecution continues : clear evidence that the real reason lies deeper than the reason given.

Moreover, it sometimes seems that these two types of social nonconformity are interchangeable. In its periods of introversion and intolerance Christian society, like any society, looks for scapegoats. Either the Jew or the witch will do, but society will settle for the nearest. The Dominicans, an international order, hate both ; but whereas in the Alps and Pyrenees they pursue witches, in Spain they concentrate on Jews. It is not that there are no witches in Spain. The Pyrenees, after all, are as much Spanish as French, and in the fourteenth and fifteenth centuries, when the Roman Inquisition operated in Aragon, the witches of northern Spain supplied many of its victims. The earliest of all general treatises on witchcraft was written in 1359 by a Dominican inquisitor-general in Aragon,[1] and in the next century Spanish witches — *bruxas* and *xorguinas* — gave as much

---

[1] Nicolas Eymeric, *Tractatus contra Daemonum Invocatores* (see Lea, *The Inquisition in the Middle Ages*, II, 175).

trouble to the champions of orthodoxy as Spanish Jews.[1] Numerous works on demonology were produced in Spain in the fifteenth and early sixteenth centuries, and Spanish expertise in such matters was exported to other countries.[2] But once the Inquisition had been firmly established, the local order of priority asserted itself. With Jews and Moors on their hands, the inquisitors had very little time for witches, and so they have won glowing tributes for their 'firmness' and 'temperate wisdom' in this respect.[3]

In Germany, on the other hand, the priorities are reversed. There, outside the Alpine regions, there is little or no persecution of witches in the fourteenth and early fifteenth centuries; but those are the years of terrible anti-Jewish pogroms. About 1450 the inquisitors begin to extend the craze down the Rhine, and this, of course, is the immediate purpose of the *Malleus*.[4] In the sixteenth century the witch gradually replaces the Jew, and in the seventeenth the reversal is almost complete. If the universal scapegoat of the Black Death in Germany had been the Jew, the universal scapegoat of the Wars of Religion will be the witch. There were exceptions to this generalization, of course. The Rostock jurist Dr Gödelmann, for instance, at the end of the sixteenth century, evidently hated Jews more than the witches about whom he explicitly wrote. He would suspend his liberal utterances about the latter in order to vent his hatred of the former: a blasphemous, impious race rightly expelled from their dominions by many Christian rulers.[5] Perhaps he was merely

---

[1] See, for instance, Hansen, *Quellen*, pp. 71, 124, 238–9, 246–51. The Spanish Franciscan Alonso de Espina, in his *Fortalicium Fidei* (Nuremberg, 1494), denounces Jews and witches (whom he calls by their Spanish names) with equal ferocity.

[2] Thus at the end of the sixteenth century Juan Maldonado and Martín del Rio, both Spaniards, taught demonology in France and Flanders respectively, and in the mid-seventeenth century we find the Spanish terms, *xurguminae* and *bruxae,* used in a work published in Hungary (J. C. Mediomontanus, *Disputatio Theologica de Lamiis et Veneficis,* Grosswardein, 1656, cited in Lea, *Materials,* p. 1254).

[3] Lea, *History of the Inquisition in Spain,* IV, 217–18. For witchcraft cases in Spain outside the Basque provinces, see also Sebastián Cirac Estopañan, *Los procesos de hechicerías en la inquisición de Castilla la Nueva* (Madrid, 1942) and the excellent introduction by Agustín Gonzales de Amezúa to his edition of Cervantes, *El casamiento engañoso y el coloquio de los perros* (Madrid, 1912).

[4] Soldan-Heppe, I, 229, 245–6.

[5] J. G. Gödelmann, *de Magis, Veneficis et Lamiis . . . Libri III* (Frankfurt, 1591), pp. 51–54.

behind the times. And really good Germans (like Luther) would contrive to hate both together: at the close of the sixteenth century the Catholic Elector of Trier and the Protestant Duke of Brunswick would set out to exterminate both. But in general the emphasis fell either on one or on the other. In our own days it has fallen back upon the Jews.

This interchangeability of victims, which suggests that both Jews and witches were persecuted rather as types of social non-conformity than for doctrinal or other given reasons, can be illustrated in many ways. In medieval Hungary, for instance, witches were sentenced, for a first offence, to stand all day in a public place, wearing a Jew's hat.[1] Witchcraft was one of the charges often made against the Jews. But the neatest instance of alternative priorities between the same two social groups is shown by the events on either side of the Pyrenees in the years 1609–10.

In those years there was a sudden panic of denunciation in the old kingdom of Navarre, which had once straddled the Pyrenees but was now divided into two parts, one governed from Paris the other from Madrid. The King of France, Henri IV, who was also King of Navarre, in response to the clamour of the noblemen and syndics of the Pays de Labourd, issued a commission to the president of the parlement of Bordeaux and to the counsellor of the parlement, Pierre de l'Ancre, to deal with the matter. In four months these energetic officials, both bigoted Catholics, burnt nearly a hundred witches, including several priests. But in describing his triumphs afterwards, and in denouncing the practices which he and his colleague had so gloriously repressed, de l'Ancre did not stop at witches. A whole section of his work is devoted to denunciation of the Jews: their absurd and indecent rites and beliefs, their cruelty, their greed, their poisoning of Christian wells, their forcible circumcision and ritual murder of Christian children. The Jews, says de l'Ancre, 'by their filth and stink, by their sabbaths and synagogues', are so disgusting to God that he has not only withdrawn from them his grace and his promise: he has also condemned them to creep about

[1] Lea, *Materials*, p. 1253.

the world 'like poor snakes', deprived of every kind of office, dignity or public employment. The Jews, he adds, are ordinarily great magicians : they turn themselves into wolves by night ; they can never be converted into good Christians. In other words, they behave just like witches.[1]

Thus in French Navarre the stereotype of the enemy of society is the witch : but the Jew is not forgotten. He comes second, to take the fag-end of persecution, or at least of denunciation. On the Spanish side of the Pyrenees the persecution is no less, but the order of priority is reversed. There in this same year, 1609, the Inquisition had achieved one of its great triumphs : the expulsion from Spain, as unassimilable heretics, of the whole Morisco population. Next year, in 1610, the Inquisition in Navarre, where there were no Moriscos, dealt with its local tensions. At a great *auto-de-fé* in Logroño, fifty-three persons were presented. Many of them were Jews, but no less than twenty-nine were presented as witches. But when the Spanish Inquisition reached the humble category of witches, its appetite was already slaked. Of those twenty-nine, six were burnt alive ; another six, having died in prison, were burnt in effigy. The remaining eighteen, having confessed and repented, were spared. As Lea remarks, under any other jurisdiction they would have been burnt. And even this relatively merciful sentence led to a commission of inquiry which concluded, in effect, that all witchcraft was an illusion, so that Spanish witches enjoyed thereafter an even greater immunity. As Michelet wrote, the Spanish Inquisition, 'exterminatrice pour les hérétiques, cruelle pour les Maures et les Juifs, l'était bien moins pour les sorciers'. Having chosen its victims elsewhere, it could afford to overlook the base, even bestial deviations of Pyrenean goatherds.[2]

So, in 1609–10, as in 1478–84, the persecution of witches can be seen as part of the same process as the persecution of Jews. That persecution was not doctrinal : it was not (whatever excuse might be given) because the victims were 'heretics'. It was not

[1] Pierre de l'Ancre, *L'Incrédulité et mescréance du sortilège pleinement convaincue* (Paris, 1622), pp. 446–501.

[2] Lea, *History of the Inquisition in Spain*, IV, 225–39 ; Jules Michelet, *La Sorcière*, p. 172.

launched merely by the personal decision of a bigot in the papal chair. Neither Sixtus IV nor Innocent VIII was a bigot — nor were Leo X and Clement VII, the Medici popes, who continued the process. Nor was the established Church bigoted. In general the established Church is opposed to the persecution. In the 1480s the established authorities — bishops and secular clergy as well as princes and city governments — disliked it. The authors of the *Malleus* found themselves obstructed by the ecclesiastical establishment in Germany and they were reduced to forging the approbation of the University of Cologne.[1] The Archbishop of Trier resisted the bull, declaring that there were no witches in his diocese.[2] (A century later it would be very different.) Even when the persecution was in full swing, the distinction is still perceptible. The Gallican Church would oppose it in France,[3] the Anglican Church in England,[4] the Catholic Church at its headquarters, Rome.[5] The pressure throughout came from a lower level, from the missionary orders who moved among the people, on the sensitive social frontier between differing communities, whether in the heart of a multi-racial society, as in Spain, or in frontier areas, the areas of missionary activity. The popes might authorize, but the pace was set by the tribunes of the people, and the tribunes in their turn responded to popular pressure, seeking a scapegoat for social frustration.

For no ruler has ever carried out a policy of wholesale expulsion or destruction without the co-operation of society. To think otherwise, to suppose that a ruler, or even a party in the state, can thus cut out part of the living tissue of society without the consent of society, is to defy the lesson of history. Great massacres may be commanded by tyrants, but they are imposed by peoples. Without general social support, the organs of isolation and expulsion cannot even be created. The social resentment of the Spanish *pueblo*, not the bigotry of Spanish kings, lay behind the foundation of the Spanish Inquisition. Spanish society

[1] See the careful examination by Hansen (summarized in Lea, *Materials*, pp. 337 ff.).
[2] Soldan-Heppe, II, 1.   [3] Lea, *Materials*, p. 1287.   [4] See below, p. 142.
[5] Practically no witches were burnt in Rome in the whole period of the witch-craze. See Nikolaus Paulus, *Hexenwahn und Hexenprozess, vornehmlich im 16ten Jahrhundert* (Freiburg-im-Breisgau, 1910), pp. 260 ff.

approved the persecution of the Jews and welcomed the expulsion of the Moriscos. French society applauded the massacre of the Huguenots in 1572 and their expulsion in 1685. German society supplied Hitler with the means of destroying the Jews. Afterwards, when the mood has changed, or when the social pressure, thanks to that blood-letting, no longer exists, the anonymous people slinks away, leaving public responsibility to the preachers, the theorists and the rulers who demanded, justified and ordered the act. But the historian must present to it too its share of the account. Individually that share may be infinitesimal but collectively it is the largest of all. Without the tribunes of the people, social persecution cannot be organized. Without the people, it cannot be conceived.[1]

So it was with the persecution of witches. If the Dominicans, by their constant propaganda, created a hatred of witches, they created it in a favourable social context. Without that context their success is inexplicable. But within that context, these tribunes played an essential part. From the very beginning it was they who detected the social pressure. It was they who mobilized it. And in order to mobilize it, they also supplied the mythology without which it could never have become a European movement. To this mythology we must now turn.

III

The mythology of the witch-craze, I have suggested, was the articulation of social pressure. In a religious society such articulation generally takes the form of heresy. But before examining any heresy it is useful to ask who in fact articulated it. Was it the heretics themselves, or was it the inquisitors who articulated it for them? This is an important question, applicable to many

imp.
see 106
127

---

[1] Is it necessary to document these statements? Then let the reader refer to the works of Américo Castro for the Spanish Inquisition; let him observe the conflict between personal humanity and social fear, in respect of the expulsion of the Moriscos, in the contemporary works of Cervantes and the Spanish *arbitristas*; let him read M. Jean Orcibal's *Louis XIV et les protestants* (Paris, 1951); and let him digest the profound and terrible book of Mr Raul Hilberg, *The Destruction of the European Jews* (Chicago, 1961).

historic heresies. It applies, among others, to the Albigensians and to the Vaudois. So, when the inquisitors discovered a new 'heresy' beneath the ruins of Albigensianism, we naturally ask the same question. Did they really discover this new heresy, or did they invent it?

It has been argued by some speculative writers that the demonology of the sixteenth century was, in essence, a real religious system, the old pre-Christian religion of rural Europe which the new Asiatic religion of Christ had driven underground but never wholly destroyed. But this is to confuse the scattered fragments of paganism with the grotesque system into which they are only long afterwards arranged. The primitive peoples of Europe, as of other continents, knew of charms and sorcery, and the concept of night-riding 'with Diana or Herodias' survived into the early Christian centuries; but the essential substance of the new demonology — the pact with Satan, the witches' sabbat, the carnal intercourse with demons, etc., etc. — and the hierarchical, systematic structure of the kingdom of the Devil, are an independent product of the later Middle Ages.[1] All the evidence makes it clear that the new mythology owes its system entirely to the inquisitors themselves. Just as anti-semites build up, out of disconnected titbits of scandal, their systematic mythology of ritual murder, poisoned wells and the world-wide conspiracy of the Elders of Zion, so the Hammerers of Witches built up their systematic mythology of Satan's kingdom and Satan's accomplices out of the mental rubbish of peasant credulity and feminine hysteria; and the one mythology, like the other, once launched,

[1] The idea that witch-beliefs were lingering relics of a systematic pre-Christian religion was first advanced by Jacob Grimm, who, in his *Deutsche Mythologie* (Göttingen, 1835), argued that the witch-cult was no other than the ancient Teutonic religion. In this form it was refuted by Soldan, who argued that, in so far as it contained pagan concepts, those concepts could be traced to Roman (and so to Greek and Oriental), not to Germanic paganism (Soldan, p. 494). The distinction may be too fine: possibly some of the coarser ingredients, though justified from literary sources, were directly derived from German paganism (see below, p. 185). But however that may be, the demonological system, as distinct from the particular details incorporated in it, is demonstrably scholastic and medieval. The fancies of the late Margaret Murray need not detain us. They were justly, if irritably, dismissed by a real scholar as 'vapid balderdash' (C. L. Ewen, *Some Witchcraft Criticisms*, 1938).

acquired a momentum of its own. It became an established folk-lore, generating its own evidence, and applicable far outside its original home.

How that folk-lore was established is clear enough to anyone who reads the successive manuals of the inquisitors. Fighting against the enemies of the Faith, they had easily divided the world into light and darkness, and having systematized the kingdom of God in a *Summa Theologiae*, what was more natural than to systematize the kingdom of the Devil in a *Summa Daemonologiae*? The method was the same : the only difference lay in the nature of the material. The basic evidence of the kingdom of God had been supplied by Revelation. But the Father of Lies had not revealed himself so openly. To penetrate the secrets of his king-dom, it was therefore necessary to rely on indirect sources. These sources could only be captured members of the enemy intelligence service : in other words, confessing witches.

So the Dominicans set to work and their efforts were soon rewarded. Since a system was presupposed, a system was found. The confessions — those disconnected fragments of truth hardly won from the enemy — were seen as the few visible projections of a vast and complex organization, and so every new confession supplied fresh evidence for deductive minds. The same logic which had constructed the great work of the Angelic Doctor would construct a series of demonological manuals confirming and extending each other. The climax, because of its timing and distribution, would be the *Malleus*. When it was published, it carried on its title-page the bold epigraph, *Haeresis est maxima opera maleficarum non credere* ('to disbelieve in witchcraft is the greatest of heresies'). It was the exact opposite of the ruling of the Church in the Dark Ages. Since the ninth century, the wheel had come full circle.

But if the theory of Satan's kingdom, with its hierarchy of demons and witches, rested ultimately on the confessions of witches, how were those confessions obtained ? This question is crucial. If the confessions were freely given, we have to admit at least the 'subjective reality' of the experiences confessed, and then the remarkable identity of those confessions, which converted many a sixteenth-century sceptic, becomes a real problem. On the other hand, if the confessions were obtained by torture, that problem hardly exists. The similarity of answers can be explained by a combination of identical questions and intolerable pain. Since some of the most distinguished historians of witchcraft have adopted this explanation,[1] we must clearly examine the whole question of the part played by judicial torture in the trial of witches.

Judicial torture had been allowed, in limited cases, by Roman law; but Roman law, and with it judicial torture, had been forgotten in the Dark Ages. In the eleventh century Roman law had been rediscovered in the west, and torture had soon followed it back into use. In 1252 Innocent IV, by the bull *Ad Extirpanda*, had authorized its use against the Albigensians. By the fourteenth century it was in general use in the tribunals of the Inquisition, and it was used, particularly, in cases of witchcraft, where evidence was always difficult to find. In 1468 the Pope declared witchcraft to be *crimen exceptum* and thereby removed, in effect, all legal limits on the application of torture in such cases. It was not, as yet, used by the secular courts; and Lea points out that certain of the more extravagant and obscene details of witches' confessions do not, at first, appear before secular tribunals, but only before the tribunals of the Inquisition. In other words, they were obtained only by the courts which used torture. But this distinction between lay and clerical practice did not last for long. At the time of the Renaissance the medieval Inquisition was everywhere in decay and, north of the Alps at least, the secular courts had taken over many of its functions. Thus cases of witchcraft in Germany and France were judged by secular lords who had higher jurisdiction. But at the same time the procedures of Roman law were adopted in the criminal law of all countries of western Europe except England. Thus England alone escaped from the judicial use of torture in ordinary criminal

[1] Soldan, Lea, and Soldan's twentieth-century editor, Max Bauer, ascribed a great deal of demonological science, but not all, to torture. Lea's disciple and biographer, G. L. Burr, seems, in his essays on witchcraft, to have gone further and to have supposed that torture created witchcraft (cf. *Life*, pp. 177–8).

cases, including cases of witchcraft.[1] It may also be observed
that some of the more extravagant and obscene details remain
absent from the confessions of English witches.[2] When we consider all these facts, and when we note that the rise and decline
of the European witch-craze corresponds generally with the rise
and decline of judicial torture in Europe, we may easily conclude
that the two processes are interdependent : that the Dark Ages
knew no witch-mania because they lacked judicial torture and
that the decline and disappearance of witch-beliefs in the eighteenth
century is due to the discredit and gradual abolition of torture
in Europe. We may also observe that, since torture has been
revived in certain European countries, absurd confessions have
returned with it.

That this general conclusion is true, is, I believe, undeniable.
The evidence supplied by Lea clearly shows that the witch-craze
grew by its own momentum ; that witches' confessions became
more detailed with the intensification of inquisitorial procedure ;
and that the identity of such confessions is often to be explained
by the identity of procedure rather than by any identity of experience : identical works of reference, identical instructions to
judges, identical leading questions supported by torments too
terrible to bear. This natural inference is also supported by
positive evidence. Accused witches often admitted to their confessors that they had wrongly accused both themselves and
others, and these admissions are the more credible since they
brought no advantage to the accused — unless they were willing,
as they seldom were, to make a formal retraction, which meant
submitting to torture again. Some judges refused to allow testimony because they knew that it had been created by torture and
was therefore unreliable ; and it was the increasing recognition
of this fact which, more than anything else, ultimately discredited

---

[1] There were exceptions — e.g. for high treason — and the English common law
provided *peine forte et dure*, or pressing to death, for refusal to plead. But these
exceptions are not germane to the present argument. There was also some non-
judicial torture in ill-regulated cases : e.g. during the civil wars, when Matthew
Hopkins and his assistants used the *tormentum insomniae*. See Wallace Notestein,
A History of Witchcraft in England, 1558–1718 (New York, 1909), pp. 204–5.

[2] England was unique in another respect too. English witches, unlike those of
Europe and Scotland, were not burnt (as for heresy), but hanged.

the whole science. As Sir George Mackenzie, the Lord-Advocate of Scotland, declared of the Scottish witches who were still being burnt in his time, 'most of all that ever were taken were tormented after this manner, and this usage was the ground of all their confession'.[1]

It might well be. When we consider the fully developed procedure at continental or Scottish witch-trials we can hardly be surprised that confessions were almost always secured. For such a crime, the ordinary rules of evidence, as the ordinary limits of torture, were suspended. For how could ordinary methods prove such extraordinary crimes ? As Jean Bodin would write, not one in a million would be punished if the procedure were governed by ordinary laws. So, in the absence of a 'grave *indicium*', such as a pot full of human limbs, sacred objects, toads, etc., or a written pact with the Devil (which must have been a rare collector's piece),[2] circumstantial evidence was sufficient to mobilize the process. And the circumstantial evidence need not be very cogent : it was sufficient to discover a wart, by which the familiar spirit was suckled ; an insensitive spot which did not bleed when pricked ; a capacity to float when thrown into water ; or an incapacity to shed tears. Recourse could even be had to 'lighter *indicia*', such as a tendency to look down when accused, signs of fear, or the mere aspect of a witch, old, ugly or smelly. Any of these *indicia* might establish a *prima facie* case and justify the use of torture to produce the confession, which was proof, or the refusal to confess, which was even more cogent proof and justified even more ferocious tortures and a nastier death.

Of the tortures used, we have plenty of evidence. Basically they were the same throughout the lands of Roman law. There were the *gresillons* (in Scottish *pennywinkis*), which crushed the tips of fingers and toes in a vice ; the *échelle* or 'ladder', a kind of rack which violently stretched the body ; and the *tortillon* which squeezed its tender parts at the same time. There was the *strappado* or *estrapade*, a pulley which jerked the body violently in

---

[1] Sir George Mackenzie of Rosehaugh, *The Laws and Customs of Scotland in Matters Criminal* (1678), p. 9.

[2] It is gravely mentioned as an *indicium* by Carpzov (cited in Lea, *Materials*, p. 826).

mid-air. There was the leg-screw or Spanish boot, much used in Germany and Scotland, which squeezed the calf and broke the shin-bone in pieces — 'the most severe and cruel pain in the world', as a Scotsman called it — and the 'lift' which hoisted the arms fiercely behind and back ; and there was the 'ram' or 'witch-chair', a seat of spikes, heated from below. There was also the 'Bed of Nails', which was very effective for a time in Styria. In Scotland one might also be grilled on the *caschielawis*, and have one's finger-nails pulled off with the *turkas* or pincers ; or needles might be driven up to their heads in the quick. But in the long run perhaps nothing was so effective as the *tormentum insomniae*, the torture of artificial sleeplessness which has been revived in our day. Even those who were stout enough to resist the *estrapade* would yield to a resolute application of this slower but more certain form of torture, and confess themselves to be witches.[1] Once a witch had confessed, the next stage was to secure from her, again under torture, a list of all those of her neighbours whom she had recognized at the witches' sabbat. Thus a new set of *indicia* was supplied, clerical science was confirmed, and a fresh set of trials and tortures would begin.

It is easy to see that torture lay, directly or indirectly, behind most of the witch-trials of Europe, creating witches where none were and multiplying both victims and evidence. Without torture, the great witch-panics of the 1590s and the late 1620s are inconceivable. But can we ascribe the whole craze, in effect, to torture, as some liberal writers seem to do ? Can we suppose that witchcraft had no other basis than the fanaticism and prurience of the inquisitors, spellbound by their own inventions ? I must confess that I find this difficult to believe. The problem

[1] Lists of tortures are given in many of the sixteenth- and seventeenth-century manuals — e.g. Benedict Carpzov, *Practica Rerum Criminalium* (1635), quoted in Lea, *Materials*, p. 823. They are also mentioned in reports of trials, e.g. Robert Pitcairn, *Criminal Trials in Scotland* (1833), I, pt. 2, 215-23. Summaries may be found, for Alsace, in Reuss, *L'Alsace au 17e siècle* ; for Lorraine in Ch. Pfister, 'Nicolas Rémy et la sorcellerie en Lorraine à la fin du 16e siècle', in *Revue historique*, 1907 ; for Germany, in B. Duhr, *Geschichte der Jesuiten in den Ländern deutscher Zunge* (Freiburg-im-Breisgau, 1907-21), II, ii, 482. For the use of *tormentum insomniae* to extract false confessions in our own time see Z. Stypulkowski's account of his own experiences in his book *Invitation to Moscow* (1951).

seems to me more complex than that. If the confessions were merely a response to torture we should have to explain why even in England, where there was no judicial torture, witches confessed to absurd crimes ; [1] why the people were so docile in the face of such a mania ; and above all, why some of the most original and cultivated men of the time not only accepted the theory of witch-craft, but positively devoted their genius to its propagation. For, as Lucien Fèbvre said, although we may dismiss Henri Boguet and many others as 'imbeciles', we have to stop before the great figure of Bodin : Bodin the Aristotle, the Montesquieu of the sixteenth century, the prophet of comparative history, of political theory, of the philosophy of law, of the quantitative theory of money, and of so much else, who yet, in 1580, wrote the book which, more than any other, reanimated the witch-fires throughout Europe.[2] To turn over the pages of Bodin's *De la démono-manie des sorciers*, to see this great man, the undisputed intellectual master of the later sixteenth century, demanding death at the stake not only for witches, but for all who do not believe every grotesque detail of the new demonology, is a sobering experience. After such an experience it is impossible, absurd, to suppose that the confessions of witches were mere clerical fabrications, imposed upon reluctant victims by instruments of torture.

Nor is the coincidence in time of judicial torture and the witch-craze in any way decisive. When we look closely at the dates, we find that the abolition of torture did not precede but often followed the disintegration of witch-beliefs. Torture was not abolished in Prussia till 1740 (although it had been brought under strict control in 1714) ; but the Prussian Land Law of 1721 had

---

[1] 'Note also', Reginald Scot wrote, 'how easily they may be brought to confess that which they never did, nor lieth in the power of man to do.' (*Discovery of Witchcraft*, 1584, epistle to Sir Thomas Scot, J.P.)

[2] L. Fèbvre, in *Annales : économies, sociétés, civilisation*, 1948, p. 15. By an unfortunate misprint, the word 'Boguet' has here been printed as 'Bossuet', and this error has since been redoubled in an attempt to make it more plausible. In the posthumously published collection of Fèbvre's essays, *Au cœur religieux du XVIe siècle*, the phrase 'un imbécile ?' has been changed into 'Bossuet ?'. No doubt the editor thought that the master had gone too far in describing Bossuet as an imbecile ; but in fact it was only the printer who had done so. The 'imbecillity' quoted is from Henri Boguet, *Examen des sorciers* (Lyon, 1602), Dedication to the Vicar-General of Besançon.

already declared that no belief could be placed in the pact with
the Devil, night-riding to the sabbat, metamorphosis, intercourse
with demons, etc. ; and since the law always lags behind the fact,
we can assume that the belief had already faded.[1] In Bavaria the
decisive blow to the belief was struck by the Theatine monk
Ferdinand Stertzinger in 1766, but torture was not abolished till
1806.[2] In France witch-beliefs died before the Revolution, torture after it. In general, it seems clear that it was the growing
disbelief in confessions produced by torture which brought
torture into discredit : in other words, that the disintegration
of witch-beliefs led to the abolition of torture, not *vice versa*.

What then is the explanation of those confessions, and of their
general identity ? When we read the confessions of sixteenth-
and seventeenth-century witches, we are often revolted by the
cruelty and stupidity which have elicited them and sometimes,
undoubtedly, supplied their form. But equally we are obliged to
admit their fundamental 'subjective reality'. For every victim
whose story is evidently created or improved by torture, there
are two or three who genuinely believe in its truth. This duality
because of
confessions,
though.
forbids us to accept single, comprehensive, rational explanations.
'Rationalism', after all, is relative : relative to the general intellectual structure of the time. The sixteenth-century clergy and
lawyers were rationalists. They believed in a rational, Aristotelean universe, and from the detailed identity of witches' confessions they logically deduced their objective truth. To the
'patrons of witches' who argued that witches were 'aged persons
of weak brains' whose melancholy natures were exploited by the
Devil, the Rev. William Perkins could reply with confidence that,
if that were so, each would have a different fantasy ; but in fact
men of learning had shown 'that all witches throughout Europe
are of like carriage and behaviour in their examinations and convictions'. Such international consistency, he argued, was evidence of central organization and truthful testimony.[3] The
not
necessarily

---

[1] Lea, *Materials*, pp. 1133, 1431–5.   [2] Lea, *Materials*, pp. 1459–61.
[3] William Perkins, *A Discourse of the Damned Art of Witchcraft* (Cambridge,
1608), pp. 187–93. The 'patron of witches' whom Perkins is attacking is clearly
Reginald Scot. The same point had been made by Bodin.

liberal scholars of the nineteenth century were also rationalists.
They knew that, objectively, the confessions of witches were
worthless. Therefore they found another explanation of their
identity. They ascribed it to the identity of the questions and the
pressure of torture. But we in the twentieth century are not
rationalists — at least in our approach to human behaviour and
human belief. We do not look only for external causes of identical expression or identical illusion. We look also for internal
causes, and we find them in human psychology and psycho-
pathology.

That external suggestion alone does not account for witches'
confessions is clear when we descend to detail. Again and again,
when we read the case histories, we find witches freely confessing
to esoteric details without any evidence of torture, and it was this
spontaneity, rather than the confessions themselves, which convinced rational men that the details were true. It was because he
had heard confessions given without torture that Paolo Grillandi,
a judge of witches in central Italy in the early sixteenth century,
was converted to the belief that witches were transported bodily
to the sabbat. Bodin too assures us that the confession which
converted him to the science of demonology and inspired him to
become its most formidable propagandist was made 'sans question ny torture'; and yet the woman, Jeanne Harvellier of Verbery near Compiègne, had been remarkably circumstantial. Not
only had she compassed the death of man and beast: she had
also had the Devil for her paramour for thirty-eight years, during
which he had visited her 'en guise d'un grand homme noir, outre
la stature des hommes, vestu de drap noir', coming to her by
night, on horseback, booted and spurred, with a sword at his
side. She had also described her visits to the sabbat in copious
detail; and here too the detail had exactly confirmed the
science of the demonologists: the long and tiring journey
which left her utterly exhausted, the adoration of a big black
man whom they called Belzebuh, the sexual promiscuity. Bodin
admits that such a story seemed strange and almost incredible
at second-hand. But he had heard it himself; he was a man
of the world; and he was personally convinced of its spon-

taneity. Who are we to doubt his conviction ?[1]

Or take the case of Françoise Fontaine, the servant-girl whose interrogation at Louviers by Loys Morel, *prévôt-général* of Henri IV in Normandy, was discovered and published in full in 1883. Here there was no question of torture : the *prévôt* was a humane man, and the story was elicited by patience, not pressure. And yet the story is the standard story, even down to the details : the visit of the Devil through the window, in the guise of 'ung grand homme tout vestu de noir, ayant une grande barbe noire et les yeux fort esclairantz et effroyables' ; the large promises made ; the oppressive solidity of his attentions, the lack of pleasure derived from them, the ice-cold contact . . . In his introduction to the document, the Vicomte de Moray has shown, from the evidence of the Salpêtrière hospital in Paris, that every detail of Françoise Fontaine's experience has its parallel today : the diabolic incubus is only the sixteenth-century form of a kind of sexual hysteria familiar to every twentieth-century psychiatrist.[2]

Only . . . ? No, not quite. For there is, in these numerous sixteenth-century and seventeenth-century cases, one ingredient which has since disappeared : the Devil. Today, every psychopath has his or her private obsession. The supposed *incubi* and *succubi* vary from patient to patient. In the past the neurotics and hysterics of Christendom centralized their illusions around the figure of the Devil, just as the saints and mystics centralized theirs around the figure of God or Christ. So, while the pious virgins, having vowed themselves to God, felt themselves to be the brides of Christ, the less pious witches, having bound themselves to Satan, felt themselves to be his concubines. The former, like St Theresa or Madame Guyon, enjoyed ecstasies of glowing pleasure piercing their inmost entrails as they clung to the mystical body of their Saviour ; the latter, like Françoise Fontaine or a hundred others who were dragged before their judges,

---

[1] Paolo Grillandi, *Tractatus de Sortilegiis*, 1536 (Lea, *Materials*, pp. 401–5). Jean Bodin, *De la démonomanie des sorciers* (Paris, 1580), Preface.

[2] *Procès-verbal fait pour délivrer une fille possédée par le malin esprit à Louviers*, ed. Armand Bénet (Paris, 1883), pp. 38–44, 87–92.

felt joyless pangs as they lay crushed in the embrace of that huge black figure who 'jettoit quelque chose dans son ventre qui estoit froid comme glace, qui venoit jusques au dessus de l'estomac et des tétins de ladite respondante'. In the former the psychopathic experience was sublimated in the theology of the Fathers, and they might be canonized ; in the latter it ran into disorder in the folk-lore of the demonologists, and they might be burnt.[1]

Here, surely, we see what the Dominican inquisitors had done, what their successors would do. They did not, of course, discover a concealed world of demons, objectively there (as they supposed). They did not even discover a systematic illusion, a false religion of paganism behind the true religion of Christ. Doubtless there were some pagan survivals in witchcraft just as there were some pagan survivals in Christianity. In Lorraine, for instance, the sabbat was ascribed, incidentally, to the old 'high places' of pre-Christian worship.[2] But what was taken over was mere fragments, not a system : it was the inquisitors who supplied the system. Nor did those inquisitors invent a purely imaginary system, in the ordinary sense of that verb : they may have used their ingenuity to create the system, but they did not create the basic evidence on which it rested. They found it in the confessions of supposed witches ; and as those confessions seemed genuine to the witches who made them, we can hardly blame the inquisitors for supposing them to be genuine too. What was 'subjective reality' to the penitent was 'objective reality' to the confessor. Out of those fragments of truth, spontaneously given if also amplified by suggestion and torture, a total picture of Satan's kingdom could, by logic, by the 'rationalism' of the time, be built up.

Thus the genesis of the sixteenth-century witch-craze can be explained in two stages. First, there is the social tension. Just

[1] There is no need to press the comparison : it is obvious to anyone who faces the evidence. Compare, for instance, the evidence in any sexual witch-trial with the evidence given in J. H Leuba, *The Psychology of Religious Mysticism* (1925) or the grotesque treatises of the sixteenth- and seventeenth-century demonologists with the hardly less grotesque lives of the baroque saints. The point is also made by the Vicomte de Moray, in *Procès-verbal*, pp. lxxxi–lxxxvii.

[2] See Étienne Delcambre, *Le Concept de la sorcellerie dans le duché de Lorraine au XVIe et XVIIe siècle* (Nancy, 1948–51), fasc. I, pp. 149–53.

as systematic anti-semitism is generated by the ghetto, the *aljama*, not by the individual Jew, so the systematic mythology of the witch-craze was generated not by individual old women casting spells in scattered villages — these had always been tolerated — but by unassimilable social groups who, like the Jews and Moors of Spain, might be persecuted into outward orthodoxy but not into social conformity, and who therefore became, as the others did not, objects of social fear. It was out of this tension that the frustrated evangelists began to manufacture the new mythology of Satan's kingdom. That that mythology was entirely fantastic need not here concern us. We may merely observe that, in this respect, it is not unique. Some of the ideas and practices ascribed to the Albigensians, and before them to other esoteric sects,[1] had been no less fantastic, and the absurdity of inquisitorial demonology should be a salutary warning to us never to trust the accounts which a persecuting society has drawn up of any esoteric heresy with which it is at war. But once the mythology had been established, it acquired, as it were, a reality of its own. Ideology is indivisible, and those who believed that there were devil-worshipping societies in the mountains soon discovered that there were devil-worshipping individuals in the plains. So the second stage of the witch-craze developed out of the first. The new mythology provided a new means of interpreting hitherto disregarded deviations, an explanatory background for apparently innocent nonconformity. Whatever seemed mysterious and dangerous (like the power of Joan of Arc), or even mysterious and merely odd, could best be explained by it. Nonconformists

---

[1] Anyone who supposes that the absurd and disgusting details of demonology are unique may profitably look at the allegations made by St Clement of Alexandria against the followers of Carpocrates in the second century A.D. (*Stromata*, III, 5–10), or by St Epiphanius against the Gnostic heretics of the fourth century A.D. (in his *Panarion*), or by St Augustine against certain Manichaean heretics (*c. Faustum*, xv, 7 ; xxii, 30 ; xx, 6 ; *de Moribus*, ii, 65 ; *de Natura Boni*, 47 ; *de Haeresibus*, 46), or indeed at the remarks of Tacitus on the early Christians (*Annals*, xv, 44) or of the orthodox Catholics on the Albigensians and Vaudois of the twelfth century and the Fraticelli of the fourteenth (see the remarks of Juan Ginés de Sepúlveda quoted in Lea, *Materials*, p. 203). In these recurrent fantasies the obscene details are often identical, and their identity sheds some light on the psychological connection between persecuting orthodoxy and sexual prurience. The springs of sanctimony and sadism are not far apart.

themselves, in search of a sustaining ideology, even deliberately took up the newly revealed doctrines ; sadists like Gilles de Raïs dignified their brutalities by giving them a satanic impulse ; helpless victims of society clutched at it for relief ; and psychopaths co-ordinated their delusions about its central theme.

In a climate of fear it is easy to see how this process could happen : how individual deviations could be associated with a central pattern. We have seen it happen in our own time. The McCarthyite experience of the United States in the 1950s was exactly comparable : social fear, the fear of a different kind of society, was given intellectual form as a heretical ideology and suspect individuals were then persecuted by reference to that heresy. In the same way, in the fourteenth and fifteenth centuries, the hatred felt for unassimilable societies was intellectualized as a new heresy and politically suspect individuals were brought to judgment by reference to it. The great sorcery trials in France and England at that time — the trials of the Templars and Joan of Arc, of the Duchess of Gloucester and the Duchess of Bedford — were political exploitations of a social fear and a social ideology, whose origins were to be found at a deeper level and in another field. The difference was that whereas McCarthyism in America lasted only a few years (although it may yet recur), the European witch-craze had a far longer history. The new ideology reached its final form in the 1480s. From the publication of the *Malleus* onwards, its basic content never changed. There was no further development. And yet equally there was no disintegration. It formed a reservoir of monstrous theory from which successive persecutions were fed : persecutions which did not diminish but were positively intensified in the course of the next two hundred years.

IV

The duration of the witch-craze is certainly surprising, for whatever forces may have created it there were others which would seem naturally to undermine it. In the fourteenth century, that century of plague and depression and social dislocation, the mental climate might be congenial; [1] but the later fifteenth century, which saw the craze formally launched, was the beginning of a period of new European expansion. Nor was the craze, even then, firmly accepted. The established Church — the bishops and the secular clergy — had no great love of the friars and their fanatical doctrines. The educated urban laity of Europe were in no mood to swallow the Alpine credulities, the monkish phantasmagoria of excited missionaries. City governments, even in what were to become the classic lands of witchcraft, resisted the craze, with varying success, even at its height.[2] Civil lawyers, the professional rivals of the clergy, were at first highly sceptical of these new doctrines. Besides, the Witch Bull and the *Malleus* appeared in an age of enlightened criticism. It was the time of Renaissance humanism, when Lorenzo Valla and Erasmus and their disciples, under the protection of princes and free cities, were using human reason to dissolve ancient superstitions and established errors. At a time when the older forgeries of the Church were being exposed and the text of Scripture critically examined, why should new absurdities escape scrutiny? Surely the Donation of Constantine and the apostolic authorship of the Apocalypse were not more obviously improbable than *succubi* and the sabbat.[3]

[1] The spread of witchcraft in fifteenth-century France is explicitly connected with the devastation of the Hundred Years War by Petrus Mamoris, canon of St Pierre of Saintes and Regent of the University of Poitiers, in his *Flagellum Maleficorum*, written about 1462 and published, without date or indication of place, about 1490 (sig. a ii verso, 'Ingressus ad Rem').

[2] Thus the magistrates of Metz, in the witch-ridden duchy of Lorraine, at least resisted the claims of the Dominican inquisitor to be sole judge in 1456 (Lea, *Materials*, p. 235). The Senate of Venice similarly opposed the operations of the Dominican inquisitors in the dioceses of Bergamo and Brescia (see the bull *Honestis petentium votis* of Leo X in 1521; cf. Soldan-Heppe, I, 555–7). The city of Cologne successfully kept down the persecution until 1629 (see below, p. 156). The city of Nuremberg was an island of safety for witches in Bavaria throughout the period (see Burr, *Life*, p. 185). The city of Strasbourg was another such island in Alsace (see R. Reuss, *La Sorcellerie au 16ᵉ et 17ᵉ siècles, particulièrement en Alsace*, Strasbourg, 1871, pp. 178–81). The city of Lübeck survived the sixteenth century almost untouched by the craze (Soldan-Heppe, I, 526–7).

[3] The attitude of Erasmus towards witchcraft is disputed. His references to it are few, and their interpretation (since he never explicitly affirms or questions its reality) depends on the amount of irony which can be detected in the tone of his voice; which in turn depends on the reader. A letter of 14 Jan. 1501 concerning

So we are not surprised to find, at the beginning, a good deal of dissent. When the Archduke Sigismund of Austria learned of the new doctrines which were to be extirpated from his Tyrolean lands, he consulted a learned civil lawyer, a doctor of Padua, now professor in Constance, to give him advice ; and the lawyer, Ulrich Müller (alias Molitor), replied with a treatise in which he insisted that although there were witches who listened to the suggestions of the Devil and who therefore deserved to die, nevertheless these witches had none of the powers which they claimed but were the victims of despair or poverty or village hatreds.[1] Such opinions were widely repeated. Lawyers like Andrea Alciati and Gianfrancesco Ponzinibio, philosophers like Cornelius Agrippa of Nettesheim and Girolamo Cardano, medical men like Antonio Ferrari, called Galateo, even Franciscan School-

a sorcerer of Meung-sur-Loire (*Des. Erasmi Opus Epistolarum*, ed. P. S. Allen, 1, 1906, 334–41) has been interpreted as showing scepticism by some (e.g. Thomasius, *de Origine ac Progressu Processu Inquisitorii contra Sagas*, Halle, 1729, pp. 52–53 ; Soldan, p. 321 ; G. Längin, *Religion und Hexenprozess*, Leipzig, 1888, p. 73), credulity by others (e.g. Paulus, *Hexenwahn und Hexenprozess*, p. 18, who is followed by Bauer in Soldan-Heppe, 1, 414). But I find it difficult to read Erasmus' accounts of the witches near Freiburg-im-Breisgau, one of whom caused a village to be burnt down, while the other conducted an amour with an inn-keeper's daughter and inundated a village with fleas, as written in a serious spirit. Erasmus himself described such stories as *vulgi fabulas* (op. cit., x, 275, 316, 324). In any case, it is clear that the general philosophy of Erasmus was sceptical, and it seems safer, with him as with Grotius, Selden, Bacon, etc. (see below, p. 180), to deduce his particular views from his known general ideas than to seek to extract evidence of belief from casual and elliptical references.

Moreover, the very silence of Erasmus is expressive. In his *Annotations on the New Testament* he avoids every opportunity of encouraging the demonologists. On all those passages from which Catholics and Protestants alike deduced the power of the Devil to intervene in human affairs (Matt. iv. 5, Luke iv. 2, Rev. xii. 12), Erasmus is almost ostentatiously unhelpful. 'Diaboli nomen', he says firmly, in connection with the temptation of Christ (and the Devil's power to transport Christ to the pinnacles of the Temple was one of the stock proofs of his power to transport witches to the sabbat) '. . . non spiritum impium sed simpliciter delatorem aut calumniatorem significare videtur'. In this, as in so much else, he is followed by Grotius. And since Erasmus regarded the encounters of the Desert Fathers, Paul and Anthony, with the Devil, though described by St Jerome, whom he revered, as imaginary, he is unlikely to have given more credit to the similar encounters of witches, as described by monks, whom he hated. De l'Ancre, incidentally, included Erasmus among the sceptics whose incredulity had culpably weakened the crusade against witches (*L'Incrédulité*, p. 23), and Weyer, the greatest opponent of the craze, was a disciple of Erasmus. See below, p. 146.

[1] Ulricus Molitor, *Tractatus de Pythonicis Mulieribus* (Strasbourg, 1489).

men like Samuel de' Cassini all agreed that the powers claimed by witches, or ascribed to them, were largely illusions. They were the hallucinations of melancholy, half-starved persons ; they should be interpreted by lay science — the science of medicine and law — not theology ; and their proper cure was not fire but hellebore, the classical cure for mere human insanity.[1] Such a view had already been advanced two centuries before by the famous medieval physician of the University of Padua, Peter of Abano, who now became widely quoted by all the enemies of the witch-craze — and as widely attacked by its promoters. Indeed, the University of Padua, the centre of Renaissance science, became the citadel of common sense against the new mythology : its doctors appealed from the new Aristotle of the Schoolmen to the original Aristotle of Stagira, and in that process the philosophical basis of witchcraft dissolved. Agostino Nifo, doctor of Padua and physician to el Gran Capitán, Gonzalo de Córdoba, and to Pope Leo X, showed that, in a true Aristotelean universe, there was no room for demons. The greatest of the Paduans, Pietro Pomponazzi, went further. Cautiously, and hedging his meaning with pious lip-service to orthodoxy (for his work on the immortality, or rather mortality, of the soul had already been publicly burnt in Venice), he argued that all the marvels which the vulgar, and the Church, ascribed to demons could be explained away by other influences. Those influences were not yet purely 'natural' forces : they were celestial bodies and hidden powers. But at least they were not diabolic interventions. Pomponazzi maintained that apparitions were natural phenomena and that men 'possessed by the devil' were merely melancholic. 'Had his views prevailed', writes the greatest authority on Renaissance magic, 'there would hardly have been any witchcraft delusion and persecution or religious wars.'[2]

If the revived and purified Aristoteleanism of the Renaissance

---

[1] Andrea Alciati, *Parergon Juris* (Lea, *Materials*, p. 374) ; Gianfrancesco Ponzinibio, *Tractatus de Lamiis et Excellentia Juris Utriusque* (ibid., p. 377) ; Girolamo Cardano, *de Subtilitate* (1550) and *de Rerum Varietate* (1557), ibid., p. 435 ; Samuel de' Cassini, *Question de le strie* (1505), ibid., p. 366.

[2] Lynn Thorndike, *History of Magic and Experimental Science*, v (New York, 1941), 110.

pointed one way out of the satanic cosmology, another very different way was pointed by the revived Platonism, or rather neo-Platonism, of Florence. The scientific revolution of the sixteenth and seventeenth centuries, it is now generally agreed, owed more to the new Platonism of the Renaissance, and to the Hermetic mysticism which grew out of it, than to any mere 'rationalism' in the modern sense of the word. Ficino, with his 'natural magic', Paracelsus for all his bombast, Giordano Bruno in spite of his 'Egyptian' fantasies, did more to advance the concept and investigation of a regular 'Nature' than many a rational, sensible, Aristotelean scholar who laughed at their absurdities or shrank from their shocking conclusions. It was precisely at the time of the Witch Bull that Platonic ideas were adopted in Italy and it was during the next century and a half that they provided the metaphysical impulse to the exploration of Nature. Nature, to the neo-Platonists, might be filled with 'demons' and charged with 'magical' forces, operating by sympathies and antipathies. It might not exclude the existence of 'witches' — creatures who, by arcane methods, contrived to short-circuit or deflect its operations. But at least it had no need of such vulgar mechanism as particular satanic compacts, with their ridiculous concomitants of carnal intercourse, 'imps', broomsticks and the witches' sabbat. It is no accident that 'natural magicians' like Agrippa and Cardano and 'alchemists' like Paracelsus and his disciples were among the enemies of the witch-craze, while those who attacked Platonist philosophy, Hermetic ideas and Paracelsian medicine were also, often, the most stalwart defenders of the same delusion.[1]

[1] Agrippa and Cardano were both frequently attacked as being themselves witches (e.g. by Bodin and James VI). So was the greatest critic of the witch-craze, Johann Weyer, who had been a pupil of Agrippa. Among Weyer's supporters was Dr Johann Ewich, a physician, who was also an advocate of 'natural magic' (although both he and Weyer opposed Paracelsus). On the other hand Thomas Erastus of Heidelberg impartially attacked Paracelsus on medicine — in his *Disputationes de Medicina Nova Paracelsi* (1572) — and Weyer on witches — in his *Disputatio de Lamiis* (1578) — and the Provençal physician Jacques Fontaine of St-Maximin was equally extreme in his diatribes against witches and against Paracelsus (see *Jacobi Fontani Sanmaxitani . . . Opera*, Cologne, 1612, pp. 313–25, 'Magiae Paracelsicae Detectio', and cf. Thorndike, *History of Magic and Experimental Science*, VI, 554). The French Huguenot Lambert Daneau showed himself

Thus it might seem that the dogmas so magisterially formulated by the *Malleus* would soon crumble against the corrosive ideas of the new century. However, they did not. The sceptics spoke only to be instantly overpowered by the defenders of faith. Those who deny the existence of *incubi* and *succubi*, declared the Dominican inquisitor of Lombardy, Sylvester Mozzolino, 'catholice non loquuntur'. These lawyers, protested Mozzolino's disciple Bartolomeo Spina, referring to Ponzinibio, are altogether ignorant of theology : they should be prosecuted by the Inquisition as the chief cause of the increase of witches. The robust Dominican Vincente Dodo announced that he would pursue the wavering Franciscan Cassini with a brandished sword. Afterwards the lay judges who inherited the mantle of the inquisitors would speak with the same voice. Peter of Abano and Alciati and Agrippa and all their followers, and all lenient judges, Bodin would write, were themselves witches, inspired by Satan in order to divert attention from their own kind and so enable them to multiply in peace.[1]

All through the sixteenth and seventeenth centuries this dialogue continued. The voice of scepticism — the scepticism of common sense, the scepticism of Paduan science, the scepticism of Platonic metaphysics — was never stilled. Every orthodox

an obscurantist Aristotelean scientist in his *Physice Christiana* (1580) and an obscurantist witch-hunter in his *de Veneficis . . . Dialogus* ([Geneva], 1574). So did the Dutch Calvinist oracle Voëtius. The French scholar Gabriel Naudé, in his *Apologie pour les grands personnages . . . soupçonnez de magie* (Paris, 1625), shows himself an admirer of the Platonists, Hermetics and Paracelsians and an opponent of witch-beliefs. The same is true of the English physician John Webster (see his *Displaying of Supposed Witchcraft . . .* 1677). This equation of Platonists and 'natural magicians' with critics of the witch-craze is not constant and some Platonists — like the 'Cambridge Platonists' Henry More and Joseph Glanvill — were also believers in witchcraft. But logically it seems to me that Renaissance Platonism and Paracelsianism were incompatible with the crude form of witch-belief which had been established on the basis of scholastic Aristoteleanism. For this reason I am not convinced by the suggestion of Fèbvre (*Annales*: *economies, sociétés, civilisations*, 1948, p. 13) that Renaissance Platonism, merely because it postulated a world of demons, positively contributed to witch-beliefs. They were a very different kind of demons. I am grateful to my friend Mr Pyarali Rattansi for illuminating discussions on this abstruse matter.

[1] For Mozzolino, known as Prierias, see Lea, *Materials*, 354 ff. ; for Spina, ibid. pp. 385 ff. ; for Dodo, ibid. p. 367. Bodin's attack on Peter of Abano and Alciati is in his *De la démonomanie des sorciers*, Preface.

writer pays reluctant tribute to it by his hysterical denunciations of the unbelievers thanks to whom witches are multiplying so terribly in the world. Nevertheless, at least until the middle of the seventeenth century, the orthodox always prevailed. The voice of dissent was powerless to stay the persecution. It could hardly be uttered in safety. Romances of chivalry could be laughed out of existence, but no Don Quixote dared to kill, by ridicule, the bizarre novelettes which the grave lawyers and divines of all Europe published about Satan's kingdom.

Why was this? Some explanations easily offer themselves. The new intellectual forces were themselves ambivalent. The humanist spirit might be critical in a Valla or an Erasmus, but it could be uncritical in others to whom the very fables of Greece and Rome were as Holy Writ: and those fables — of Circe, of Pegasus, of the amours of gods with men — could be called in to sustain the witch-beliefs. The pseudo-Aristoteleanism of the Church had the support of a vested interest which the true Aristoteleanism of Padua had not. The gulf between the neo-Platonic demons, which filled and animated all Nature, and the diabolic hierarchy of the inquisitors might be very deep and logically impassable, but to the common eye — and even to some uncommon eyes — it was also very narrow and could be jumped. When Ficino and Pico della Mirandola, Reuchlin and Cardano, Copernicus and Paracelsus, Giordano Bruno and Campanella all believed, or seemed to believe, that men, by arcane knowledge, might make angels work for them and so control the movements of heaven, it was not unreasonable for ordinary men to suppose that witches, by a baser acquisition of power, might make devils work for them and so interfere with events on earth. or vice versa,

However, in matters of ideology, it is not generally the ideas which convince. Between two interpretations of any philosophy it is often external events which make the decision. Therefore if we are to ask why the witch-craze, established in its final form in the 1480s, was proof against all criticism for nearly two hundred years, we should perhaps turn back again from its intellectual content to its social significance. We may begin by considering

its history : the timing, in relation to external events, of its great
outbreaks.

Once we do this, we soon see that a pattern emerges. The
fourteenth and fifteenth centuries had been periods of spectacular
individual persecutions, but not, outside the Alps and the
Pyrenees, of mass-crazes. What we have seen, in those centuries,
is the formulation of doctrine on the basis of Alpine and Pyrenean
experience and the application of it in particular trials, often of a
political character. The Witch Bull and the *Malleus* mark the
final presentation of the doctrine and help to extend it beyond
its original frontiers. They demand a renewed crusade in the
mountain areas, but at the same time they carry it outside those
areas and call upon the support of secular as well as clerical
authorities. In particular, they extend it, or seek to extend it, to
lower Germany : that Germany which is already showing signs
of the impending revolt from Rome, and in which the great
adversaries of Luther would be the Dominicans.[1]

In the immediately following generation we can see the results.
The crusade against the Alpine peoples is renewed. There is
intenser persecution in Styria and the Tyrol. Then, from 1500
to 1525, there is a real social war, disguised as witch-hunting, in
the Italian Alps. According to the Dominican inquisitor in the
diocese of Como, a thousand witches were tried and a hundred
burnt in his area every year. In the end the population took up
arms and appealed to the bishop. The bishop sent a lawyer to
report, and the lawyer convinced himself, and told the bishop,
that very few of the persecuted peasants were really witches. In
1520 this crusade in the mountains was extended from the Alps
to the Apennines and a long persecution soon began in the diocese
of Bologna. Simultaneously it spread to the Pyrenees and Spanish
inquisitors set to work in Guipúzcoa and Vizcaya. Meanwhile, in
Germany, obedient to the bull, the secular powers began to take up
the task which the inquisitors had been powerless to carry out.[2]

[1] For the leading part played by the Dominicans in the struggle against Luther
in Germany, see especially Nikolaus Paulus, *Die deutschen Dominikaner im Kampf
gegen Luther 1518–1563* (Freiburg-im-Breisgau, 1903).
[2] For the crusade in the Alps and Apennines, see Hansen, *Zauberwahn*, pp. 500–1,
Quellen, pp. 310–12. The lawyer was Andrea Alciati, who describes his mission in

But apart from occasional activity in Germany, the first half of the sixteenth century, outside the Alps and Pyrenees, was a period of relative calm. The witch-hunt, it seemed, had passed its peak, or perhaps the sceptics were prevailing. In France, after the spectacular trials of the fifteenth century, witchcraft seemed forgotten.[1] Even in Germany, in spite of the *Malleus* and the inquisitors, the persecution remained slight.[2] Moreover, the law refused to make witchcraft in itself punishable by death. Luther and the Dominicans might vie with each other in credulous ferocity, but the imperial constitution of 1532, the *Constitutio Criminalis Carolina*, if it generalized the Roman law against witchcraft, also insisted on the old Roman distinction between the 'good' and the 'bad' witch. Punishment could only be for harm done by witchcraft : merely to be a witch was not enough.[3] Even in Switzerland, in those years, persecution was negligible. Geneva, that mercantile city, the seat of international fairs and an educated *bourgeoisie*, had long been free from witch-trials. In Schwyz they were unknown till 1571. Zürich, under Zwingli, was mild : Zwingli himself never showed any sign of belief in witchcraft. Erasmian Basel listened to the witch-stories of the surrounding mountains with polite amusement.[4]

Parergon Juris, printed in his *Opera* (Basel, 1558). For the inquisitors in the Spanish Pyrenees, see J. Caro Baroja, *The World of the Witches*, pp. 145–52.

[1] For the increase in witch-trials in Germany after the bull, see G. Längin, *Religion und Hexenprozess*, pp. 76 ff. Bodin implies that witchcraft was of recent introduction in France in his time (Lea, *Materials*, p. 576). Similarly the author of the pamphlet *Les Sorcelleries de Henri de Valoys et les oblations qu'il faisoit au Diable dans le bois de Vincennes* (Paris, 1587) says that France was free from the abominable science of magic in the time of François I and Henri II, and indeed until the time of Henri III and the *Sainte Ligue*.

[2] Sigmund Riezler, *Geschichte der Hexenprozessen in Baiern* (Cotta, 1896). Weyer states that, before 1562, the craze had died down in Germany (*de Praestigiis Daemonum*, 1563, Dedication).

[3] The *Carolina* was based on the *Constitutio Bambergensis* of 1507, which had been compiled by Johann Freiherr zu Schwarzenberg u. Hohenlandsberg. The article of the Carolina on witchcraft (art. 109) was taken bodily from the Bambergensis. The relevant Roman law is the law of Constantine *de Maleficis et Mathematicis*, incorporated in the Code of Justinian.

[4] For Zürich, see Paul Schweizer, 'Der Hexenprozess und seine Anwendung in Zürich', in *Zürcher Taschenbuch*, 1902 ; Nikolaus Paulus, *Hexenwahn und Hexenprozess*, § VIII, 'Der Hexenwahn bei den Zwinglianern des 16ten Jahrhundert'. (But Paulus' attempt to prove Zwingli a persecutor *ex silentio* seems to me special pleading.) For Schwyz, see A. Dettling, *Die Hexenprozesse im Kanton Schwyz* (Schwyz, 1907).

But if the sceptics thought that they were prevailing, they were
soon to know better. If the Catholic evangelists had launched
the craze, the Protestant evangelists would soon revive and
extend it. Already, in the 1540s, there had been warning signs.
In 1540, in Luther's Wittenberg, four witches were burnt. On
this subject Luther himself was as credulous as any Dominican,
and as he grew older, he contrived to believe more: *succubi*,
incubi, night-flight and all. Witches, he declared, should be burnt
even if they did no harm, merely for making a pact with the
Devil.[1] In Zürich, Zwingli's successors did not imitate his
restraint.[2] In Geneva, Calvin held the same language as Luther.
'The Bible', he declared, preaching to the Elect on the Witch
of Endor, 'teaches us that there are witches and that they must
be slain . . . God expressly commands that all witches and
enchantresses shall be put to death ; and this law of God is an
universal law.' The law of God was stated most explicitly in
Exodus xxii. 18 : 'thou shalt not suffer a witch to live'. On
this savoury text the Protestant clergy — Lutheran, Calvinist,
Zwinglian — were to preach, with grim relish, for the next century ; and they did not fail to point out that the law of God,
unlike the law of the Emperor, made no exception in favour of
'the good witch'.[3]

Wherever they went, they carried the craze with them. It was
Lutheran preachers who first brought it to Denmark,[4] Calvinist

[1] Paulus, *Hexenwahn und Hexenprozess*, § II, 'Luthers Stellung zur Hexenfrage',
shows the growing credulity of Luther. Luther based his beliefs explicitly on the
Bible and old wives' tales, but he was, of course, a renegade friar, and although
he does not avow such a source, he was no doubt familiar with the more systematic
demonology of the inquisitors.

[2] Paulus, *Hexenwahn und Hexenprozess*, § VIII. The decline of the Zwinglian
Church from the liberalism of its founder is further emphasized in the next century.
See the account of Bartholomäus Anhorn, *Magiologia* (Basel, 1674), in Lea, *Materials*,
p. 747.

[3] Paulus, *Hexenwahn und Hexenprozess*, § IV, 'Die Bibel als Autorität für protestantische Hexenverfolgung', gives many instances of the use of this happy text.
For the undeniable effect of Calvinism, see the summary in G. L. Burr, 'New
England's Place in the History of Witchcraft', in *Proceedings of the American Anti-
quarian Society*, 1911, reprinted in Burr, *Life*, pp. 352–77.

[4] The Danish oracle was Niels Hemmingsen (Hemmingius), who published his
Admonitio de Superstitionibus Magicis Vitandis at Copenhagen in 1575. He had
studied at Wittenberg under Luther's successor, Melanchthon, and shows some

missionaries who implanted it in Transylvania.[1] Like the Dominicans before them, the Protestant evangelists introduced the
systematic mythology of the Inquisition into countries which
hitherto had known only the disconnected superstitions of the
countryside. It was Lutheran preachers who brought the witch-
craze in the 1560s into Brandenburg, Württemberg, Baden,
Bavaria, Mecklenburg. It was the Calvinist revolution which
brought the first witch-law to Scotland in 1563 and thus inaugurated a century of terror. In the previous year the first
general witch-law had been passed by the English Parliament.
In both Scotland and England the pressure came from the
'Marian exiles' — the Protestant clergy who, in the days of
persecution, had sat at the feet of Calvin or other Reformers, in
Switzerland and Germany.[2]

The responsibility of the Protestant clergy for the revival of
the witch-craze in the mid-sixteenth century is undeniable. It has
led some commentators to argue that Protestantism has a special
responsibility for such beliefs. But this is absurd : it is to judge
on far too narrow a basis. To dispose of such a conclusion, we
need only look back to the Dominicans. We may equally look
forward to the Jesuits.

For if the Dominicans had been the evangelists of the medieval

of the good sense of his master. But he is firm on the subject of the 'good'
witch; 'similis est impietas nocere et prodesse arte magica'; and he explicitly
rejects the old distinction of Roman Law.

[1] F. Müller, *Beiträge zur Geschichte des Hexenglaubens und des Hexenprozesses in
Siebenburgen* (Brunswick, 1854), pp. 16 ff.

[2] For Scotland, see G. F. Black, 'Witchcraft in Scotland 1510–1727', in *Bulletin
of the New York Public Library*, XLI, no. 11 (Nov. 1937). For England, Notestein,
History of Witchcraft in England . Notestein points out that the first prosecutions
under the new law were explicitly related, by the magistrate concerned, to the
opinions brought by Jewel from Switzerland : 'there is a man of great cunning and
knowledge come over lately unto our Queen's Majesty which hath advertised her
what a company and number of witches be within England ; whereupon I and
other of her Justices have received commission for the apprehending of as many
as are within these limits' (p. 46). It may be added that the first manual of witch-
beliefs to be published in England also came from Switzerland. It was Lambert
Daneau's *de veneficis* . . . *Dialogus*, of which Thomas Twyne published a translation
in 1575. Daneau's work had been written at Gien, near Orléans, where he was
a Huguenot pastor ; but it was published in Geneva, whither he had fled after
the massacre of St Bartholomew and where he had formerly learned his doctrines
from Calvin himself.

against Renaissance humanism *against Protestantism*

Counter-Reformation, the Jesuits were the evangelists of the sixteenth-century Counter-Reformation, and if Protestant evangelists carried the craze to the countries which they conquered for Reform, these Catholic evangelists carried it equally to the countries which they reconquered for Rome. Some of the most famous of Jesuit missionaries distinguished themselves in propagating the witch-craze : St Peter Canisius, the apostle of Germany ; Peter Thyraeus, the oracle of the witch-burning Archbishop of Mainz ; Fr. Schorich, the court-preacher of the Duke of Baden ; Gregor von Valentia, the theologian of Ingolstadt ; Jerome Drexel, court-preacher to the insatiable Duke of Bavaria ; Georg Scherer, the court-preacher of the Emperor in Vienna. It was the Catholic reconquest which brought the witch-craze in a terrible form to Bavaria, where dukes William V and Maximilian I, great patrons of the Jesuits, kept the witch-fires burning. It was the Catholic reconquest which decimated the Rhineland in the 1590s, and the Jesuits who stood behind its greatest executioners, the Archbishop of Trier and his terrible suffragan, Bishop Binsfeld. It was the Catholic reconquest which introduced witch-burning into Flanders, and the Jesuit del Rio who would keep it up. Philip II's letters patent of 1590, declaring witchcraft the scourge and destruction of the human race, inaugurated a long reign of terror in Flanders. The Counter-Reformation brought the witch-craze to Poland as the Reformation had brought it to Hungary. The restitution of clerical power in 1600 led to the renewal of witch-trials in Franche-Comté. Special powers granted by the Pope in 1604 enabled the Duke Maximilian to intensify the crusade in Bavaria. Pierre de l'Ancre, the gleeful executioner of the Pays de Labourd in 1609, gloried in his Jesuit education.[1]

Thus, if we look at the revival of the witch-craze in the 1560s

[1] For the Jesuits in Germany, see especially Duhr, *Geschichte der Jesuiten in den Ländern deutscher Zunge*, II, ii, 498, etc. ; Riezler, *Geschichte der Hexenprozessen in Baiern*. The admissions of the Jesuit historian are as telling as any of the accusations of the Protestant. For Franche-Comté, see the documents published by F. Bavoux in *La Sorcellerie en Franche-Comté : Pays de Quingey* (Monaco, 1954) and *Hantises et diableries dans la terre abbatiale de Luxeuil* (Monaco, 1956). See also Lea, *Materials*, pp. 1218–19. For Flanders, see J. B. Cannaert, *Procès des sorcières en Belgique sous Philippe II et le gouvernement des archiducs* (Ghent, 1847). For Poland, Soldan-Heppe, I, 427.

in its context, we see that it is not the product either of Protestantism or of Catholicism, but of both : or rather, of their conflict. Just as the medieval Dominican evangelists had ascribed witch-beliefs to the whole society which resisted them, so both the Protestant and Catholic evangelists of the mid-sixteenth century ascribed the same beliefs to the societies which opposed them. The recrudescence of the absurd demonology of the *Malleus* was not the logical consequence of any religious idea : it was the social consequence of renewed ideological war and the accompanying climate of fear. The parties drew on a mythology which was already there, elaborated out of a similar situation by their medieval predecessors. Perhaps, on the eve of the Reformation, that mythology was on the way out. Who can say what might have happened if Erasmus had triumphed instead of Luther and Loyola ? Then the Renaissance might have led direct to the Enlightenment and the witch-craze have been remembered as a purely medieval lunacy. But that was not to be. The frontal opposition of Catholics and Protestants, representing two forms of society incompatible with each other, sent men back to the old dualism of God and the Devil and the hideous reservoir of hatred, which seemed to be drying up, was suddenly refilled.

The recrudescence of the witch-craze from about 1560 can be documented from innumerable sources. We can trace it geographically, watch it, country by country, as the Protestant or the Catholic missionaries declare war on the obstinate. We can see it in literature, in the series of grotesque encyclopaedias in which writer after writer repeated and amplified the fantasies of the *Malleus*. We can see it in its legal form, in the gradual change of law and practice to meet the alleged multiplication of witches, and in the gradual acquiescence of the lawyers in a new and profitable branch of their business.[1] One of the new practices was

---

[1] It is interesting to observe the change in the legal attitude towards witchcraft in the course of the sixteenth century. At first the lawyers were generally hostile to the new mythology — as Mozzolino (see above, p. 133), Francisco de Vitoria (*Relectiones XII Theologicae*, ch. x, cited in Hansen, *Quellen*, pp. 354–7) and others admit. But from mid-century they generally support the witch-hunters, and by 1600 they are more savage and pedantic than the clergy. The same conservative spirit which had once resisted the novelty now venerated the established doctrine.

like English trial by ordeal with Assize of Clarendon — 1166

THE EUROPEAN WITCH-CRAZE

the 'cold-water test', the throwing of a suspected witch into a
pond or river to see whether she would float or not.[1] If she did,
diabolic aid was proved and she was burnt as a witch. If she
sank, innocence could be presumed, although perhaps, by that
time, she had drowned. The literature of the time shows that
this test was invented, or revived, in the 1560s.[2] At the same
time the law itself received an important modification : under
clerical pressure it abandoned the old and humane distinction
between the 'good' and the 'bad' witch.

In 1563 the Scottish witch-law, obedient to the voice of Calvin,
prescribed death for all witches, good or bad, and for those who
consulted them.[3] In 1572 Augustus the Pious, Elector of Saxony,
introduced a new criminal code, the *Consultationes Saxonicae*,
according to which even the 'good' witch was to be burnt,   *see 137*
merely for having made a pact with the Devil, 'even if she has
harmed nobody with her sorcery'. This provision was the result
of organized pressure by the lawyers and clergy of Luther's
Wittenberg.[4] The same provision was adopted ten years later in
the Palatinate by its Lutheran Elector Ludwig, and by a number
of other princes. Where the Catholic, Lutheran or Calvinist
Churches ruled the practice was the same.[5] In Elizabethan

[1] So called to distinguish it from the 'hot-water test', which involved thrusting
the suspect's arm into boiling water and measuring guilt or innocence by the effect.
[2] See the controversy on the subject provoked by Adolf Schreiber (Scribonius),
de Examine et Purgatione Sagarum . . . Epistola (Lemgo, 1583). Schreiber was a
physician of Marburg and advocated the test as scientific. His critics included
Johann Ewich, state physician of the city of Bremen, and Hermann Neuwaldt, a
physician of Brunswick. Ewich described the cold-water test as 'indicium recens
repertum sed nunc quoque passim usitatum' (*De Sagarum . . . Natura, Arte, Viribus
et Factis*, Bremen, 1584, sig D.3) ; Neuwaldt as a test which he had observed
'nunc denuo vires resumere' (*Exegesis Purgationis sive Examinis Sagarum*, Helmstedt,
1585). It is mentioned in Weyer's *de Praestigiis Daemonum* (Lea, *Materials*, pp. 524–
525). Most lawyers — even Bodin — condemned the cold-water test (see Gödelmann, *de Magis*, I, ch. v, nn. 21, 23, 26–30). But their condemnation was vain :
the custom, once adopted, became a new sport with country people, as popular as
bear- or bull-baiting. See Francis Hutchinson, *An Historical Essay on Witchcraft*
(1718), p. 175. For its use in France, see *Papiers d'état du chancelier Séguier* (Paris,
1964), I, 636–7. I owe this last reference to Mrs Menna Prestwich.
[3] *Acts of the Parliament of Scotland*, II, 539.
[4] Paulus, *Hexenwahn und Hexenprozess*, pp. 55–57.
[5] Thus Melchior Goldast, a Calvinist lawyer, in a memorial submitted to the
Catholic Elector of Trier in 1629, declares that witches, whether harmful or not,

England the law preserved the old distinction and indeed the Anglican Church has an honourable record of sanity and modera-tion.[1] Its teacher had been Bucer, the disciple of Erasmus, whose influence also kept Strasbourg as an island of sense in the Rhine-land. But even in England the Calvinist clergy pressed for con-formity with the pure 'schools of Christ' abroad. Their oracle was the Cambridge preacher and casuist William Perkins, who lectured on the subject in Emmanuel College in the 1590s. He impressed upon his hearers — and indirectly on the founding fathers of New England Puritanism, who were to prove apt pupils[2]— the standard view of the godly that by the law of Moses, 'the equity whereof is perpetual', and from which there are no exceptions, the witch must be put to death. Whoever has made a pact with the Devil, even to do good, must die. Indeed, said Perkins, 'the good witch' was 'a more horrible and detestable monster than the bad'; so if 'death be due to any', as we know that it is due to all, 'then a thousand deaths of right belong to the good witch'.[3] A few years later, the royal demonologist, James VI of Scotland, came to reign in England. Brought up as a good Calvinist and committed to all the absurdities of con-tinental science, he did not like the mild Elizabethan law. He 'found a defect in the statutes', we are told, ' . . . by which none died for witchcraft but they only who by that means killed, so that such were executed rather as murderers than witches'.

must be burnt, and gives a list of princes and cities, Catholic, Lutheran and Calvinist, that have adjusted their laws accordingly (*Rechtliches Bedencken von Confiscation der Zauberer- und Hexen-Güther* (Bremen, 1661)). See also Lea, *Materials*, p. 805 ; Paulus, *Hexenwahn und Hexenprozess*, p. 78.

[1] 'The singularly favourable contrast which the Anglican Church presents both to continental Catholicism and to Puritanism' is mentioned both by W. E. H. Lecky, *History of the Rise and Influence of . . . Rationalism in Europe*, I, 124–6, and by White, *The Warfare of Science with Theology*, I, 362. Lest religious bias be suspected, it may be added that White was a Baptist. The same point had been made by Francis Hutchinson, *An Historical Essay on Witchcraft*, Dedication : 'in the main, I believe, our Church of England and its clergy, have as little to answer for, in this respect, as any'. The Erasmian *via media*, the lukewarmth of a non-evangelizing Church, has something to commend it. For Strasbourg, see Lea, *Materials*, pp. 1081, 1208 ; Reuss, *La Sorcellerie*, pp. 178–81.

[2] For the influence of Perkins on the New England Puritans, see Burr, *Life*, p. 366.

[3] Perkins, *A Discourse on the Damned Art of Witchcraft*, pp. 173–8, etc.

So he had the law changed. Henceforth death was the legal penalty, even in England, for the 'good' witch.[1]

That this recrudescence of the witch-craze in the 1560s was directly connected with the return of religious war is clear. It can be shown from geography : every major outbreak is in the frontier-area where religious strife is not intellectual, a dissent of opinion, but social, the dissidence of a society. When Bishop Palladius, the Reformer of Denmark, visited his diocese, he declared those who used Catholic prayers or formulas to be witches ; and witches, he said, 'in these days of pure Gospel-light', must be burnt.[2] When Bishop Jewel, fresh from Switzerland, told Queen Elizabeth that witches and sorcerers 'within these last few years are marvellously increased within this your Grace's realm', and demanded action against them, he was declaring Protestant war on the Catholic England of Mary Tudor.[3] The persecution in England was sharpest in Essex and in Lancashire — two counties where Catholicism was strong and the Puritan evangelists particularly energetic. The Scottish Calvinists, when they obtained their witch-law, were similarly declaring war on Catholic society. Germany and Switzerland were also countries where the two religions faced each other in sharp social opposition : in Germany the persecution remained most persistent in Westphalia, the seat of medieval heresy and sixteenth-century Anabaptism,[4] while in Switzerland the Calvinist

[1] For the witch-law of James I, passed in 1604, see Notestein, *History of Witchcraft in England*, pp. 101-4.

[2] See J. Janssen, *A History of the German People at the Close of the Middle Ages*, trans. by M. A. Mitchell and A. M. Christie (1896-1925), XVI, 307.

[3] Notestein, *History of Witchcraft in England*, p. 116.

[4] H. A. Meinders, writing in Lemgo (Westphalia) in 1716, refers to terrible abuses in witch-prosecutions in Westphalia from 1600 to 1700 in which whole towns, especially Herford and Lemgo, have been laid waste (cited in Lea, *Materials*, p. 1432 ; cf. also the remarks of Jacob Brunnemann, ibid. p. 429). But the persecution had begun well before 1600. It was in Lemgo, in 1583, that Scribonius had published his arguments in favour of the cold-water test, now generally used 'in hisce nostris regionibus, praesertim vero in Westphalia'. He dedicated his works to the magistrates of Lemgo and Osnabrück whom Ewich and Neuwaldt afterwards accused of 'iniquity and injustice' against witches. The Westphalian jurist Anton Praetorius, who wrote against the craze in 1598-1602, had been driven to protest by the executions he had witnessed there. (See Paulus, *Hexenwahn und Hexenprozess*, § x, 'Der calvinische Prediger Anton Praetorius, ein Bekämpfer der

cities made war on the obstinate peasantry of the country.[1]   In
France the geographical antithesis was no less clear.   The same
areas which had accepted the medieval heresies became, in the
sixteenth century, the solid base of the Huguenots : in the Wars
of Religion the Protestant south opposed the Catholic north and
the last redoubt of Protestantism was the last redoubt of Albigensianism, Languedoc.   It was therefore natural that witches
should be found in Protestant islands like Orléans or Normandy ;
that by 1609 the entire population of 'Protestant' Navarre should
be declared to be witches ;[2]   and that the capital of the witch-
burners should be the great centre of vindictive Catholic orthodoxy, Toulouse.[3]

The same connection can be shown from chronology.   The
recrudescence in the 1560s marks the period of Protestant

Protestants as witches (margin note)

Hexenverfolgung').   For statistical evidence of the persecution in Osnabrück in
the 1580s and 1590s, see Hansen, *Quellen*, p. 545, n. 1.
  [1] Thus, in the areas ruled by the Protestant, German-speaking city of Bern, the
victims came principally from the Catholic, French-speaking Pays de Vaud : see
F. Treschsel, *Das Hexenwesen im Kanton Bern* (1870) and H. Vuilleumier, *Histoire de
l'Église réformée du Pays de Vaud sous le régime bernois* (Lausanne, 1927–33), II, 642–721.
  [2] This is repeatedly stated by de l'Ancre, *L'Incrédulité*.
  [3] Toulouse has preserved a constant character of intolerance.   It was the centre
from which the Albigensian heresy was exterminated ; it played a sanguinary part
in the suppression of the Huguenots of Languedoc ; and it was no less brutal in
the war against witches.   The first witch known to have confessed to sexual intercourse with the Devil was burnt in Toulouse in 1275 (Lea, *Inquisition in the Middle
Ages*, III, 384).   From the time of Pope John XXII, it was the scene of continual
and ferocious witch-trials (Lea, *Materials*, pp. 222, 230–2, etc.) ; and in the single
year 1577, according to Pierre Grégoire, a civil lawyer of Toulouse (*Syntagma Juris
Universi . . .* Lyon, 1582), the parlement of Toulouse burnt 400 witches.   The
same authority would burn Giulio Cesare Vanini for intellectual heresy in 1619
and break Jean Calas on the wheel for being a Huguenot in 1762.   The cathedral
of Albi, the University of Toulouse, and the thaumaturgical apparatus of Lourdes
mark the successive triumphs of an intolerant orthodoxy over spirit, mind and
common sense.
  The same character of intolerance, regardless of the nature of the heresy, can be
detected in Bavaria.   The oppressive nature of the Counter-Reformation in Bavaria
is well known.   Max Bauer, the editor of Soldan-Heppe's *Geschichte der Hexenprozesse*, printed as motto to the book a peculiarly revolting song of Bavarian
orthodoxy :

> Die Teutschen wurden wohlgemut,
> Sie giengen in der Ketzer Plut
> Als wers ein Mayentawe.

(The Germans were high-spirited : they waded in the blood of heretics as though
it were summer dew.)   In our time Bavaria was the cradle of Nazism.

evangelism. Thereafter, almost every local outbreak can be
related to the aggression of one religion upon the other. The
Wars of Religion introduce the worst period of witch-persecution
in French history. The outbreak in the Basque country in 1609
heralds the Catholic reconquest of Béarn. The terrible outbreaks
in Germany, in Flanders and the Rhineland in the 1590s, and
again in 1627-9, mark the stages of Catholic reconquest. Under-
standably, the Catholic historians of Germany dwell with unction
on the persecutions of the 1560s and 1570s, when the witch-
burners were Protestant.[1] Protestants can take their revenge by
looking back to the Dominican campaign of the later Middle
Ages, or forward to the Catholic triumphs of the early seventeenth
century.

Was there any difference between the Catholic and the Protestant craze? Theoretically, yes. The Catholics inherited the
whole medieval tradition of the later Fathers and the Schoolmen
while the Protestants rejected everything which a corrupt papacy
had added to the Bible and the primitive Fathers. Theoretically,
therefore, they should have rejected the whole demonological
science of the Inquisitors; for no one could say that *succubi* and
incubi, 'imps' or werewolves, cats or broomsticks were to be
found in the Bible. This point was constantly made by isolated
Protestant critics, but it had no effect on their official theorists.
Some Calvinist writers might be more intellectual and austere
in detail,[2] but in general Catholics and Protestants vied with
each other in credulity. The authority of Luther transmitted
all the fantasies of the Dominicans to his disciples, and the

[1] Thus the burden of all Nikolaus Paulus' scholarly essays, printed as *Hexenwahn und Hexenprozess*, is to show (*a*) that before the Reformation all men, including the humanists, believed in witchcraft, so that the Catholic inquisitors deserve no special blame; (*b*) that in the late sixteenth century the Protestants were great burners of witches. Although Paulus carries his interest in Protestant persecution down to the end of the seventeenth century, he shows no interest in the persecutions from 1590 to 1630, which were mainly Catholic.

[2] Thus Perkins (*A Discourse on the Damned Art of Witchcraft*) does not mention *succubi* or *incubi* — which are absent also from English witch-trials — and rejects anything which might be regarded as popish 'conjuring'; but he accepts the pact with the Devil and the power of the Devil, by God's permission, to work whatever miracles he likes; from which all else can logically flow, even without the Dominican learning.

confessions of witches were regarded as an untainted supple-
ment to Holy Writ. So, in the end, Catholics and Protestants
agreed on the facts and drew on each other for details. The
Catholic Binsfeld cites the Protestants Erastus and Daneau ; the
Calvinist Voëtius and the Lutheran Carpzov cite the Dominican
Malleus and the Jesuit del Rio. They all also agreed in denouncing
those infamous sceptics who insisted on telling them that supposed witches were merely deluded, 'melancholic' old ladies and
that the Bible, in denouncing death to 'witches', had not referred
to persons like them. From either side, terrible denunciations
fell upon these neuters in the holy war, these 'patrons of witches',
who, together with lenient judges, were regularly declared to be
witches themselves, equally deserving of the bonfire and the stake.

And who were these sceptics ? The most famous of them was
Johann Weyer, a survivor from the civilized days of Erasmus, a
pupil of the Platonist Cornelius Agrippa of Nettesheim, a doctor
of medicine who had studied in the humanist France of François I
and practised in Erasmian Holland. In 1550 he had been invited
to Cleves by the tolerant, Erasmian Duke of Cleves-Jülich-Berg-
Marck, William V,[1] and it was under his protection, and with
his encouragement, that he wrote, in 1563, at the age of forty-
eight, his famous, or notorious work, *de Praestigiis Daemonum*.
In this, while accepting the reality of witchcraft and the whole
Platonic world of spirits, he argued that all the activities to which
witches confessed, and for which they were now being burnt
throughout Germany, were illusions created in them either by
demons or by disease. Having written his work, Weyer sent
copies to his friends and awaited the reaction.

[1] William V's father, John III, had carried out an Erasmian reform in his duchies,
and had secured, as William's tutor, Erasmus' friend Conrad von Heresbach (see
A. Wolters, *Conrad von Heresbach*, Elberfeld, 1867). Carl Binz, *Doctor Johann
Weyer* . . . 2nd ed. (Berlin, 1896), p. 159, describes William V as 'der in den Grund-
sätzen des Erasmus erzogene Herzog'. Weyer's own attitude is illustrated by the
fact that the whole of his chapter xviii is an extract from Erasmus' *Apologia adversus
articulos aliquot per monachos quosdam in Hispaniis exhibitos* (Basel, 1529). Weyer was
himself a Protestant, but his Protestantism has to be deduced : it is never stated
either by him or his enemies — further evidence of his Erasmian moderation.
(See Janssen, *A History of the German People*, XVI, 320-1.) On Weyer see also
Leonard Dooren, *Doctor Johannes Wier, Leven en Werken* (Aalten, 1940).

The reaction was formidable. Weyer had chosen to publish his book precisely at the moment when the witch-craze, after a long lull, was beginning again. That, indeed, was what had provoked him to write. But this Erasmian Platonist — 'the father of modern psychiatry' as he has been called — was no longer heard by a generation that had repudiated Erasmus. A fellow-physician might hail him as a prophet of enlightenment, a Hercules triumphant over superstition,[1] but his other readers thought differently. Weyer was told by his friends that his book must be destroyed or rewritten ; by his enemies that he was a 'Vaudois', a Wycliffite, a lunatic. His work was denounced by the French Calvinist Lambert Daneau, burnt by the Lutheran University of Marburg, and put on the Index by the Catholic governor of the Netherlands, the Duke of Alba, who would ultimately secure Weyer's dismissal from the Court of Cleves. However, the book was read, and in 1577 Weyer published a sequel in which he had congratulated himself on its salutary effect. Unfortunately, he had to add, the tyrants had now resumed their murderous persecution, and so he sought, once again, to expose their errors. This second book happened to come into the hands of Jean Bodin just as Bodin was working himself into a lather of indignation at the leniency of French judges and the infamous neutrality of the French court : the 'Erasmian', 'Platonic' Court of Catherine de Médicis.[2] As if he had not written rubbish enough, Bodin hastily added an appendix denouncing Weyer as an infamous patron of witches, a criminal accomplice of the Devil.

There were sceptics after Weyer, but none of them improved materially on his work. Just as the demonology of the

[1] This fellow-physician was Johann Ewich, whose letter was printed by Weyer. See above, p. 141, n. 1.

[2] Bodin attacked Charles IX as a patron of witches in his *De la démonomanie des sorciers*. Henri III was regularly attacked on the same grounds in the *Ligueur* pamphlets of 1589. See, for instance, *La Vie et faits notables de Henri de Valois* ; *L'Athéisme de Henri de Valoys* ; *Les Sorcelleries de Henri de Valoys* ; *Charmes et caractères de sorcelleries de Henri de Valoys trouvez en la maison de Miron, son premier médecin*. The Erasmianism of the Court of Catherine des Médicis is well brought out by Frances Yates, *The Valois Tapestries* (*Studies of the Warburg Institute*, 1959), pp. 102–8. For Henri III as patron of Platonic 'magicians', see Frances Yates, *Giordano Bruno* (1964), p. 180.

witch-hunters, Catholic or Protestant, was laid down in final form in the *Malleus*, so the basic philosophy of the sceptics, Catholic or Protestant, was laid down by Weyer, and neither the one nor the other was modified by the argument of a century. Every champion of demonological science from Daneau and Bodin onwards took care to attack the 'vain ravings' of Weyer; no sceptic, at least in print, did more than repeat his arguments. The most famous of his successors, the Englishman Reginald Scot, if he was inspired by his own experiences, accepted the arguments of Weyer, and thereafter Weyer and Scot feature together, as an infamous couple, in the books of the orthodox. King James VI of Scotland himself wrote his treatise on *Demonologie* to refute Weyer and Scot; when he came to the English throne one of his earliest acts was to have Scot's work sent to the bonfire; and the Dutch Calvinist Voëtius, equally enraged against both sceptics, is able to dismiss their arguments by appealing to unassailable authority: Weyer was refuted by King James and Scot 'by the public burning of all copies of his book'.[1]

The enemies of Weyer, Scot and other sceptics always accused them of denying the reality of witchcraft. Their defenders impatiently insisted that this was not true. Nor was it. Weyer believed implicitly in the power of Satan, but not that old women were his agents. 'Truly I deny not that there are witches', Scot had written, '. . . but I detest the idolatrous opinions conceived of them.' To the end of the witch-craze, although we always hear it said that there are some who disbelieve the very existence of witches,[2] we never actually hear the denials. To the last the most radical argument against the witch-craze was not that witches

[1] *Gisberti Voetii Selectarum Disputationum Theologicarum . . . Pars Tertia* (Utrecht, 1649), pp. 539–632, 'de Magia'. It is amusing to note this stern Calvinist's deference to public authority: he never mentions Scot without adding 'eius liber titulo *Discoverie of Witchcraft* in Anglia combustus est', 'fuit tamen liber ille publica auctoritate combustus', or some such phrase: e.g. pp. 544, 451, 564.

[2] 'Witches, if there be such creatures' is a phrase which crops up in casual records — e.g. in the remarks of an English soldier in Scotland (see *Letters and Papers illustrating the Relations between Charles II and Scotland in 1650*, Scottish History Society, 1894, p. 136). Edward Fairfax, in *A Discourse of Witchcraft . . .* (1621), refers to such as 'think that there be no witches at all', of whom he has heard that there are many, 'some of them men of worth, religious and honest'. But this absolute disbelief is not found in reasoned writing.

do not exist, not even that the pact with Satan is impossible, but simply that the judges err in their identification. The 'poor doting women', as Scot called them, who are haled before the law courts, and who may confess — whether through torture or delusion — to being witches, have not in fact made any pact with the Devil, or surrendered to his charms, or harmed man or beast. They are 'melancholic'. This was a very tiresome doctrine, and it drove successive orthodox commentators into tantrums of indignation. It could not be refuted. But equally it could not refute the witch-craze. Logically, it left it untouched.

The powerlessness of the critics, a full century after the Witch Bull, is clearly shown by the terrible events which accompanied the Catholic reconquest in Germany. If the Protestant princes and petty lords had waged war on witches in Württemberg and Baden, Brandenburg and Saxony, in the 1560s, 'out of respect for law and evangelic piety',[1] the Catholic princes and prince-bishops (who exercised the same power) outdid them in their turn from 1580 onwards. In one German state after another the craze was then taken up, and no prince was too insignificant to qualify for the competition. The Prince-Abbot of Fulda, for instance, Balthasar von Dernbach, had been driven out by his Protestant subjects. When he came back in 1602, he took his revenge. He gave a free hand to his minister, Balthasar Ross, who styled himself *Malefizmeister* or 'witchmaster' and conducted 'a travelling inquisition' round the principality, falling unexpectedly on villages where he scented a rich prey. He invented new tortures, was paid by results, and in three years, out of 250 victims, had made 5393 gulden.[2] Other instances could be given. But perhaps the most spectacular example, in those first years of reconquest, was given by the pious Archbishop-Elector of Trier, Johann von Schöneburg.

Johann von Schöneburg began his reign in 1581. 'Wonderfully addicted' to the Jesuits, for whom he built and endowed a

---

[1] It was 'aus habendem Recht und evangelischer Frommigkeit' that the Protestant Count Ulrich and Count Sebastian von Helfenstein tortured and burnt sixty-three witches in 1562–3 (see Paulus, *Hexenwahn und Hexenprozess*, p. 110).

[2] Lea, *Materials*, pp. 1075, 1079, 1232; Soldan, pp. 312–13.

splendid college, he showed his devotion in militant fashion too. First he rooted out the Protestants, then the Jews, then the witches : three stereotypes of nonconformity. Thanks to his patronage the campaign of Trier was 'of an importance quite unique in the history of witchcraft'. In twenty-two villages 368 witches were burnt between 1587 and 1593, and two villages, in 1585, were left with only one female inhabitant apiece.[1] Among the victims were men, women and children of noble birth and public position. Such was Dietrich Flade, rector of the university and chief judge of the electoral court. Unconvinced by the confessions which had been extracted by torture, he judged the victims leniently. Consequently the prince-archbishop had him arrested, accused of witchcraft himself, tortured till he confessed whatever was put to him, strangled and burnt. This put a stop to leniency by judges, and the population of Trier continued to shrink. As it shrank, the executioner, like some solitary cannibal, swelled in pride and sleekness, and rode about on a fine horse, 'like a nobleman of the court, dressed in silver and gold, while his wife vied with noblewomen in dress and luxury'.[2]

The craze in Trier was spectacular ; but it was by no means isolated. All through the Rhineland and in south Germany, in those years, the example was followed, and the unrestrained secular and clerical jurisdiction of the princes was capable of terrible abuse. Moreover, like the good kings of Israel whom they strove to emulate, each prince also had his prophet to fire his zeal and keep it on fire. The Archbishop of Trier had his suffragan Peter Binsfeld, whose two sanguinary works, published in 1589 and 1591, were of great help in sustaining and guiding

[1] *Gesta Trevirorum*, ed. J. H. Wyttenbach and M. F. J. Müller (Trier, 1839), III, 47–57. This fearful account of the persecution in Trier is by a canon of the cathedral who was shocked by its excesses. Parts of it are quoted by Soldan, pp. 358–61 ; Lea, *Materials*, pp. 1188–91 ; G. L. Burr, *Translations and Reprints from the Original Sources of European History : The Witch Persecutions* (Philadelphia, 1897). The remark about the unique significance of the persecution in Trier is by Burr.

[2] For the persecution in Trier, see Lea, *Materials*, pp. 1075, 1189–90 ; G. L. Burr, 'The Fate of Dietrich Flade', *American Historical Association Papers*, v (1891), 3–57 (partly reprinted in Burr, *Life*, pp. 190–233). For the similar prosperity of the executioner in Schongau, Bavaria, see Riezler, *Geschichte der Hexenprozessen in Baiern*, p. 172. Other instances in Soldan, pp. 314 ff.

the persecution. The Archbishop of Mainz had his Jesuit Peter Thyraeus, who went to press in 1594. The Duke of Lorraine had the lawyer Nicholas Rémy, whose *Daemonolatreia*, published in 1595, was hailed as the greatest Catholic encyclopaedia of witchcraft since the *Malleus*. The Cardinal-Archbishop of Besançon in the Spanish Franche-Comté had another lawyer, Henri Boguet, whose *Examen des sorciers* was published in 1602, its soundness attested by the rector of the Jesuit College of Besançon. Meanwhile the Spanish authorities in Flanders were encouraged by the huge success of their local product. This was the massive encyclopaedia of Martín del Rio, Spaniard turned Fleming, lawyer turned Jesuit. It was first published in 1599–1600, at Louvain, and quickly replaced Rémy's work as the new Catholic *Malleus*. When we consider that these same years, 1580 to 1602, the years from Bodin to Boguet, also saw the Protestant *Demonologie* of King James in Scotland, the work of the Calvinist Perkins in England, the translation of Bodin's work into Latin by the Dutch Calvinist Franciscus Junius,[1] and the Lutheran manuals of Henning Gross in Hanover and Johann Georg Gödelmann in Mecklenburg, as well as a hundred lesser works, we see what batteries of learning were ready to quench the thin and feeble voice of dissent.

To read these encyclopaedias of witchcraft is a horrible experience. Each seems to outdo the last in cruelty and absurdity. Together they insist that every grotesque detail of demonology is true, that scepticism must be stifled, that sceptics and lawyers who defend witches are themselves witches, that all witches, 'good' or 'bad', must be burnt, that no excuse, no extenuation is allowable, that mere denunciation by one witch is sufficient evidence to burn another. All agree that witches are multiplying incredibly in Christendom, and that the reason for their increase is the indecent leniency of judges, the indecent immunity of Satan's accomplices, the sceptics. Some say, writes Binsfeld, that the increase of witches is an argument for leniency. What a suggestion! The only answer to increased crime is increased

[1] Franciscus Junius (François du Jon) was French by birth, but naturalized in the Netherlands.

punishment : as long as there are witches, enchanters, sorcerers in the world, there must be fire ! fire ! fire ! Rémy thought that not only the lawyers but also the law was too mild. By law, children who were said to have attended their mother to the sabbat were merely flogged in front of the fire in which their parent was burning. Rémy would have had the whole seed of witches exterminated and pointed (to show that Catholics too could quote the Bible) to the fate of the irreverent children whom Elisha had very properly caused to be devoured by bears. Boguet was reduced to an agony of hysteria when he thought of the fate of Christendom unless the epidemic were checked. Already, he calculated, the witches of Europe could raise an army bigger than that of Xerxes. And all around him he saw signs of their increase. Germany was almost entirely occupied in building bonfires for them — he was looking, no doubt, towards Trier and Mainz. Switzerland had had to wipe out whole villages in order to keep them down — in the last decade at least 311 witches had been burnt, in steadily increasing batches, in the Pays de Vaud alone.[1] Travellers in Lorraine may see thousands and thousands of stakes — the stakes to which Nicolas Rémy was sending them. 'We in Burgundy are no more exempt than other lands . . . Savoy has not escaped this pest' : indeed, it was from the mountains of Savoy that they descended into Franche-Comté — Savoy, as the Calvinist Daneau had written, which could produce an army of witches able to make war and defeat great kings.[2] All over Europe, cried Boguet, 'that miserable and damnable vermin' 'was multiplying on the land like caterpillars in a garden . . . I wish they all had but one body, so that we could burn them all at once, in one fire !'

When we read these monstrous treatises, we find it difficult to see their authors as human beings. And yet, when we look at their biographies, what harmless, scholarly characters they turn out to be ! Rémy was a cultivated scholar, an elegant Latin poet, the devoted historian of his country. When he died in 1616,

[1] Vuilleumier, *Histoire de l'Église réformée*, II, 655–6.

[2] Daneau, *de Veneficis . . . Dialogus*, p. 11. Savoy was still one of the main centres of the craze a century later. See P. Bayle, *Réponse aux questions d'un provincial* (Rotterdam, 1704), I, 285.

having sent (we are told) between two and three thousand victims
to the stake, he was universally respected. His dedication of his
Daemonolatreia to Cardinal Charles of Lorraine showed touching
personal solicitude : the cardinal suffered from rheumatism,
which he ascribed to the machinations of witches.[1] Boguet was
similarly a scholar, widely read in the classics and in history.
De l'Ancre, the hammer of the Basque witches, is an enchanting
writer who gives us an idyllic account of his country house at
Loubens, with its grotto and chapel of oyster-shells, poised on
a hill overhanging the Garonne, 'the Mount Parnassus of the
Muses'. This old anti-semite and witch-burner, who had retired
thither to devote himself to the Muses, was desolated when gout
detained him at Bordeaux and prevented him from showing his
'chapel of grottos and fountains' to Louis XIII.[2] The Jesuit
del Rio was also a universally respected figure, dedicated to quiet
scholarship from his earliest days, when he had provided himself
with a specially constructed combination of desk and tricycle in
order to dart, with all his papers, from folio to folio in great
libraries. Thanks to such labour-saving devices, he produced
an edition of Seneca at the age of nineteen, citing 1100 authorities,
and was hailed by no less a scholar than Justus Lipsius as 'the
miracle of our age'. He knew nine languages, was marvellously
chaste, refusing, when young, to share the bed of a very illustrious
man, was devoted to the Virgin Mary, was feared as much by
heretics as Hector by the Greeks or Achilles by the Trojans, and
died, almost blind with the intensive study which he had devoted
to the detection and exposure of witches.[3]

Society, it is clear, approved of Rémy and Boguet, de l'Ancre
and del Rio, and they themselves were entirely content with their
work. They, after all, were the scholars, the rationalists of the
time, while the sceptics were the enemies of reason. Such sceptics
were Platonists, Hermetics, Paracelsians — in which case they
were witches themselves and deserved to be burnt, as Giordano

[1] For an account of Rémy, see Ch. Pfister, in *Revue historique*, 1907.
[2] P. de l'Ancre, *L'Incrédulité*, Dedication, etc.
[3] See *Martini Antonii Delrio e Soc. Jesu . . . Vita brevi commentariolo expressa*
(Antwerp, 1609).

Bruno and Vanini were — or they were 'Epicureans', 'libertines', 'Pyrrhonists', who distrusted human reason and reduced its finest constructions to a powder of doubt. Such was Montaigne, who, having attended a witch-burning at some petty Court in Germany, remarked that 'it is rating our conjectures highly to roast people alive for them'.[1] Against such fancies the guardians of reason and education naturally stood firm, and orthodoxy was protected, impartially, by the miracle of Catholic learning, the Jesuit del Rio, and the Protestant Solomon, King James.

Indeed, the more learned a man was in the traditional scholarship of the time, the more likely he was to support the witch-doctors. The most ferocious of witch-burning princes, we often find, are also the most cultured patrons of contemporary learning. The Catholic Prince-Bishop of Würzburg, Julius Echter von Mespelbrunn, who introduced the craze into his territory in the 1590s, was a universal man of the time, polite, learned and enlightened — with the enlightenment of the Counter-Reformation.[2] His contemporary, Heinrich Julius, Duke of Brunswick, is described as 'unquestionably the most learned prince of his time' — and he was a contemporary of our James I. He was skilled in mathematics, chemistry, natural science, Latin, Greek and Hebrew. He was a jurist who preferred the Pandects to the Bible and read the Codex rather than a romance; an architect who designed the buildings of his new University of Helmstedt; a poet and a playwright. In his plays he dwelt with unction on the moral duty of princes to burn witches, and throughout his reign (which he began by expelling the Jews from his state) he never failed in that duty. In his lifetime, says a chronicler, the Lechelnholze Square in Wolfenbüttel looked like a little forest, so crowded were the stakes; works of gross superstition were gratefully dedicated to him;[3] and at his

---

[1] Montaigne, *Essais*, liv. III, § II.

[2] See Götz Freiherr von Pölnitz, *Julius Echter von Mespelbrunn* (Munich, 1934).

[3] E.g. Hemming Gross (Grosius), *Magica seu mirabilium historiarum de Spectris . . . Libri* II (Eisleben, 1597). In his dedication Gross, a Hanoverian bookseller, offers servile gratitude to the prince for his exterminating justice against witches in these days when Satan is more than ever discharging his abominable poison through Christendom.

death, his court-preacher, enumerating his virtues, dwelt especially on his zeal in burning witches 'according to God's
word'.[1]

The European witch-craze of the 1590s, which elicited so many
screams of orthodoxy, did at least elicit one protest. In 1592,
eight years after Scot's protest in England, Cornelis Loos, a devout
Catholic, ventured to suggest that night-flying and the sabbat
were imaginary, that *incubi* and *succubi* did not exist, and that confessions extracted by torture were a means of shedding innocent
blood. But Loos, unlike Scot, never reached the public. The
Cologne printer to whom he offered his book sensed the danger.
Loos was denounced, imprisoned and forced to a humiliating
recantation. The good Bishop Binsfield was present at his recantation and the good Jesuit del Rio published the text of it as
a prophylactic 'lest some evil demon should succeed' in printing
the views which the benevolent authorities had so far suppressed.
In fact the prophylactic was unnecessary. In spite of repeated
efforts, which cost him further imprisonment, until death by
plague saved him from the stake, Loos' book was never published. It remained locked up for three centuries in the Jesuit
college at Trier and his shocking views were known only from
his officiously published recantation.[2]

But if the orthodox contrived to suppress the critics, they did
not succeed in reducing the witches. After 1604 the campaign
abated, at least for a time : the return of peace to Europe no
doubt helped, and King James himself, having settled down in
England, gradually forgot his Scottish ferocity against witches.[3]
In those years the main persecution was once again in the
Pyrenees. But the reservoir of fear remained even when it was
not in use ; those mountain streams continued to feed it ; and
when religious war returned to Europe the witches were suddenly found, once again, to have increased alarmingly during the

---

[1] A. Rhamm, *Hexenglaube und Hexenprozesse, vornämlich in den braunschweigischen
Landen* (Wolfenbüttel, 1882). Cf. Soldan-Heppe, ii, 59 ff.

[2] The manuscript was discovered in 1886 by G. L. Burr. See his account published in *The Nation* (New York), 11 Nov. 1886.

[3] For King James' conversion, see Notestein, *History of Witchcraft in England*
pp. 137–45.

years of peace. In the 1620s, with the destruction of Protestantism
in Bohemia and the Palatinate, the Catholic reconquest of Germany was resumed. In 1629, with the Edict of Restitution, its
basis seemed complete. Those same years saw, in central Europe
at least, the worst of all witch-persecutions, the climax of the
European craze.

All over Europe (as a Jesuit historian admits) the witch-trials
multiplied with the Catholic reconquest.[1] In some areas the lord
or bishop was the instigator, in others the Jesuits. Sometimes
local witch-committees were set up to further the work. Among
prince-bishops, Philipp Adolf von Ehrenberg of Würzburg was
particularly active : in his reign of eight years (1623–31) he burnt
900 persons, including his own nephew, nineteen Catholic priests,
and children of seven who were said to have had intercourse
with demons.[2] The years 1627–9 were dreadful years in Baden,
recently reconquered for Catholicism by Tilly : there were 70
victims in Ortenau, 79 in Offenburg. In Eichstatt, a Bavarian
prince-bishopric, a judge claimed the death of 274 witches in
1629. At Reichertsofen an der Paar, in the district of Neuburg,
50 were executed between November 1628 and August 1630. In
the three prince-archbishoprics of the Rhineland the fires were
also relit. At Coblenz, the seat of the Prince-Archbishop of
Trier, 24 witches were burnt in 1629; at Schlettstadt at least
30 — the beginning of a five-year persecution. In Mainz, too,
the burnings were renewed. At Cologne the City Fathers had
always been merciful, much to the annoyance of the prince-
archbishop, but in 1627 he was able to put pressure on the city
and it gave in.[3] Naturally enough, the persecution raged most
violently in Bonn, his own capital. There the chancellor and his
wife and the archbishop's secretary's wife were executed, children
of three and four years were accused of having devils for their

[1] Duhr, *Geschichte der Jesuiten*, II, ii, 498. The point had already been made, in
an indirect way, by the witch-burning Bishop Forner of Bamberg, when he inquired,
in his *Panoplia Armaturae Dei* (see below, p. 157, n. 3), why it was that there were
so many witches in Catholic lands and so few in Protestant. And cf. Soldan-Heppe,
I, 426–7.
[2] See Friedrich Merzbacher, *Die Hexenprozesse in Franken* (Munich, 1957).
[3] Lea, *Materials*, pp. 1203–4.

paramours, and students and small boys of noble birth were sent to the bonfire.[1]

The craze of the 1620s was not confined to Germany: it raged also across the Rhine in Alsace, Lorraine and Franche-Comté. In the lands ruled by the abbey of Luxueil, in Franche-Comté, the years 1628–30 have been described as an 'épidémie démoniaque'. 'Le mal va croissant chaque jour', declared the magistrates of Dôle, 'et cette malheureuse engeance va pullulant de toutes parts.' The witches, they said, 'in the hour of death accuse an infinity of others in fifteen or sixteen other villages'.[2]

But the worst persecution of all, in those years, was probably at Bamberg. There the prince-bishop was Johann Georg II Fuchs von Dornheim, known as the *Hexenbischof* or 'Witch-bishop'. He built a 'witch-house', complete with torture-chamber adorned with appropriate biblical texts, and in his ten-year reign (1623–33) he is said to have burnt 600 witches. He, too, had his Court-prophet, his suffragan, Bishop Forner, who wrote a learned book on the subject.[3] One of their victims was the bishop's chancellor, Dr Haan, burnt as a witch for showing suspicious leniency as a judge. Under torture he confessed to having seen five burgomasters of Bamberg at the sabbat, and they too were duly burnt. One of them, Johannes Julius, under fierce torture confessed that he had renounced God, given himself to the Devil, and seen twenty-seven of his colleagues at the sabbat. But afterwards, from prison, he contrived to smuggle a letter out to his daughter Veronica, giving a full account of his trial. 'Now my dearest child', he concluded, 'you have here all my acts and confessions, for which I must die. It is all falsehood and invention, so help me God. . . . They never cease to torture until one says something. . . . If God sends no means of bringing the truth to light, our whole kindred will be burnt.'[4]

Johannes Julius' *cri de cœur*, which must represent hundreds of

[1] This was reported by a correspondent of Count Werner von Salm. The document is quoted in W. v. Waldbrühl, *Naturforschung u. Hexenglaube* (Berlin, 1867).
[2] See Bavoux, *Hantises et diableries dans la terre abbatiale de Luxueil*, pp. 128–9.
[3] *Panoplia Armaturae Dei adversus . . . Magorum et Sagarum Infestationes* (1625).
[4] For the persecution in Bamberg, see Johann Looshorn, *Geschichte des Bisthums Bamberg* (Munich, 1886), v, 55 ; Merzbacher, *Die Hexenprozesse in Franken*, pp. 42 ff.

unuttered cries from inarticulate victims, found one response. The terrible persecution of the 1620s caused a crisis within the very order which did so much to direct it : the Jesuits. Already, in 1617, Adam Tanner, a Jesuit of Ingolstadt, had begun to entertain very elementary doubts which had raised an outcry against him in his order. Now another Jesuit, Friedrich Spee, was more radically converted by his experience as a confessor of witches in the great persecution at Würzburg. That experience, which turned his hair prematurely white, convinced him that all confessions were worthless, being based solely on torture, and that not a single witch whom he had led to the stake had been guilty. Since he could not utter his thoughts otherwise — for, as he wrote, he dreaded the fate of Tanner — he wrote a book which he intended to circulate in manuscript, anonymously. But a friend secretly conveyed it to the Protestant city of Hameln and it was there printed in 1631 under the title *Cautio Criminalis*.

Spee's work was not the only critical work produced by the massacres of the 1620s ; [1] but it was the most eloquent protest against the persecution of witches that had yet appeared. Like Tanner and all the early enemies of the craze, he did not doubt the reality of witchcraft. But he was convinced that, although 'all Germany smokes everywhere with bonfires which obscure the light', he had not yet seen a real witch, and that 'however much the Princes burn, they can never burn out the evil'. It was torture, and torture alone, which caused denunciation and confession. The whole 'science' of the witch-doctors was based on torture. 'All that Rémy, Binsfeld, del Rio and the rest tell us is based on stories extracted by torture.' Torture proves nothing, nothing at all. 'Torture fills our Germany with witches and unheard-of wickedness, and not only Germany but any nation that attempts it . . . If all of us have not confessed ourselves witches, that is only because we have not all been tortured.' And who, he asked, were the men who demanded these tortures ?

---

[1] Other protests include Theodor Thumm, *Tractatus Theologicus de sagarum impietate* . . . (Tübingen, 1621) ; the anonymous *Malleus Judicum*, of about 1626 (Lea, *Materials*, p. 690 ; but see also Paulus, *Hexenwahn und Hexenprozess*, pp. 193–4) ; Justus Oldekop, *Cautelarum Criminalium Sylloge* (Brunswick, 1633), on which see Burr's note in Lea, *Materials*, p. 850.

Jurists in search of gain, credulous villagers and 'those theologians and prelates who quietly enjoy their speculations and know nothing of the squalor of prisons, the weight of chains, the implements of torture, the lamentations of the poor — things far beneath their dignity.' We think at once of Nicolas Rémy, writing elegant verses in his fine house at Les Charmes in Lorraine, of Pierre de l'Ancre retiring with his Muses to the grotto of his *cottage orné* on the Garonne, of Fr. del Rio in his devout cell, growing blind with study of the Fathers and stiff with prayer to the Virgin.

We might also at this time think of another, and this time a Lutheran scholar. In 1635, four years after the publication of Spee's book, Benedict Carpzov published his great work, *Practica Rerum Criminalium*, dealing with the trial of witches. Carpzov had probably read Spee. He admitted that torture was capable of grave abuse and had led to thousands of false confessions throughout Europe. But he concluded that, *suadente necessitate*, it should still be used, even on those who seemed innocent ; and his view of innocence was not liberal. He maintained that even those who merely believed that they had been at the sabbat should be executed, for the belief implied the will. From 'the faithful ministers of the Devil, who bravely defend his kingdom' — i.e. sceptics like Weyer with their 'frivolous' arguments — he appeals to the Catholic authorities : the *Malleus*, Bodin, Rémy, del Rio. And having thus restated the sound doctrine — his book became 'the *Malleus* of Lutheranism' — he would live to a ripe old age and look back on a meritorious life in the course of which he had read the Bible from cover to cover fifty-three times, taken the sacrament every week, greatly intensified the methods and efficacy of torture, and procured the death of 20,000 persons.

Thus Spee, for all his eloquence, achieved no more than Loos or Scot or Weyer before him. His attack, like theirs, was not upon the belief in witches — indeed, he was less radical than Weyer, who, though the earliest, was the boldest of them all. By his personal influence he may have reduced the savagery of the persecution in the next generation, for the most enlightened of seventeenth-century prince-bishops of Würzburg, Johann Philipp von Schönborn, Elector of Mainz, the friend and patron of Leibniz, was convinced by him and worked to undo the damage wrought by his predecessors.[1] But if the witch-craze of the 1620s died down in the 1630s that was largely due to extraneous causes : war and foreign domination. The French in Lorraine and Franche-Comté, the Swedes in Mecklenburg, Franconia and Bavaria, put a stop to this social war among the natives, just as the English, in the 1650s, would do in Scotland. They did so not necessarily because they were more liberal — the spectacular French witch-trial of Urbain Grandier took place in the 1630s, Matthew Hopkins would have a free hand in England in the 1640s, and the witch-craze would break out in Sweden in the 1660s — but simply because they were foreign, and witch-trials were essentially a social, internal matter. And anyway, the stop was not permanent. Once the hand of the foreigner was removed, the natives would return to their old ways. As in Scotland, relieved of English occupation in the 1660s, so in Mecklenburg after the withdrawal of the Swedes, so in Lorraine after the departure of the French, the old persecution would break out again. Indeed, in some areas the persecution was worse at the end of the seventeenth than at the end of the sixteenth century. In 1591 the Rostock professor of law, J. G. Gödelmann, had urged liberalism and clemency on the Mecklenburg judges. A century later his successor Johann Klein asserted in print the reality of *succubi* and *incubi* and demanded (and secured) death by burning for those who were accused of intercourse with them, and his arguments were supported in print by the dean of the faculty of theology at Rostock thirty years later. As late as 1738 the dean of the faculty of law at Rostock demanded that witches be extirpated by 'fire and sword' and boasted of the number of stakes he had seen 'on one hill'.[2]

Thus the intellectual basis of the witch-craze remained firm

---

[1] According to Leibniz, Philipp von Schönborn 'fit cesser ces brûleries aussitôt qu'il parvint à la Régence ; en quoi il a été suivi par les ducs de Brunswic et enfin par la plupart des autres princes et états d'Allemagne' (*Théodicée*, 1, 144–5, § 97).

[2] Paulus, *Hexenwahn und Hexenprozess*, § VI ; Ernst Boll, *Mecklenburgische Geschichte . . . neu bearbeitet von Dr. Hans Witte*, II (Wismar, 1913), pp. 123 ff.

all through the seventeenth century. No critic had improved on the arguments of Weyer; none had attacked the substance of the myth; all that successive sceptics had done was to cast doubt on its practical interpretation: to question the value of confessions, the efficacy of torture, the identification of particular witches. The myth itself remained untouched, at least in appearance. Artificial though it was, recent though it was, it had become part of the structure of thought, and time had so entwined it with other beliefs, and indeed with social interests, that it seemed impossible to destroy it. In happy times men might forget it, at least in practice. In the early sixteenth century there had seemed a good chance that it might be forgotten — that is, dissolve again into scattered peasant superstitions. But those happy times had not lasted. The ideological struggle of Reformation and Counter-Reformation — that grim struggle which was so disastrous in European intellectual history — had revived the dying witch-craze just as it had revived so many other obsolescent habits of thought: biblical fundamentalism, theological history, scholastic Aristoteleanism. All these had seemed in retreat in the age of Erasmus and Machiavelli and Ficino; all returned a generation later to block the progress of thought for another century.

Every crucial stage in the ideological struggle of the Reformation was a stage also in the revival and perpetuation of the witch-craze. In the 1480s the Dominicans had made war, as they thought, on the relics of medieval heresy. That was the time of the Witch Bull and the *Malleus*, and the renewed persecution in those 'Alpine valleys cold' in which del Rio would afterwards see the eternal source of witchcraft and Milton the ancient cradle of Protestantism. In the 1560s the Protestant missionaries had set out to evangelize the countries of northern Europe whose rulers had accepted the new faith, and at once the witch-craze had been renewed by them. From 1580 the Catholic Counter-Reformation had begun to reconquer northern Europe and the craze became, once again, a Catholic terror, with the new Jesuits replacing the old Dominicans as evangelists. It was then that the Spaniard Francisco Peña, a canon lawyer in the Roman Curia,

collected and summarized the conclusions of the Roman inquisitors : for no subject, he wrote, was now more frequently
discussed by the Catholic clergy than sorcery and divination.[1]
Finally, the Thirty Years War, the last stage of the ideological
struggle, brings with it the worst persecution of all : the 'epi-
démie démoniaque' which reached its climax in the year of
Catholic restoration, 1629.

Admittedly there are exceptions to this general rule. In
England, for instance, the persecution of witches was always
trivial by continental standards[2] and its closest student has been
able to detect no pattern in it. 'There was in fact', writes Ewen,
'no clearly defined periodic wave of witch-mania sweeping
through the country, but rather a succession of sporadic outbreaks. The underlying current of superstition, always present,
manifested itself unpleasantly whenever and wherever fanaticism
was unusually rampant, the influence of one man being sufficient
to raise the excess of zeal to the danger point.'[3] Perhaps this may
safely be said of England, where persecution, thanks to the
absence of judicial torture, never became a craze. But does not
such an answer, even there, beg the question ? For why was
fanaticism, at some times, 'unusually rampant' ? Why did 'one
man', like Matthew Hopkins, appear in 1645 rather than in 1635 ?
In fact, when we compare England with the Continent, we see
that the rhythm of English persecution follows very closely that
of the continental craze of which it is a pale reflection. On the

[1] 'Nulla est fere hodie frequentior disputatio quam quae de sortilegiis et divina-
tionibus suscipitur.' For Peña, see Hansen, *Quellen*, pp. 357–9. He concluded that
incubi and *succubi* were real and that the night-flight to the sabbat was proved beyond
doubt.

[2] The figures commonly given for the execution of witches in England are
grotesquely exaggerated. Lea himself, in his *History of the Inquisition in Spain*,
IV, 247, estimated the number of victims in Britain as 90,000, 'of whom about a
fourth may be credited to Scotland'. But Mr C. L. Ewen's careful study of the
records of the Home Circuit has discredited all such wild guesses. He concludes
that between 1542 and 1736 'less than one thousand' persons were executed for
witchcraft in England' (*Witch Hunting and Witch Trials*, 1929, p. 112). The executions in Scotland, where torture was used, were not less but far more numerous :
probably 4400 in the ninety years from 1590 to 1680 (see Black, in *Bulletin of New
York Public Library*, XLI, no. 11 (Nov. 1937), p. 823).

[3] Ewen, *Witch Hunting and Witch Trials*, p. 113.

Continent, the great persecutions are after 1560, when the Protestant evangelists carry it northwards; after 1580 as the Counter-Reformation overtakes them, and especially in the 1590s, those years of general economic depression and European plague; and in the 1620s, during the Catholic reconquest of the Thirty Years War. In England persecution similarly begins in the 1560s with the return of the Marian exiles; it similarly takes new life in the 1580s and 1590s, the years of Catholic plots, war and fear; and thereafter, if its course is different — if it virtually ceases for the duration of the Thirty Years War — this very divergence is perhaps the exception which proves the rule. For England — to her shame, cried the Puritans — was uninvolved in the Thirty Years War. In the 1640s, when civil and ideological war came to England, witches were persecuted in England too.[1]

Another exception which may yet prove the general rule is supplied by Sweden. The Swedish Lutheran Church, like the Anglican Church, was neither a persecuting nor a proselytizing body, at least in its first century. When it came in contact with the Lapps of the north, it found — as the Roman Church had found in the Pyrenees and the Alps — a different society, racially as well as socially different, half-pagan in religion, given over, it seemed, in that Arctic cold, to bizarre witch-beliefs.[2] But as it did not seek to assimilate these harmless dissenters, their beliefs

[1] The trials of witches in England fell off markedly after 1617, when James I, in Fuller's words, 'receding from what he had written in his *Demonologie*, grew first diffident of, and then flatly to deny, the workings of witches and devils, as but falsehoods and delusions'. (Notestein, *History of Witchcraft in England*, pp. 142–4; Ewen, *Witch Hunting and Witch Trials*, pp. 98 ff.; but see also G. L. Burr's review of Ewen in *American Historical Review*, xxxv, 1929–30, 844 ff.) Under the personal rule of Charles I executions for witchcraft ceased altogether in England, at least in the counties of the Home Circuit (Ewen, op. cit.), and were at least severely cut down in Scotland: one of the articles of complaint against the Scottish bishops in 1638 was for 'staying' such proceedings (W. L. Mathieson, *Politics and Religion. A Study in Scottish History from the Reformation to the Revolution*, Glasgow, 1902, II, 157–9). However, the events of 1640 changed all that. The Scottish General Assembly of 1640, having got rid of the bishops, required all ministers to nose out witches and urge the enforcement of the law against them (ibid. p. 159), which they did, to some tune; and in 1645 more witches were executed in England than in any year before or since.

[2] The Lapland witches were first reported in Olaus Magnus, *de Gentibus Septentrionalibus* (Rome, 1555), pp. 119–28; thereafter they became famous in Europe. Cf. Milton, *Paradise Lost*, II, 665.

were not persecuted, and the Lapland witches remained always outside the general European witch-craze. In 1608 Sweden, like other Lutheran countries, adopted the Mosaic penalties for offences previously punished by the Church courts; but even this provision, which was used to justify witch-burning elsewhere, had no such consequence in Sweden. There witch-trials remained sporadic and episodic, and no great native witch-doctor, like King James in Scotland, or Perkins in England, or Hemmingsen in Denmark, or Gödelmann in Mecklenburg, sought to erect in Sweden the full-blown demonology of Europe. Indeed, as we have seen, in the Thirty Years War the Swedish generals, obeying explicit orders from Queen Christina, suppressed the witch-fires in Germany. It was not till the 1660s that a change came to Sweden, and then it was in circumstances which recall the European outbreaks.

For in the 1660s the established Lutheran Church in Sweden became intolerant. Like the established Calvinist Church in Scotland, it had shaken itself free from alliance with other, more liberal Protestant parties, and its Puritan leaders prepared to advertise their purity by a great witch-hunt. In 1664 it branded as heretical the Syncretist Movement — the movement of Pan-Protestantism which had been so useful in the Thirty Years War. In 1667 it put out a new declaration of orthodoxy, 'the most rigorous of the century', against the subtle menace of Cartesianism : that Cartesianism which Descartes himself had brought to the Court of Queen Christina. Now that Queen Christina was an exile in Rome, the frightened Church of Sweden resolved to assert itself; its preachers became zealots of their faith, eager to sniff out and condemn heresy; and in the same year the witch-craze was fired by panic fears in the province of Dalårna. 'It is something more than an accident', writes Hr Sundborg, 'that the victory of orthodoxy in 1664 was followed so closely by the outbreak of the persecutions.'[1] The same might be said of all the previous European crazes.

[1] Bertil Sundborg, 'Gustaf Rosenhane och Trolldomsväsendet', in *Lychnos* (Uppsala), 1954-5, pp. 203-64. I am indebted to Professor Michael Roberts for his help in interpreting the Swedish evidence.

Why did social struggle, in those two centuries, invariably *imp,* revive this bizarre mythology ? We might as well ask, why has economic depression in Germany, from the Middle Ages until this century, so often revived the bizarre mythology of anti-semitism : the fables of poisoned wells and ritual murder which were spread at the time of the Crusades, during the Black Death, in the Thirty Years War, and in the pages of Julius Streicher's Nazi broadsheet, *der Stürmer*? The question is obviously not simple. It carries us beyond and below the realm of mere intel-lectual problems. We have here to deal with a mythology which is more than a mere fantasy. It is a social stereotype : a stereo-type of fear. *"collective conscience"*

Any society is liable, at times, to collective emotion. There is the exalted 'messianism' which is common in rural societies in medieval Europe ; in southern Italy, Spain and Portugal in early modern times ; in modern Brazil. There is also the undefined 'great fear', such as ran through rural France at the beginning of the revolution of 1789. And these emotions tend to take stereo-typed form. How such stereotypes are built up is a problem in itself; but once they are built up, they can last for generations, even centuries. The stereotype in German society has long been the Jewish conspiracy. In England, from the days of the Spanish Armada till the days of the 'Papal Aggression' of 1851 and the 'Vaticanism' of 1870, it has been the Popish Plot.[1] In America today it seems to be the Red scare. In continental Europe, in the two centuries after the Witch Bull, it was the witch-craze. So firmly had the mythology of Satan's kingdom been established *see* in the declining Middle Ages that in the first centuries of 'modern' Europe — to use a conventional notation of time — it became the standard form in which the otherwise undefined fears of society became crystallized. Just as psychopathic individuals in those years centred their separate fantasies (or, as the seventeenth-century

106
115
127
177

[1] Apart from the Gunpowder Plot of 1605 and the Popish Plot of 1679, there was the imaginary Popish Plot reported by Andreas ab Habernfeld in 1640, which was kept alive for many years afterwards ; the Irish Massacre of 1641 which still curdled the blood of John Wesley in the next century ; the *canard* that it was the Papists who had burnt London in 1666 ; the myth of the Warming-pan in 1688 ; the Gordon Riots of 1780 ; etc. etc.

doctors would say, their 'melancholy') on the Devil, and thus gave an apparent objective identity to their subjective experiences, so societies in fear articulated their collective neuroses about the same obsessive figure, and found a scapegoat for their fears in his agents, the witches. Both the individual and the society made this identification because the Devil, his kingdom and his agents had been made real to them by the folk-lore of their times; but both, by this identification, sustained and confirmed the same centralizing folk-lore for their successors.

Thus the mythology created its own evidence, and effective disproof became ever more difficult. In times of prosperity the whole subject might be ignored except on a village level, but in times of fear men do not think clearly: they retreat to fixed positions, fixed prejudices. So social struggle, political conspiracy, conventual hysteria, private hallucination were all interpreted in the light of a mythology which, by now, had been extended to interpret them all, and the craze was renewed. At each renewal, some bold and humane dissenter would seek to challenge the collective hysteria and cruelty. Ponzinibio would challenge the Dominican inquisitors, Weyer the Protestant persecutors of the 1560s, Loos and Scot the Catholic and Protestant persecutors of the 1590s, Spee the Catholic torturers of the 1620s and 1630s. But none of these would do more than question the esoteric details of the myth and the identification of the victims. The basis of the myth was beyond their reach. They might convince educated princes, as Weyer convinced the Duke of Cleves and Spee, the future Prince-Bishop of Würzburg and Elector of Mainz; and no one should underestimate the influence that a prince might have to extend or suppress the effect of the craze.[1] But their opponents appealed against them to a lower level — to

---

[1] Thus Weyer states that witches were not burnt in the dominions of the Duke of Cleves, and he names several other princes who were equally firm and equally effective, e.g. the Elector Frederick of the Palatinate and Duke Adolf of Nassau. The princes of Hesse, Philip the Magnanimous and William V, the Wise, similarly controlled the persecution in their lands. Cf. the effect of James I's conversion in England. On the other hand the extension of the persecution when princes gave free rein, or positively encouraged it, is obvious: perhaps nowhere so obvious as in the prince-bishoprics of Germany.

petty magistrates and clerical tribunes [1] — and on that lower level
kept the craze alive. It remained alive until the eighteenth-
century Enlightenment, defended by clergymen, lawyers and
scholars, and capable of being reanimated by any sudden coincidence of forces, when politicians or judges surrendered to social
fear. The great outbreaks in Sweden in 1668–77, in Salzburg in
1677–81, in Mecklenburg after 1690 and in colonial New England
in 1692 show that if the Thirty Years War was the last occasion of
international mania, national mania could still be aroused. The
fire still lurked beneath the cinders.

Nevertheless, after the Thirty Years War something had happened. It was not merely that the war was over. The stereotype
itself had weakened. In Protestant and Catholic countries alike
the myth has lost its force. In the 1650s Cyrano de Bergerac could
write in France as if it were already dead, at least among educated
men.[2] Twenty years later, in 1672, the law would recognize its
death when Colbert abolished the charge of *sorcellerie sabbatique*.
In Cromwellian England the 1650s saw an outbreak of books
repudiating witch-trials; the frequent discovery and execution
of witches, Francis Osborne told his son in 1656, 'makes me
think the strongest fascination is encircled within the ignorance
of the judges, malice of the witnesses, or stupidity of the poor
parties accused'.[3] In Calvinist Geneva, once so ferocious, the
last witch was burnt in 1652 : the urban aristocracy had by now

---

[1] Thus, while Weyer relied on the Duke of Cleves and Weyer's supporters
Johann Ewich and Hermann Neuwaldt on Count Simon of Lippe-Redtburg and
(vain hope!) Heinrich Julius of Brunswick-Lüneburg, their critic Schreiber dedicated
his works to the magistrates of Lemgo and of Osnabrück 'dominis suis et fautoribus
optimis'. In general, local magistrates remained the guarantors of the craze, while
the best hope of reformers was to secure the support of a prince. Cf. the statements
of the magistrates of Dôle, in Franche-Comté (above, p. 157) and the protests of
the parlement of Rouen against Colbert's order prohibiting witch-trials (Lecky,
History of the Rise and Influence of . . . Rationalism in Europe, I, 98–99). In Mecklenburg — as in Scotland — the triumph of the witch-burners coincided with the
triumph of the Estates over the prince. The Swedish outbreak of 1667 took place
while the power of the Crown was in abeyance.

[2] See Lucien Fèbvre, in *Annales : économies, sociétés, civilisation*, 1948, p. 15.

[3] Francis Osborne, *Advice to his Son* [1656], ed. E. A. Parry (1896), p. 125. Among
books against witch-trials at that time are [Sir Robert Filmer], *An Advertisement to
the Jury-men of England touching Witches* (1653) ; Thomas Ady, *A Candle in the Dark*
(1656).

reduced the clergy to order. At the same time the magistrates of Bern issued an ordinance to restrain the witch-judges. In 1657 even the Church of Rome, which had put all critical books on the Index, issued 'a tardy *instructio* urging her inquisitors to circumspection'.[1] From now on, in spite of local recrudescence and intellectual support, the climate of opinion has changed, and the assertors of witchcraft, but recently so confident, find themselves on the defensive. While the social stereotypes of the Jew in Germany and the Popish Plot in England retain their plausibility, that of the witch is failing, and we have to ask, how did this happen? Why did a mythology which, against all likelihood, had been prolonged for two centuries, suddenly lose its force? For although the old laws may remain on the statute book and the old beliefs will linger in school and cloister, the systematic mythology and the social force which it inspired, is crumbling. By 1700 the 'craze' is over: the infidels, as John Wesley was to lament, 'have hooted witchcraft out of the world'.

why it ended:

V

The decline and apparently final collapse of the witch-craze in the late seventeenth century, while other such social stereotypes retained their power, is a revolution which is surprisingly difficult to document. We see the controversies continue. Important names appear on both sides — but the greater names, at least in England, are on the side of the craze, not against it. How can the obscure and tipsy Oxford scholar John Wagstaffe or the crochety Yorkshire surgeon-parson John Webster compete with the names of Sir Thomas Browne and Richard Baxter and the Cambridge Platonists Ralph Cudworth, Henry More and Joseph Glanville? And yet on neither side are the arguments new: they are the arguments which have always been used. On the side of orthodoxy some caution can be observed: the grosser and more preposterous details of the demonologists are silently

[1] Lea, *Materials*, pp. 743–4; Burr, *Life*, p. 186. For the effect of the Roman Instruction in Poland, see Lea, *Materials*, pp. 1232, 1273.

dropped (although continental and Scottish lawyers and clergy continued to assert them) and the argument is given a more philosophic base. But on the sceptical side there is no advance. Webster is no more modern than Weyer. Nevertheless, without new argument on either side the intellectual belief quietly dissolved. The witch-trials, in spite of a few last outbursts, came to an end. The witch-laws were repealed, almost without debate.

It has been pointed out that, in this reform, Protestant countries led the way. England and Holland were regarded, in 1700, as countries long since emancipated while the Catholic prince-bishops of Germany were still burning away. Inside Germany, says a German scholar, the Protestant states abandoned persecution a full generation before the Catholic.[1] In mixed societies, like Alsace, the Catholic lords had always been fiercer than the Protestant.[2] And certainly Catholic manuals continued to insist on demonological doctrine when the Protestant writers had conveniently forgotten it. However, in view of the undoubted part played by the Protestant Churches in forwarding the craze after 1560, we should perhaps be chary of claiming any special virtue for Protestantism in resisting it after 1650. Calvinist and Lutheran doctrines were as uncompromising, Calvinist and Lutheran clergy as ferocious as Catholic; and where the Calvinist or Lutheran clergy had effective power — as in Scotland or Mecklenburg — the craze continued as long as in any Catholic country. To the very end, honours remained even between the two religions. If the last witch-burning in Europe was in Catholic Poland in 1793, that was an illegal act: witch-trials had been abolished in Poland in 1787. The last legal execution was in Protestant Glarus, in Switzerland, in 1782. Appropriately the craze which had been born in the Alps retreated thither to die.

But if the power of the clergy, Protestant or Catholic, prolonged the craze, their weakness hastened its end; and the clergy were undoubtedly weaker in some Protestant than in most Catholic countries. This was particularly true in the United Netherlands.

[1] Riezler, *Geschichte der Hexenprozessen in Baiern,* p. 282.
[2] Reuss, *L'Alsace au 17e siècle*, II, 105.

The Dutch Calvinist clergy, the *Predikants*, were notoriously intolerant ; but unlike their Scottish brethren, they were never allowed to exercise or influence jurisdiction. This was discovered even during the national revolution. In 1581 Lambert Daneau, the most important Huguenot preacher after his masters Calvin and Beza, and incidentally, like them, a formidable witch-hunter, received a call to a chair in the new University of Leiden. He answered the call. But he had not been long in Leiden before his theocratic pretensions brought him into trouble. The Council of Leiden, he was told, would resist the inquisition of Geneva no less than that of Spain ; and he found it prudent to leave the Netherlands to rule over a more submissive flock in Pyrenean France.[1] In the next century the Dutch Calvinist clergy continued to demand death for witchcraft. Their intellectual oracles, Junius, Rivetus, Voëtius, were unambiguous on this point.[2] The greatest and latest of them was Voëtius, professor and rector of the University of Utrecht. He denounced, with equal assurance, the theories of Galileo, Harvey and Descartes and marshalled a series of massive arguments to show that there are witches and that they should not be suffered to live. It particularly infuriated him that Scot's work, though rightly burnt in England, had been translated into Dutch and had corrupted many readers in the republic, already only too full of 'libertines' and 'semi-libertines'.[3] He was no doubt thinking of 'Arminians' like Hugo Grotius, who would put authority in matters of religion in the hands of lay magistrates and declared that the Mosaic penalties were no longer binding ; or Episcopius, who denied the reality of the witch's pact with Satan, the very basis of witchcraft ; or Johann Greve, who, like Weyer, came from Cleves and urged the aboli-

---

[1] P. de Félice, *Lambert Daneau, sa vie, ses ouvrages, ses lettres inédites* (Paris, 1882).
[2] Both Junius and Rivetus expressed their views in commentaries on Exod. xxii. 18 : Franciscus Junius, *Libri Exodi Analytica Explicatio* (Leiden, 1598) ; Andreas Rivetus, *Commentarius in Exodum* (Leiden, 1634). Junius also translated Bodin's *Démonomanie*.
[3] *Gisberti Voëtii Selectarum Disputationum Theologicarum . . . Pars Tertia*, pp. 539–632, 'de Magia'. Voëtius, who dominated Utrecht till his death in 1678, at the age of eighty-seven, first wrote this work in 1636 and amplified it in later editions. His arguments were repeated with approval by Johann Christian Frommann, *Tractatus de Fascinatione Novus et Singularis* (Nuremberg, 1675).

tion of torture in witch-trials.[1] It was an Arminian too, 'the
Arminian printer' Thomas Basson, the printer of Grotius and
Arminius himself, who had translated Scot's book and published
it in Leiden ; and it was the Arminian historian Pieter Schrijver,
or Scriberius, who had set him on.[2] The Calvinist clergy succeeded in condemning Arminianism, procured the exile of Grotius
and hounded Greve from his parish at Arnhem. But they were
never able to capture criminal jurisdiction from the lay magistrates,
and it was clearly for this reason, not because of any virtue in their
doctrine, that no witch was burnt in Holland after 1597.[3]

Was the collapse of the witch-craze then due merely to the
victory of the laity over the clergy : a victory that was more easily
won in Protestant countries, where the clergy had already been
weakened, than in Catholic countries where it had retained its
power ? The inference is natural, and no doubt partly true : but
it can only be partly true. For whence did the laity acquire their
ideas ? The witch-craze may have been first formulated by the
clergy, but by 1600 it was being perpetuated by the lawyers.
Bodin, Boguet, de l'Ancre, Carpzov were lay magistrates, not
clergymen. We have seen the lay magistrates of Lemgo, in
Westphalia, imposing the new cold-water test, and those of
Dôle, in Franche-Comté, demanding fiercer penalties for the
growing pest of witchcraft. It was the lay magistrates of Essex,
under the chairmanship of the Puritan Earl of Warwick, who in
1645 condemned a record number of witches to death at Chelms-
ford assizes and it was the lay magistrates of Rouen who protested
against Colbert's order suspending witch-trials. When we compare these laymen with clergy like the Arminian Greve or the
Jesuit Spee, or the Anglican bishops of James I and Charles I,
or the Gallican bishops of Richelieu and Mazarin,[4] we have to
admit that there are laity and laity, clergy and clergy. No doubt

[1] See Johann Greve [Graevius], *Tribunal Reformatum* (Hamburg, 1624). Greve
was influenced by Weyer whom he often quotes. See Binz, *Doctor Johann Weyer*.
[2] J. A. von Dorsten, *Thomas Basson, 1555–1613, English Printer at Leiden* (Leiden,
Sir Thomas Browne Institute, 1961), pp. 49–54.
[3] Jacobus Scheltema, *Geschiedenis der Heksenprocessen . . .* p. 258 (Haarlem, 1828).
[4] See, for instance, the enlightened letter sent by Léonor d'Estampes de Valençay,
Archbishop and Duke of Reims, to the chancellor, Séguier, on 28 July 1644, quoted
in *Lettres et mémoires du chancelier Séguier*, ed. Roland Mousnier (Paris, 1964), I, 636–7.

the independent laity of mercantile cities or great courts have a more liberal outlook than the legal caste of provincial towns or petty principalities. But is not the same true of the clergy? Ultimately, the difference is a difference of ideas. The independent laity — educated merchants, officials, gentry — may be freer to receive new ideas than clergy or lawyers; they may give social content and social force to such ideas; but the ideas themselves, as often as not, are generated among the clergy. The Reformation itself, that great social revolution, began as 'une querelle de moines'.

We can see the resistance of the laity to the witch-craze all through its course. It was a resistance to which every witch-doctor paid indignant tribute. But it was a limited resistance : a resistance of scepticism, of common sense, not of positive disbelief or opposite belief. Men revolted against the cruelty of torture, against the implausibility of confessions, against the identification of witches. They did not revolt against the central doctrine of the kingdom of Satan and its war on humanity by means of demons and witches. They had no substitute for such a doctrine. And because that doctrine was established, even accepted, it had provided the central pillar around which other doctrines, other experiences had entwined themselves, adding to its strength. Sceptics might doubt. They might even protest. But neither doubt nor protest was enough. In fair weather the luxury of scepticism might be allowed; but when the storm returned, men fell back again on the old faith, the old orthodoxy.

If the witch-craze were to be attacked at its centre, not merely doubted at its periphery, it was clearly necessary to challenge the whole conception of the kingdom of Satan. This neither Weyer nor Scot nor Spee had done. All through the sixteenth and seventeenth centuries it had been an axiom of faith that the Church was engaged in a life-and-death struggle with Satan. The writers of the *Malleus* had referred, in lamentable tones, to the impending end of the world whose disasters were everywhere visible,[1]

---

[1] 'Cum inter ruentis seculi calamitates, quas (proh dolor !) non tam legimus quam passim experimur . . . mundi vespere ad occasum declinante et malicia hominum excrescente . . .' etc. etc. *Malleus Maleficarum* (Apologia).

and the Protestant writers, reactionary in this as in all else, had used, and intensified, the same language. In the early seventeenth century millenary ideas, forgotten since the Middle Ages, were revived, and the greatest discovery of a scientific century was declared to be the calculation by a future Fellow of the Royal Society, of the hitherto elusive number of the Beast.[1] But at the very end of the century one writer did attempt to challenge the whole idea of Satan's kingdom. This was the Dutch minister Balthasar Bekker, who in 1690 published the first version of the first volume of his de Betoverde Weereld, 'the Enchanted World'.

Both at the time and since Bekker was regarded as the most dangerous enemy of witch-beliefs. The orthodox denounced him in unmeasured tones. Like Greve, seventy years before, he was persecuted by the Calvinist clergy of Holland and ultimately, though protected by the city of Amsterdam, driven out of the ministry. The first two volumes of his book, it is said, sold 4000 copies in two months and it was translated into French, German and English. Pamphlets were poured out against him. He was held responsible for the cessation of witch-burnings in England and Holland [2] — although witches had never been burnt in England and burnings had long ceased in Holland. Bekker, it has been regularly said, struck at the heart of the witch-craze by destroying belief in the Devil.[3]

Perhaps he did in theory ; but did he in fact ? When we look closer, we find reasons for doubt. Bekker's foreign reputation seems largely a myth. The controversy over his work was conducted almost entirely in the Dutch language.[4] And that controversy was evidently soon over. In 1696 a Frenchman declared that Bekker's disciples were already falling away, disappointed

[1] See the lyrical exclamations of the celebrated Puritan divine William Twisse in his Preface to Joseph Mede's Key of the Revelation (1643) and cf. Twisse's letter to Mede in Mede's Works, ed. John Worthington (1664), II, 70–71.

[2] Jacob Brunnemann, Discours von betrüglichen Kennzeichen der Zauberey (Stargard, 1708), cited in Lea, Materials, p. 1427.

[3] This point was made by Soldan in 1843 and has been repeated ever since.

[4] A. van der Linde, Balthasar Bekker Bibliographie (The Hague, 1869), lists 134 contemporary works concerning Bekker. Apart from one in French (see next note) and two in Latin, all are in Dutch.

by his later volumes ; and this opinion is confirmed by the fact that the English translation never got beyond the first volume.[1] An Englishman who wished to refute Bekker a few years later, and who sent to Holland 'for all that was writ against him and any replies he had made', could obtain only one small volume in French.[2] The German translation was declared by a good judge to be worthless : the translator, it was said, understood neither Dutch nor German nor his author.[3] By 1706 Bekker seemed forgotten. His work had enjoyed a *succès de scandale* only. And anyway, he had not repudiated belief in the Devil. He merely believed that the Devil, on his fall from Heaven, had been locked up in Hell, unable further to interfere in human affairs. This purely theological point was not likely to cause a revolution in thought. In his particular arguments about witches Bekker was inspired, as he admitted, by Scot, and did not go beyond Scot.

Moreover, Bekker's radicalism was disowned by later, and perhaps more effective, opponents of the witch-craze. If any group of men destroyed the craze in Lutheran Germany it was the Pietists of the University of Halle whose leader, in this respect, was Christian Thomasius, the advocate of the vernacular language. In a series of works, beginning with a university thesis in 1701, Thomasius denounced the folly and cruelty of witch-trials. But he was careful to dissociate himself from Bekker. There is a Devil, Thomasius protests, and there are witches : this 'cannot be denied without great presumption and thoughtlessness'. But Weyer and Scot and Spee have shown that the witches who are tried in Germany are quite different from those witches whose death is prescribed in the Bible, that the demonology of the Church is a mixture of pagan and Jewish superstition,

---

[1] Benjamin Binet, *Traité historique des dieux et des démons* (Delft, 1696). The English translation of Bekker's work appeared under the title *The World turn'd upside down . . .* (1700).

[2] John Beaumont, *An Historical, Physiological and Theological Treatise of Spirits* (1705). This work is not mentioned by van der Linde.

[3] Eberhard David Hauber, *Bibliotheca Acta et Scripta Magica* (Lemgo, 1739), I, 565. Hauber was a liberal Lutheran clergyman whose work — reprints of earlier texts illustrating the witch-craze — helped to liberalize the public opinion of Germany. But, like Thomasius, he was critical of Bekker.

and that confessions produced by torture are false. Again and again Thomasius protests that he is falsely accused of disbelieving in the Devil. He believes in the Devil, he says, and that he still operates, externally and invisibly : he only disbelieves that the Devil has horns and a tail ; and he believes in witches : he only disbelieves in their pact with the Devil, the sabbat, *incubi* and *succubi*. When we examine his arguments we find that neither he nor his friends at Halle went beyond Scot or Spee or those English writers, Wagstaffe and Webster, whose works they caused to be translated into German.[1] And yet it is equally clear that the arguments which had been advanced in vain by Scot and Spee were effective when advanced by Thomasius. The witch-craze did not collapse because Bekker dislodged the Devil from his central position : the Devil decayed quietly with the witch-belief ;[2] and why the witch-belief decayed — why the critical arguments which were regarded as unplausible in 1563 and in 1594 and in 1631 were found plausible in 1700 — is mysterious still.

The nineteenth-century liberal historians did indeed offer an answer. They saw the controversy as a straight contest between superstition and reason, between theology and science, between the Church and 'rationalism'. The Englishman Lecky, the Americans White, Lea and Burr, the German Hansen, write as if the irrationality of the witch-beliefs had always been apparent to the natural reason of man and as if the prevalence of such beliefs could be explained only by clerical bigotry allied with political power. This bigotry, they seem to say, was artificially created. The persecution began, says Burr, because the Inquisition, having fulfilled its original purpose of destroying the Albigensian

[1] A German translation of Wagstaffe's *Question of Witchcraft Debated* (1669) was published at Halle, dedicated to Thomasius, in 1711. Thomasius himself wrote a preface to a German translation of Webster's *The Displaying of Supposed Witchcraft*, which was also published at Halle in 1719.

[2] How little Bekker had to do with the destruction of belief among the Dutch laity is shown by the remarks of a French officer who visited Holland with Condé in 1673 — nearly twenty years before Bekker wrote. He reported that at that time most Dutchmen regarded Hell as a 'phantom' and Paradise as 'an agreeable chimera' invented by the clergy to encourage virtue. See G.-B. Stoppa, *La Religion des Hollandois* . . . (Paris, 1673), p. 88.

heretics, found itself with nothing to do and so 'turned its idle hands to the extirpation of witches'.[1] From that time onwards, these writers suggest, the 'rationalists' fought a long battle against clerical and conservative bigotry. At first it was a losing battle, but at last persistence brought its reward : the tide turned and the battle was ultimately won. And yet, these writers seem to be saying, even now it is not quite won. As long as there is religion, there is a danger of superstition, and superstition will break out in these and such forms. The world — so Hansen ended his great work — will not be free till the still undefeated residue of superstition has been expelled from the religious systems of the modern world.

Today such a distinction between 'reason' and 'superstition' is difficult to maintain. We have seen the darkest forms of superstitious belief and superstitious cruelty springing again not out of half-purged religious systems, but out of new, purely secular roots. We have seen that social stereotypes are more lasting than religious systems — indeed, that religious systems may be only temporary manifestations of a more deep-seated social attitude. We have also come to distrust too rational explanations. The picture of the Inquisition using up its idle machinery against witches simply to prevent it from rusting cannot convince us. Finally, we can no longer see intellectual history as a direct contest between reason and faith, reason and superstition. We recognize that even rationalism is relative : that it operates within a general philosophic context, and that it cannot properly be detached from this context.

The liberal historians of the nineteenth century supposed that it could be so detached : that those men who, in the sixteenth and seventeenth centuries, were revolted by the cruelty of witch-trials, or rejected the absurdities of witch-beliefs, ought to have seen that it was not enough to protest against these incidental excesses : they should have seen that the whole system had no rational basis. In their impatience with the critics of the past, these liberal historians sometimes seem to us absurdly anachron-

[1] Burr, *Translations and Reprints*, p. 1.

istic. When he examines the work of Weyer, Lea becomes positively snappish. Why, he asks, is Weyer so 'illogical'? Why cannot he see 'the fatal defect' in his own reasoning? Weyer, he exclaims, was 'as credulous as any of his contemporaries': his work is an extraordinary mixture of 'common sense' and 'folly'; 'nothing can exceed the ingenious perversity' of his views, his belief in magic and demons while he rejects the sabbat and *succubi*. No wonder 'his labours had so limited a result'.[1] It is clear that, to Lea, 'reason', 'logic', is a self-contained, independent system of permanent validity. What is obvious in nineteenth-century Philadelphia must have been equally obvious in sixteenth-century Germany. We are reminded of Macaulay's remark that 'a Christian of the fifth century with a Bible is neither better nor worse situated than a Christian of the nineteenth century with a Bible' and that the absurdity of a literal interpretation was 'as great and as obvious in the sixteenth century as it is now'.[2]

But the difficulty of the men of the sixteenth and seventeenth centuries was that witch-beliefs were not detachable from their general context. The mythology of the Dominicans was an extension, with the aid of peasant superstition, feminine hysteria and clerical imagination, of a whole cosmology. It was also rooted in permanent social attitudes. In order to dismantle this grotesque mental construction, it was not enough — it was not possible — to look at its component ideas in isolation. They could not be so isolated, nor was there yet an independent 'reason' detached from the context of which they too were a part. If men were to revise their views on witchcraft, the whole context of those views had to be revised. Then, and then only, this extension — the weakest part of it, but theoretically essential to it — would dissolve. Until that had happened, all that men could do was to doubt its more questionable details. Even then, even when that had happened, the repudiation would not be complete: for it would be merely intellectual. Unless there were also a social transformation, the social basis of the belief

---

[1] Lea, *Materials*, pp. 494–6, 511, etc.
[2] The passage is in Macaulay's essay on Ranke's *History of the Popes*.

would remain — although a new stereotype would have to be devised in order to express the hostility which it had embodied. *and fear*

How inseparable the witch-beliefs were from the whole philosophy of the time is clear when we look at the demonologists as a class, and at their whole intellectual output, not merely at their treatises on witches and witchcraft. Some of them, of course, are specialists, like Boguet, or are concerned, as lawyers, with witchcraft as an object of the criminal law. But the majority of them are philosophers in a wider field. To St Thomas Aquinas, the greatest of medieval Dominicans, as to Francisco de Vitoria, the greatest of Spanish Renaissance Dominicans,[1] demonology is but one aspect of the world which they seek to understand. Scribonius, who defended the cold-water test, was a professor of philosophy who wrote on natural science and mathematics. The Zwinglian Erastus was a physician, a theologian, a political philosopher as well as a writer on witches. The Lutheran Heinrich Nicolai, professor of philosophy at Danzig in the mid-seventeenth century, wrote on 'the whole of human knowledge' before coming to the specialized department of witchcraft.[2] The Calvinists Daneau and Perkins and Voëtius were the encyclopaedists of their party in France, England and Holland : Daneau wrote on Christian physics and Christian politics as well as on witches and every other subject; Perkins was an oracle on all moral questions ; Voëtius, like Bacon, took all learning for his province — only, unlike Bacon, in every direction, he resisted its advancement. Bodin was the universal genius of his age. King James and del Rio were men of multifarious, if conservative learning. When we look at the work of these men as a whole, we see that they wrote upon demonology not necessarily because they had a special interest in it, but because they had to do so.

---

[1] Vitoria was the greatest of the philosophers of Salamanca : see Marjorie Grice-Hutchinson, *The School of Salamanca* (Oxford, 1952). He dealt with witchcraft in his *Relectiones XII Theologicae* (Relectio X 'de Arte Magica'), written about 1540 and first published at Lyon in 1557.

[2] H. Nicolai, *de Cognitione Humana Universa, hoc est de omni scibili humano* (Danzig, 1648) ; *de Magicis Actionibus* (Danzig, 1649). Nicolai was a 'syncretist', and therefore relatively liberal.

Men who sought to express a consistent philosophy of nature could not exclude what was a necessary and logical, if unedifying extension of it. They would not have agreed with the modern historian of magic that 'these off-scourings of the criminal courts and torture-chamber, of popular gossip and local scandal, are certainly beneath the dignity of our investigation'.[1] Rather, they would have agreed with Bertrand Russell that to flinch from such necessary consequences of their professed beliefs, merely because they were disagreeable or absurd, would be a sign of 'the intellectual enfeeblement of orthodoxy'.

Equally, those who questioned witch-beliefs could not reject them in isolation. Pomponazzi, Agrippa, Cardano are universal philosophers, Weyer and Ewich medical men with a general philosophy of Nature. If they reject witch-beliefs, it is because they are prepared to question the accepted philosophy of the natural world, of which witch-beliefs were an extension, and to envisage a completely different system. But few men, in the sixteenth century, were prepared to make that effort. Failing such an effort, there were only two ways in which a man could express his dissent from the orthodox demonologists. He could accept the basic philosophic orthodoxy of his time and confine his criticism to the validity of particular methods or particular interpretations. This was the way of Scot and Spee, who believed in witches, but not in the modern methods of identifying them. Or he could recognize that the science of demonology rested firmly on human reason, but doubt the infallibility of such reason and so reserve a liberty of 'Pyrrhonist' scepticism. This was the way of Montaigne, who dared to refer to the unanswerable conclusions of scholastic reason as 'conjectures'.

Neither of these methods was radical enough, by itself, to destroy the intellectual belief in witches. The criticism of a Scot or a Spee might be acceptable in fair times, but it did not touch the basis of belief and with the return of a 'great fear' it would soon be forgotten. The scepticism of a Montaigne might undermine orthodoxy, but it could equally sustain it — as it often did — by undermining heresy. Montaigne himself was claimed as

[1] Thorndike, *History of Magic and Experimental Science*, v, 69.

an ally by his witch-burning friend de l'Ancre.[1] The greatest of
French sceptics, Pierre Bayle, left the witch-craze exactly where
he found it, and his English contemporary, Joseph Glanvill,
used scepticism positively to reinforce belief in witchcraft.[2] What
ultimately destroyed the witch-craze, on an intellectual level, was
not the two-edged arguments of the sceptics, nor was it modern
'rationalism', which could exist only within a new context of
thought. It was not even the arguments of Bekker, tied as they
were to biblical fundamentalism. It was the new philosophy, a
philosophical revolution which changed the whole concept of
Nature and its operations. That revolution did not occur within
the narrow field of demonology, and therefore we cannot use-
fully trace it by a study which is confined to that field. It occurred
in a far wider field, and the men who made it did not launch
their attack on so marginal an area of Nature as demonology.
Demonology, after all, was but an appendix of medieval thought,
a later refinement of scholastic philosophy. The attack was
directed at the centre ; and when it had prevailed at the centre,
there was no need to struggle for the outworks : they had been
turned.

This, it seems to me, is the explanation of the apparent silence
of the great thinkers of the early seventeenth century, the philosophers of natural science, natural law, secular history. Why, we
are asked, did Bacon, Grotius, Selden not express disbelief in
witchcraft ? Their silence, or their incidental concessions to
orthodoxy, have even been taken, by some, to argue belief. But
this, I suggest, is a wrong inference. The writers who make it
are, once again, treating the subject in isolation. If we wish to

---

[1] P. de l'Ancre (*Tableau de l'inconstance des mauvais anges et démons*, Paris, 1613,
p. 77) remarks that 'le cœur et l'âme du sieur de Montaigne' was the fashionable
Jesuit Maldonado, who used scepticism only in the cause of orthodoxy. Maldonado
preached against witches in Paris and was the acknowledged teacher (*meus quondam
doctor*) of del Rio. See Martin del Rio, *Disquisitionum Magicarum Libri VI*, Louvain,
1599–1600, 'Proloquium', and I, 210 ; J. Maldonado, 'Praefatio de Daemonibus
et eorum praestigiis', printed in H. M. Prat, '*Maldonat et l'Université de Paris*' (Paris,
1856), pp. 567 ff. ; Clément Sclafert, 'Montaigne et Maldonat', *Bulletin de Littérature
Ecclésiastique* LII (Toulouse, 1951), pp. 65–93, 129–46.

[2] P. Bayle, *Réponse aux questions d'un provincial*, ch. xxxv–xliv ; J. Glanvill, *Some
Philosophical Considerations touching the being of witches* (1666) ; etc.

interpret reticence, the correct method is not to examine, with rabbinical exactitude, particular breaches of reticence, but first to consider the whole context of a man's thought. When we do that, the explanation, I believe, becomes clear. Bacon, Grotius, Selden may have been reticent on witches. So, for that matter, was Descartes. Why should they court trouble on a secondary, peripheral issue ? On the central issue they were not reticent, and it is in their central philosophy that we must see the battle that they were fighting : a battle which would cause the world of witches, ultimately, to wither away.[1]

Nevertheless, what a struggle it had been for the centre ! No mere scepticism, no mere 'rationalism', could have driven out the old cosmology. A rival faith had been needed, and it therefore seems a little unfair in Lea to blame the earliest and greatest opponent of the craze for being hardly less 'credulous' than his adversaries.[2] The first rival faith had been Renaissance Platonism, 'natural magic' : a faith which filled the universe with 'demons', but at the same time subjected them to a harmonious Nature whose machinery they served and whose laws they operated. Ultimately, Renaissance Platonism had been left with its demons, and the Cambridge Platonists, insulated in their fenland cloister, were to provide some of the last intellectual defenders of witch-

[1] Bacon's few observations on witches, noncommittal in general, incredulous in particular, are cited in Lea, *Materials*, p. 1355. For his positive views on 'magic', see P. Rossi, *Francesco Bacone, dalla magia alla scienza* (Bari, 1951). Selden has been credited with reactionary beliefs on account of one lawyerly observation in his *Table-Talk*, which in fact indicates scepticism, not belief : his real 'Platonic' views on Nature can be seen in his *de Diis Syris* (1617), Syntagma, 1, cap. 2. Grotius not only believed generally in a universal order of Nature : specifically he rejected the penalties of the Mosaic law, which were the basis of witch-persecution in Protestant countries (*de Jure Belli ac Pacis*, lib. 1, cap. 1, xvi 'Jure Hebrae-orum numquam obligatos fuisse alienigenas') ; repudiated biblical fundamentalism (much to the indignation of good Calvinists) ; and in his Annotations on the Old and New Testament followed the example of Erasmus in omitting to comment on the passages customarily cited in support of witch-beliefs.

[2] Lea's lack of sympathy with any rationalism but his own is shown by his remarks on Erastus and Paracelsus. Erastus, he says, 'was superior to many of the superstitions of the age, as is shown in his criticism of Paracelsus, and yet a believer in witchcraft' (*Materials*, p. 430). It evidently did not occur to Lea that the rationalism of Erastus entailed belief in witchcraft, while the 'superstition' of Paracelsus might create the context of a new rationalism which would dispense with it.

beliefs.[1] But the impulse which it had given was continued by other philosophers : by Bacon with his 'purified magic', by Descartes with his universal, 'mechanical' laws of Nature, in which demons were unnecessary. It was Descartes, Thomasius and his friends agreed, who dealt the final blow to the witch-craze in western Europe [2] — which perhaps explains, better than the original Protestantism of Colbert, the early suspension of witch-trials in France. Queen Christina of Sweden, who ordered the witch-trials to cease in the Swedish-occupied parts of Germany,[3] had herself been the pupil of Descartes. Gustaf Rosenhane and the physician Urban Hiärne, who resisted the great Swedish witch-craze of 1668–77, were both Cartesians.[4] So was Bekker himself in Holland, though his critics insisted that he had muddled the teaching of his master.[5] But the final victory, which liberated Nature from the biblical fundamentalism in which Bekker himself had still been imprisoned, was that of the English deists and the German Pietists,[6] the heirs of the Protestant heretics of the seventeenth century, the parents of that eighteenth-century Enlightenment in which the duel in Nature between a Hebrew God and a medieval Devil was replaced by the benevolent despotism of a modern, scientific 'Deity'.

[1] The Cambridge Platonists adopted neo-Platonic ideas just at the time when Platonism, from a liberating, was turning into a reactionary force. But Cambridge itself was in many ways cut off from the Baconian and Cartesian ideas which were accepted in Oxford in the 1650s. Even Newton was in many ways imprisoned in the backward-looking Puritan theology of Restoration Cambridge.

[2] Thomasius, *de Crimine Magiae* (Halle, 1701, § XLVII). Cf. F. M. Brahm, *Disputatio Inauguralis* . . . (1701), in Lea, *Materials*, p. 1406.

[3] See her order of 1649 in Hauber, *Bibliotheca* . . . *Magica*, III, 250.

[4] Bertil Sundborg, in *Lychnos*, 1954–5, pp. 204–64.

[5] Even the sympathetic Hauber made this criticism (op. cit. I, 565).

[6] It is perhaps unfair to isolate Thomasius from the other Pietists, just as it would be unfair to isolate Bekker from other Cartesians. The founder of the Pietist movement, P. J. Spener, had preceded Thomasius in opposing witch-beliefs in his *Theologische Bedencken* (1700) ; Gottfried Arnold, who defended the heretics of the past in his *Unparteyische Kirche- und Ketzerhistorie* (1699), co-operated with Thomasius ; and it was from the university press of Halle, the centre of Pietism, that nearly all the German books against the witch-craze were sent forth.

VI

I have suggested that the witch-craze of the sixteenth and seventeenth centuries must be seen, if its strength and duration are to be understood, both in its social and in its intellectual context. It cannot properly be seen, as the nineteenth-century liberal historians tended to see it, as a mere 'delusion', detached or detachable from the social and intellectual structure of the time. Had it been so — had it been no more than an artificial intellectual construction by medieval inquisitors — it is inconceivable that it should have been prolonged for two centuries after its full formulation; that this formulation should never afterwards have been changed; that criticism should have been so limited; that no criticism should have effectively undermined it; that the greatest thinkers of the time should have refrained from openly attacking it; and that some of them, like Bodin, should even have actively supported it. To conclude this essay I shall try to summarize the interpretation I have offered.

First, the witch-craze was created out of a social situation. In its expansive period, in the thirteenth century, the 'feudal' society of Christian Europe came into conflict with social groups which it could not assimilate, and whose defence of their own identity was seen, at first, as 'heresy'. Sometimes it really was heresy: heretical ideas, intellectual in origin, are often assumed by societies determined to assert their independence. So Manichaean ideas, carried — it seems — by Bulgarian missionaries, were embraced by the racially distinct society of Pyrenean France and 'Vaudois' ideas, excogitated in the cities of Lombardy or the Rhône, were adopted in the Alpine valleys where 'feudal' society could never be established. The medieval Church, as the spiritual organ of 'feudal' society, declared war on these 'heresies', and the friars, who waged that war, defined both orthodoxy and heresy in the process. We know that the doctrines which they ascribed both to the Albigensians and to the Vaudois are not necessarily the doctrines really professed by those 'heretics', whose authentic documents have been almost entirely destroyed by their persecutors. The inquisitors ascribed to the societies which they opposed at once a more elaborate cosmology and a more debased morality than we have any reason to do. In particular, they ascribed to the Albigensians an absolute dualism between God and the Devil in Nature, and orgies of sexual promiscuity — a charge regularly made by the orthodox against esoteric dissenting societies. Both these charges would be carried forward from the first to the second stage of the struggle.

For the first stage was soon over. Orthodox 'feudal' society destroyed the 'Albigensian' and reduced the 'Vaudois' heresies. The friars evangelized the Alpine and Pyrenean valleys. However, the social dissidence remained, and therefore a new rationalization of it seemed necessary. In those mountain areas, where pagan customs lingered and the climate bred nervous disease, the missionaries soon discovered superstitions and hallucinations out of which to fabricate a second set of heresies : heresies less intellectual, and even less edifying, than those which they had stamped out, but nevertheless akin to them. The new 'heresy' of witchcraft, as discovered in the old haunts of the Cathari and the Vaudois, rested on the same dualism of God and the Devil ; it was credited with the same secret assemblies, the same promiscuous sexual orgies ; and it was described, often, by the same names.

This new 'heresy' which the inquisitors discovered beneath the relics of the old was not devised in isolation. The Albigensians, like their Manichaean predecessors, had professed a dualism of good and evil, God and the Devil, and the Dominicans, the hammers of the Albigensians, like St Augustine, the hammer of the Manichees, had adopted something of the dualism against which they had fought. They saw themselves as worshippers of God, their enemies as worshippers of the Devil ; and as the Devil is *simia Dei*, the ape of God, they built up their diabolical system as the necessary counterpart of their divine system. The new Aristotelean cosmology stood firmly behind them both, and St Thomas Aquinas, the guarantor of the one, was the guarantor of the other. The two were interdependent ; and they depended not only on each other, but also on a whole philosophy of the world.

The elaboration of the new heresy, as of the new orthodoxy,

was the work of the medieval Catholic Church and, in particular, of its most active members, the Dominican friars. No argument can evade or circumvent this fact. The elements of the craze may be non-Christian, even pre-Christian. The practice of spells, the making of weather, the use of sympathetic magic may be universal. The concepts of a pact with the Devil, of night-riding to the sabbat, of *incubi* and *succubi*, may derive from the pagan folk-lore of the Germanic peoples.[1] But the weaving together of these various elements into a systematic demonology which could supply a social stereotype for persecution was exclusively the work, not of Christianity, but of the Catholic Church. The Greek Orthodox Church offers no parallel. There were peasant superstitions in Greece : Thessaly was the classic home of ancient witches. There were encyclopaedic minds among the Greek Fathers : no refinement of absurdity deterred a Byzantine theologian. The same objective situation existed in the east as in the west : Manichaean dualism was the heresy of the Bogomils of Bulgaria before it became the heresy of the Albigensians of Languedoc. But even out of the ruins of Bogomilism, the Greek Orthodox Church built up no systematic demonology and launched no witch-craze. By the schism of 1054 the Slavonic countries of Europe — with the exception of Catholic Poland, the exception which proves the rule — escaped participation in one of the most disreputable episodes in Christian history.[2]

Such, it seems, was the origin of the system. It was perfected in the course of a local struggle and it had, at first, a local application. But the intellectual construction, once complete, was, in itself, universal. It could be applied anywhere. And in the fourteenth century, that century of increasing introversion and intolerance, among the miseries of the Black Death and the Hundred Years War in France, its application was made general.

[1] This is stated by Weiser-Aall in Bächtold-Stäubli, *Handwörterbuch des deutschen Aberglauben III* (Berlin and Leipzig, 1930–1), pp. 1828 ff., s.v. 'Hexe'.

[2] This point is made by Riezler, *Geschichte der Hexenprozessen in Baiern*, p. 51, and by Hansen, *Quellen*, p. 71. It may be remarked that the one great Church Father who wrote before the schism and who provided an intellectual basis for the later witch-craze, St Augustine, had little or no influence in Byzantium. This was no doubt partly because he wrote in Latin. Without Augustine, without Aquinas, the Greek Church lacked the cosmological infrastructure of the witch-craze.

The first of the Avignon popes, themselves bishops from recalci-
trant Languedoc, gave a new impulse to the craze. The weapon
forged for use against nonconformist societies was taken up to
destroy nonconformist individuals : while the inquisitors in the
Alps and the Pyrenees continued to multiply the evidence, the
warring political factions of France and Burgundy exploited it to
destroy their enemies. Every spectacular episode increased the
power of the myth. Like the Jew, the witch became the stereotype of the incurable nonconformist ; and in the declining Middle
Ages, the two were joined as scapegoats for the ills of society.
The founding of the Spanish Inquisition, which empowered the
'Catholic Kings' to destroy 'judaism' in Spain, and the issue of
the Witch Bull, which urged cities and princes to destroy witches
in Germany, can be seen as two stages in one campaign.

Even so, the myth might have dissolved in the early sixteenth
century. The new prosperity might have removed the need for
a social scapegoat. The new ideas of the Renaissance might have
destroyed its intellectual basis. We have seen that in the years
1500–50, outside its Alpine home, the craze died down. In those
years the purified Aristoteleanism of Padua corrected the extravagance of scholastic physics ; the neo-Platonism of Florence
offered a more universal interpretation of Nature ; the new
criticism of the humanists pared down medieval absurdities. All
these intellectual movements might, in themselves, be ambivalent, but they might, together, have been effective. In fact
they were not. In the mid-sixteenth century, the craze was
revived and extended and the years from 1560 to 1630 saw the
worst episodes in its long history. It seems incontestable that
the cause of this revival was the intellectual regression of Reformation and Counter-Reformation, and the renewed evangelism of
the rival Churches. The former gave new life to the medieval,
pseudo-Aristotelean cosmology of which demonology was now
an inseparable part. The latter carried into northern Europe the
same pattern of forces which the Dominicans had once carried
into the Alps and Pyrenees — and evoked a similar response.

The Reformation is sometimes seen as a progressive movement. No doubt it began as such : for it began in humanism.

But in the years of struggle, of ideological war, humanism was soon crushed out. The great doctors of the Reformation, as of the Counter-Reformation, and their numerous clerical myrmidons, were essentially conservative : and they conserved far more of the medieval tradition than they would willingly admit. They might reject the Roman supremacy and go back, for their Church system, to the rudimentary organization of the apostolic age. They might pare away the incrustations of doctrine, the mon-asticism, the 'mechanical devotions', the priestcraft of the 'corrupted' medieval Church. But these were superficial dis-avowals. Beneath their 'purified' Church discipline and Church doctrine, the Reformers retained the whole philosophic infra-structure of scholastic Catholicism. There was no new Protestant physics, no exclusively Protestant view of Nature. In every field of thought, Calvinism and Lutheranism, like Counter-Reforma-tion Catholicism, marked a retreat, an obstinate defence of fixed positions. And since demonology, as developed by the Domini-can inquisitors, was an extension of the pseudo-Aristotelean cosmology, it was defended no less obstinately. Luther might not quote the *Malleus* ; Calvin might not own a debt to the Schoolmen ; but the debt was clear, and their successors would admit it. Demonology, like the science of which it was a part, was a common inheritance which could not be denied by such conservative Reformers. It lay deeper than the superficial dis-putes about religious practices and the mediation of the priest.[1]

But if the Reformation was not, intellectually, a progressive movement, it was undoubtedly an evangelical movement. Like the Dominicans of the Middle Ages the Lutheran and Calvinist

[1] Paulus (*Hexenwahn und Hexenprozess*, § iv), in his attempts to spare the medieval Catholic Church, argues that the Protestant Reformers derived their demonology not from their Catholic predecessors but direct from Germanic mythology. This argument (which is also used by the Catholic apologist Janssen) depends, once again, on an improper isolation of witch-beliefs from general cosmology. If Luther had rejected the Aristotelean cosmology while accepting witch-beliefs, then it *might* be said that he derived those beliefs from pagan sources — although even then the argument would be very strained. But since he, like Calvin, accepted the basic cosmology of the medieval Church, there is no need for such ingen-uity. When the front door is wide open, why make a detour in search of a back passage ?

clergy set out to recover for the faith — for their version of the faith — the peoples of northern Europe whom the Catholic Church had almost lost. In the first generation after Luther this evangelical movement had hardly begun. Luther's appeal was to the Christian princes, to the Christian nobility of Germany. As in the England of Henry VIII, Reform had begun as an affair of state. But by 1560 the princes, or many of them, had been won, and the immediate need was for preachers to establish religion among their people. So the second generation of Reformers, the missionaries formed in Wittenberg or Geneva, poured into the lands of hospitable princes or estates and the Word was preached not only in the ears of the great but in rural parishes in Germany and Scandinavia, France, England and Scotland.

Of course the triumph of the preachers was not always easy. Sometimes they found individual opposition ; sometimes whole societies seemed obstinately to refuse their Gospel. Just as the Dominican missionaries had encountered stubborn resistance from the mountain communities of the Alps and Pyrenees, so the Protestant missionaries found their efforts opposed by whole communities in the waste lands of the neglected, half-pagan north. The German preachers found such dissidence in West-phalia, in Mecklenburg, in Pomerania : areas, as a German physician later observed, where the peasants live miserably on thin beer, pig's meat and black bread ; [1] the more tolerant Swedish clergy found it, though they did not persecute it, in the racially distinct societies of Lapland and Finland ; the Scottish Kirk found it, and persecuted it, among the Celtic Highlanders. Sometimes this opposition could be described in doctrinal terms, as 'popery'. The Scottish witches who set to sea in a sieve to inconvenience King James were declared to be 'Papists', and Lancashire, of course, was a nest of both Papists and witches. Sometimes it was too primitive to deserve doctrinal terms, and

[1] Friedrich Hoffmann, *Dissertatio Physico-Medica de Diaboli Potentia in Corpora* (Halle, 1703), quoted in Lea, *Materials*, p. 1466 ; and see Lea's note *ad loc*. Cf. also Brunnemann, *Discours von betrüglichen Kennzeichen der Zauberey*, cited in Lea, *Materials*, p. 1429, which also gives Westphalia, Pomerania and Mecklenburg as the home of witches.

then a new explanation had to be found. But this time there was no need to invent a new stereotype. The necessary stereotype had already been created by the earlier missionaries and strengthened by long use. The dissidents were witches.

With the Catholic reconquest a generation later, the same pattern repeats itself. The Catholic missionaries too discover obstinate resistance. They too find it social as well as individual. They too find it in particular areas : in Languedoc, in the Vosges and the Jura, in the Rhineland, the German Alps. They too describe it now as Protestant heresy, now as witchcraft. The two terms are sometimes interchangeable, or at least the frontier between them is as vague as that between Albigensians and witches in the past. The Basque witches, says de l'Ancre, have been brought up in the errors of Calvinism. Nothing has spread this pest more effectively through England, Scotland, Flanders and France, declares del Rio (echoing another Jesuit, Maldonado) than *dira Calvinismi lues*. 'Witchcraft grows with heresy, heresy with witchcraft', the English Catholic Thomas Stapleton cried to the sympathetic doctors of Louvain.[1] His argument — his very words — were afterwards repeated, with changed doctrinal labels, by Lutheran pastors in Germany.[2] Whenever the missionaries of one Church are recovering a society from their rivals, 'witchcraft' is discovered beneath the thin surface of 'heresy'.

Such, it seems, is the progress of the witch-craze as a social movement. But it is not only a social movement. From its social basis it also has its individual extension. It can be extended deliberately, in times of political crisis, as a political device, to see p.28 destroy powerful enemies or dangerous persons. Thus it was used in France in the fourteenth and fifteenth centuries. It can

[1] 'Crescit cum magia haeresis, cum haeresi magia.' Thomas Stapleton's dissertation on the question 'Cur magia pariter cum haeresi hodie creverit', delivered on 30 Aug. 1594, is printed in *Thomae Stapleton Angli S.T.D. Opera Omnia* (Paris, 1620), II, 502–7.

[2] Hauber (*Bibliotheca . . . Magica*, II, 205) states that he possessed a copy of Stapleton's dissertation as emended for delivery in a Lutheran university during the great witch-craze of the late 1620s. The words 'Luther' and 'Lutherans' had been changed into 'the Pope' and 'the Jesuits' ; otherwise no alteration had been thought necessary : a nice commentary on the intellectual originality of both sides. The good Lutheran had left Stapleton's abuse of the Calvinists intact.

also be extended blindly, in times of panic, by its own momentum. When a 'great fear' takes hold of society, that society looks naturally to the stereotype of the enemy in its midst ; and once the witch had become the stereotype, witchcraft would be the universal accusation. It was an accusation which was difficult to rebut in the lands where popular prejudice was aided by judicial torture : we have only to imagine the range of the Popish Plot in England in 1679 if every witness had been tortured. It is in such times of panic that we see the persecution extended from old women, the ordinary victims of village hatred, to educated judges and clergy whose crime is to have resisted the craze. Hence those terrible episodes in Trier and Bamberg and Würzburg. Hence also that despairing cry of the good senator de l'Ancre, that formerly witches were 'hommes vulgaires et idiots, nourris dans les bruyères et la fougière des Landes', but nowadays witches under torture confess that they have seen at the sabbat 'une infinité de gens de qualité que Satan tient voilez et à couvert pour n'estre cognus'.[1] It is a sign of such a 'great fear' when the *élite* of society are accused of being in league with its enemies.

Finally, the stereotype, once established, creates, as it were, its own folk-lore, which becomes in itself a centralizing force. If that folk-lore had not already existed, if it had not already been created by social fear out of popular superstition within an intellectually approved cosmology, then psychopathic persons would have attached their sexual hallucinations to other, perhaps more individual figures. This, after all, is what happens today. But once the folk-lore had been created and had been impressed by the clergy upon every mind, it served as a psychological as well as a social stereotype. The Devil with his nightly visits, his *succubi* and *incubi*, his solemn pact which promised new power to gratify social and personal revenge, became 'subjective reality' to hysterical women in a harsh rural world or in artificial communities — in ill-regulated nunneries as at Marseilles, at Loudun, at Louviers, or in special regions like the Pays de Labourd, where

[1] P. de l'Ancre, *Tableau de l'inconstance des mauvais anges et démons* (Paris, 1613), dedication to Mgr de Sillery, chancelier de France.

THE EUROPEAN WITCH-CRAZE

(according to de l'Ancre) the fishermen's wives were left deserted for months. And because separate persons attached their illusions to the same imaginary pattern, they made that pattern real to others. By their separate confessions the science of the Schoolmen was empirically confirmed.

Thus on all sides the myth was built up and sustained. There were local differences of course, as well as differences of time ; differences of jurisdiction as well as differences of procedure. A strong central government could control the craze while popular liberty often let it run wild. The centralized Inquisition in Spain or Italy, by monopolizing persecution, kept down its production, while north of the Alps the free competition of bishops, abbots and petty lords, each with his own jurisdiction, kept the furnaces at work. The neighbourhood of a great international university, like Basel or Heidelberg, had a salutary effect,[1] while one fanatical preacher or one over-zealous magistrate in a backward province could infect the whole area. But all these differences merely affected the practice of the moment : the myth itself was universal and constant. Intellectually logical, socially necessary, experimentally proved, it had become a *datum* in European life. Rationalism could not attack it, for rationalism itself, as always, moved only within the intellectual context of the time. Scepticism, the distrust of reason, could provide no substitute. At best, the myth might be contained as in the early sixteenth century. But it did not evaporate : it remained at the bottom of society, like a stagnant pool, easily flooded, easily stirred. As long as the social and intellectual structure of which it was a part remained intact, any social fear was likely to flood it, any ideological struggle to stir it, and no piecemeal operation could effectively drain it

[1] The University of Heidelberg deserves particular credit, for it maintained critical standards in a strongly Calvinist country. In 1585, or just before, the faculty of law at Heidelberg opposed the death penalty for witchcraft, saying that it was 'billicher zu Seelsorgern führen dann zur Marten und zum Todte' — better to cure the soul than to torture and kill the body (cited in Binz, *Doctor Johann Weyer*, pp. 101-2). One of the most powerful opponents of the craze, the Calvinist Hermann Wilchen or Witekind, who wrote under the name 'Lerchheimer von Steinfelden', was professor of mathematics at Heidelberg (see Janssen, *A History of the German People*, XVI, 326). On the other hand the famous Daniel Erastus, professor of medicine, was a firm believer.

away. Humanist critics, Paduan scientists, might seek to correct the philosophic base of the myth. Psychologists — medical men like Weyer and Ewich and Webster — might explain away its apparent empirical confirmation. Humane men, like Scot and Spee, by natural reason, might expose the absurdity and denounce the cruelty of the methods by which it was propagated. But to destroy the myth, to drain away the pool, such merely local operations no longer sufficed. The whole intellectual and social structure which contained it, and had solidified around it, had to be broken. And it had to be broken not at the bottom, in the dirty sump where the witch-beliefs had collected and been systematized, but at its centre, whence they were refreshed. In the mid-seventeenth century this was done. Then the medieval synthesis, which Reformation and Counter-Reformation had artificially prolonged, was at last broken, and through the cracked crust the filthy pool drained away. Thereafter society might persecute its dissidents as Huguenots [1] or as Jews. It might discover a new stereotype, the 'Jacobin', the 'Red'. But the stereotype of the witch had gone.

[1] Thus in 1685 Louis XIV expelled the Huguenots from France as an unassimilable group, but as far as I know, the charges of witchcraft so furiously hurled at the Huguenots of the south in 1609 were not repeated. The Huguenot became again, *per se*, the stereotype of social hatred, and so remained long afterwards, as shown by the Calas affair in 1762. The social significance of that affair is well brought out in David D. Bien, *The Calas Affair : Persecution, Toleration and Heresy in 18th-century Toulouse* (Princeton, 1960).

4 The Religious Origins of the Enlightenment

I

It is commonly said that the intellectual, no less than the industrial revolution of modern Europe has its origins in the religious Reformation of the sixteenth century : that the Protestant Reformers, either directly, by their theology, or indirectly, by the new social forms which they created, opened the way to the new science and the new philosophy of the seventeenth century, and so prepared the way for the transformation of the world. Without the Protestant Reformation of the sixteenth century, we are told, we should have had no Enlightenment in the eighteenth century : without Calvin we should have had no Voltaire.

This theory has often been questioned, but it is hard to destroy. Generation after generation finds in it an irresistible plausibility. It is part of the philosophy of action without which any study of history seems remote and academic. In the past it has been a Whig theory. In the nineteenth century the 'Whig' Protestant writers — Guizot in France, Macaulay in England — looking forward to change in the future, transferred their ideas into the past and saw the Protestants of the sixteenth century, the Whigs of the seventeenth, not merely as the party of radical action (which is one thing), but also as the party of economic, social and intellectual progress (which is another). Today the same theory is a Marxist theory. The Marxists, having replaced the Whigs as the party of radical action, similarly look to their pedigree, and attach themselves to an older radical tradition. In order to replace the Whigs, they borrow their philosophy. To them too progress is synonymous with political radicalism — and progress includes intellectual progress. Whoever is politically radical, they seem to say, is also intellectually right.

It is interesting to observe the continuity, in this respect, between the political radicals of yesterday and today : to see the torch, so nearly dropped from the failing hands of the last Whigs, skilfully caught and carried on by their successors, the first Marxists. This transfer of the same formula to different hands, this neat theoretical lampadophory, occurred at the close of the last century. It was then that the theory of the exclusively Protestant origin of progress, of modern thought, of modern society, having long been argued in political terms by the *'bourgeois'* thinkers of Europe, received its new, social content from the work of Max Weber and, being thus refloated, sailed triumphantly into the new age. Today, in this new form, it is as strong as ever. The Puritan Revolution in England, we are now assured, was not merely the 'constitutional' revolution : it was also the *'bourgeois'* revolution : and the *bourgeois* revolution was, in turn, the intellectual revolution. The new science, the new philosophy, the new historiography, the new economy were all the work of 'radical Protestants' — the more radical the more progressive ; [1] and a distinguished non-Marxist modern historian, reviewing a history of modern Scotland, can casually remark, as a truism that needs no argument, that the Scottish Enlightenment of the eighteenth century, the Scottish industry of the nineteenth century, would have been inconceivable in an episcopalian country.[2]

How simple history would be if we could accept these convenient rules of thumb ! But, alas, I find that I cannot. Admittedly the new philosophy was established in England in the 1650s. Admittedly Scotland was Presbyterian in the seventeenth century, enlightened in the eighteenth. But before we conclude that one fact determines the other, that *post hoc* is the same as *propter hoc*, it is essential to test the links of the argument. Is it clear that the new philosophy would not have triumphed in England in the 1650s if Charles I had continued to rule ? Is it

[1] See, for instance, Christopher Hill, *Intellectual Origins of the Puritan Revolution* (Oxford, 1965). I have expressed my criticisms of Mr Hill's argument in *History and Theory*, v, 1 (1966).

[2] A. J. P. Taylor, review of George Pryde, *Local and Central Government in Scotland since 1707* (1960), in the *New Statesman*.

certain that Scotland would have remained backward, even in the eighteenth century, if its Church had continued to be governed by bishops, as under Charles I and Charles II ? These hypothetical questions are perhaps unanswerable in themselves ; but they cannot be entirely jumped. We must at least consider them. Even if a direct answer is impossible, there is always the comparative method. Before accepting a conclusion on the imperfect evidence of one society, we can look aside to the evidence of another. We may note that the new philosophy triumphed in France in the 1650s although Louis XIV crushed the Fronde. Why then, we may ask, should the ruin of Charles I have been a necessary condition of its triumph, at the same time, in England ? Calvinism did not create Enlightenment in seventeenth-century Transylvania, nor did episcopacy stifle it in the England of Wren and Newton. Why then should we leap to conclusions about eighteenth-century Scotland ?

So we may object ; and yet, to our objections, we can already foresee the answers. They are the answers which the men of the Enlightenment themselves would have given. Voltaire might not have had much good to say of the Protestant Reformers or the Protestant clergy. He might detest Calvin, 'cet âme atroce' ; he might dismiss the founding fathers of the Reformation as 'tous écrivains qu'on ne peut lire' ; and he might prefer the society of sophisticated Parisian *abbés* to the dull, worthy prelates of Protestant England. But objective facts had to be faced. Intellectual life was undeniably freer, heresy was undeniably safer in Protestant than in Catholic countries. This had always been true, and it was no less true in the eighteenth century. The exceptions did but prove the rule. Giannone might succeed in publishing his great work in Naples, but what a scandal followed its publication, what disastrous consequences to author and printer alike ! To avoid persecution, and to reprint his work, Giannone was ultimately driven to take refuge in Protestant Geneva, only to be treacherously lured into Catholic Savoy, kidnapped by Catholic agents, and to disappear for the rest of his life into a Catholic prison. Montesquieu and Voltaire might escape such physical dangers, but they took no risks. Voltaire saw his

Lettres philosophiques burnt in Paris and thought it prudent to live abroad, or at least within easy reach of the Swiss frontier. Montesquieu sought to meet trouble half-way by squaring the censors — and failed at the last. And both published their works in Protestant cities, in Calvinist Holland or Calvinist Switzerland. Admittedly discussion was free in Catholic countries. Admittedly the censorship was imperfect. Admittedly social eminence limited clerical power. But the basic fact remained. Hume might insist that as much real freedom could be found in Catholic France as in Calvinist Scotland. It was difficult to argue with him, since he had experience of both. But in the end, when the best has been said about the one and the worst about the other, the difference between the intellectual life of the two societies cannot be overlooked. It was the difference which caused Gibbon to describe the exceptions to the rule as 'the *irregular* tendency of papists towards freedom' and 'the *unnatural* gravitation of protestants towards slavery'.[1]

Moreover, if we look at the stages of the Enlightenment, the successive geographical centres in which its tradition was engendered or preserved, the same conclusion forces itself upon us. The French Huguenots, we are told,— Hotman, Languet, Duplessis-Mornay and their friends — created the new political science of the sixteenth century. Calvinist Holland brought forth the seventeenth-century concept of natural law and provided a safe place of study for Descartes. Cromwellian England accepted the scientific programme of Bacon and hatched the work of Hobbes and Harrington. The Huguenots in Calvinist Holland — Pierre Bayle, Jean Leclerc — created the Republic of Letters in the last years of Louis XIV. Switzerland — Calvinist Geneva and Calvinist Lausanne — was the cradle of the eighteenth-century Enlightenment in Europe : it was in Geneva that Giannone and Voltaire would seek refuge ; it was a Calvinist pastor of Geneva, Jacob Vernet, who would be the universal agent of the movement : the correspondent of Leclerc, the friend and translator of Giannone, the friend and publisher of Montesquieu, the agent of Voltaire ; and it was to Calvinist Lausanne that Gibbon would

[1] E. Gibbon, *Vindication* . . ., in *Miscellaneous Works* (1814), I, 75.

owe, as he would afterwards admit, his whole intellectual formation. Finally, after Switzerland, another Calvinist society carried
forward the tradition. The Scotland of Francis Hutcheson and
David Hume, of Adam Smith and William Robertson carried
on the work of Montesquieu and created a new philosophy, a
new history, a new sociology. Thither, as Gibbon wrote, 'taste
and philosophy seemed to have retired from the smoke and hurry
of this immense capital', London ; and Thomas Jefferson would
describe the University of Edinburgh and the Academy of Geneva
as the two eyes of Europe.

Calvinist Holland, Puritan England, Calvinist Switzerland,
Calvinist Scotland. . . . If we take a long view — if we look at
the continuous intellectual tradition which led from the Renaissance to the Enlightenment — these Calvinist societies appear as
the successive fountains from which that tradition was supplied,
the successive citadels into which it sometimes retreated to be
preserved. Without those fountains, without those citadels what,
we may ask, would have happened to that tradition ? And yet
how easily the fountains might have been stopped, the citadels
overrun ! Suppose that the Duke of Savoy had succeeded in
subjugating Geneva — as so nearly happened in 1600 — and that
the Bourbons, in consequence, had imposed their protectorate
on the remaining French cantons of Switzerland. Suppose that
Charles I had not provoked an unnecessary rebellion in Scotland,
or even that James II had continued the policy of his brother and
perpetuated a high-flying Tory Anglican government in England.
If all this had happened, Grotius, Descartes, Richard Simon,
John Locke, Pierre Bayle would still have been born, but would
they have written as they did, could they have published what
they wrote ? And without predecessors, without publishers,
what would have happened to the Enlightenment, a movement
which owed so much of its character to the thought of the
preceding century and to its own success in propaganda and
publicity ?

No doubt this supposition is unfair, as all hypothetical questions, except the simplest, always are. The easy answer is that if

[1] *The Letters of Edward Gibbon*, ed. J. E. Norton (Oxford, 1956), II, 100.

Catholicism had triumphed in Europe, the whole terms of the problem would have been different : the ideological struggle would have been relaxed in victory, and ideas which had been excluded and suppressed by a society in tension might well have been tolerated by a society at ease. But on the facts it is clear that there is at least a *prima facie* case for the view that Calvinism was in some way essential to the intellectual revolution which led to the Enlightenment. The question therefore remains, in what way ? Was it a direct or an accidental connection ? Did Calvinism provide an essential mental or moral discipline ? Did its theological doctrines, when translated into secular terms, produce a new philosophy ? Or is the connection rather a social connection, independent of ideas ? In order to answer these questions it is best to begin not by presupposing the connection, but by asking what was the religious tradition which led to the Enlightenment. What philosophical precursors did the men of the Enlightenment themselves recognize ? When we have answered this question, when we have defined the continuing intellectual tradition, we may examine the relation between this tradition and the equally continuous tradition of European Calvinism.

II

The answer to this first question is, I think, reasonably clear. When Voltaire looked back in history, he recognized, of course, numerous predecessors at all times for various elements in his philosophy. But when he sought the beginnings of modernity, of his modernity, of the process which gradually and unevenly built up the new philosophy of which he was the prophet, he found them not in the Reformation, which he hated, but in the period before the Reformation, 'the century which ends with Leo X, François I and Henry VIII' : in other words, in the period of the late Renaissance and the Pre-Reform, the age of Valla and Erasmus, Machiavelli and Guicciardini, that liberal era which was overwhelmed and eclipsed by the hateful struggles of religion. That was the time, Voltaire wrote, when a new spirit, spreading over Europe from Italy, caused a revival of letters, an efflorescence of the arts, a softening of manners. The human mind, in those years, experienced a revolution 'which changed everything, as in our own world'.[1]

Unfortunately it did not last. With the Reformation came the Wars of Religion, which destroyed all, or nearly all, the intellectual achievements of the recent past, making the second half of the century frightful and bringing upon Europe 'une espèce de barbarie que les Hérules, les Vandales et les Huns n'avaient jamais connue'. It was not till the end of the sixteenth century, till the reign of Voltaire's constant hero, Henri IV, that the progress of mankind, which those wars had interrupted, could be resumed. This was the second stage of the Renaissance, the time when 'philosophy began to shine upon men' with the discoveries of Galileo and the enlarged vision of Lord Chancellor Bacon. But this second stage, Voltaire lamented, was also cut short by wars of religion. The quarrels of 'two Calvinist doctors' about grace and free will brought enlightened Holland back to dissension, persecution and atrocity. The newly restored civility of Europe foundered in the Thirty Years War. In England, polished and enlightened under James I, 'les disputes du clergé, et les animosités entre le parti royal et le parlement, ramenèrent la barbarie'.[2]

Throughout the middle years of the seventeenth century, as Voltaire saw them, barbarism prevailed. It was not till the personal reign of Louis XIV that it began to give way. Then, in the generation immediately preceding his own, Voltaire discovered the period of victory. In the middle of the seventeenth century 'la saine philosophie commença à percer un peu dans le monde'; by the end of it, thanks above all to the great English writers Locke and Newton, the Moderns had won their 'prodigieuse supériorité' over the Ancients. Today, wrote Voltaire, there is not a single ancient philosopher who has anything to say

[1] Voltaire, 'Conseils à un journaliste sur la philosophie, l'histoire, le théâtre', in *Mélanges*, ed. L. Moland, tome I, vol. XXII, 241 ; *Essai sur les mœurs*, ch. cxviii, cxxi.
[2] *Essai sur les mœurs*, ch. cxxi, clxxix, clxxxvii.

to us. They have all been superseded. Between Plato and Locke, there is nothing, and since Locke, Plato is nothing.[1]

To Voltaire, in effect, there are three periods since the gothic Middle Ages which he can recognize as pointing forward to the 'philosophy' and civilization of the Enlightenment. These are, first, the period before the Reformation; then the brief era of Henri IV and James I; and finally the period from the later seventeenth century onwards. These three periods can be summarized as the age of Erasmus, the age of Bacon and the age of Newton.

From France we turn to England, from Voltaire the propagandist to Gibbon the philosopher of history. Gibbon's attitude to the past was different from that of Voltaire. He had more respect for scholarship, a greater sense of the relativity of ideas, less confidence in the universal validity of 'reason'. But his interpretation of the stages of modern 'philosophy' is precisely the same as that of Voltaire. When he traces the development of 'philosophic history', of that 'philosophy and criticism', that 'reason' which achieved its fulfilment in 'the full light and freedom of the eighteenth century', the essential links are the same. Machiavelli and Guicciardini, he writes, 'with their worthy successors Fra Paolo and Davila', are justly esteemed the founders of modern history 'till, in the present age, Scotland arose to dispute the prize with Italy herself'. Again, in theology, he writes, 'Erasmus may be considered as the father of rational theology. After a slumber of a hundred years it was revived by the Arminians of Holland, Grotius, Limborch and Leclerc; in England by Chillingworth, the latitudinarians of Cambridge, Tillotson, Clarke, Hoadly, etc.'[2] Again and again, in his footnotes and miscellaneous observations, Gibbon shows the pedigree of his philosophy, and we see his masters grouped, mainly, in three periods. First, there is the age of the Pre-Reform, of Erasmus, Machiavelli, Guicciardini. Then there is the beginning of the seventeenth century, the age of Grotius and Bacon, Paolo Sarpi and de Thou. Finally there is the end of the same century

---

[1] Voltaire, *Siècle de Louis XIV* (1751), ch. xxxiv, xxxvi.
[2] Gibbon, *Decline and Fall of the Roman Empire*, ed. J. B. Bury (1909), VI, 128, and VII, 296.

and the beginning of the next : the age of Newton and Locke, Leibniz and Bayle. These three periods are distinct phases of light separated from each other, the first two by 'a slumber of a hundred years', the second and third by the heart of the seventeenth century.

What is the common character of these three periods in which the men of the Enlightenment agreed to recognize their predecessors ? The first and most obvious fact is that they are all periods of ideological peace. The first period, the age of Erasmus, is the last age of united Christendom in which the rational reform of an undivided Church seemed possible. The second period, the age of Grotius, the Dutch heir of Erasmus, is the period of *las Pazes*, the lull between the wars of Philip II and the Thirty Years War. The last age, the age which merges in the eighteenth-century Enlightenment, begins with the end of that war. It is not a period of peace, any more than the age of Erasmus had been ; but the wars of Louis XIV were not, like the wars of the late sixteenth and early seventeenth century, ideological wars : they were not characterized by that shrivelling of the mind, that narrowing of vision and severance of communication which is the peculiar quality of doctrinal strife.

Secondly, we may observe that these three periods are periods, and their intellectual leaders are often protagonists, not only of ideological peace but of theological reconciliation. Erasmus wore himself out preaching peace and a reform of the Church which would forestall and prevent the violent schism threatened by Luther. Grotius worked for a reunion of the Churches on an Arminian — that is, an Erasmian — base. Leibniz devoted much of his universal energy to the same end and was supported by allies in all countries and of all religions : the Catholic Spinola and Molanus, the Anglican Archbishop Wake, the Lutheran Praetorius, the Calvinist Jablonski, the Arminian Leclerc. In these projects of reunion, as in so much of the public activity of Leibniz, there was much of state policy also. But the spirit behind them was that which led ultimately to the deism of the eighteenth century, enabling Gibbon, and many others, to acquiesce 'with implicit belief in the tenets and mysteries which are adopted by the general consent of Catholics and Protestants'.

Finally, these three periods, so happily exempt from ideological war, hot or cold, were all, for that reason, periods of cosmopolitan intellectual correspondence. The correspondence of Erasmus knew no frontiers, geographical or ideological. It extended from Scotland to Transylvania, from Poland to Portugal. The struggles of the later sixteenth century broke up this intellectual unity, but the peace of the early seventeenth century restored it. The Jacobean age — if we may use this parochial but convenient term — was indeed one of the great ages of free exchange in the intellectual world. Lipsius and Casaubon, de Thou and Sarpi, Camden and Grotius, Gruter and Peiresc were nodal points in a vast network of intellectual contact which took no account of national or religious differences. It was then that the phrase 'the Republic of Letters' first came into use. It was a phrase which, at that time, had a missionary content. The *élite* of that new Republic, like the Erasmian *élite* before them, knew that they were not merely enjoying a delightful international conversation : they were also working together to lay the intellectual foundations of a new world. To Bacon, the reign of James I in England coincided with a European Renaissance comparable only with the golden ages of Greece and Rome. It was a time when ancient literature had been revived, when 'controversies of religion, which have so much diverted men from other sciences', had happily dried up, and peace, navigation and printing had opened the prospect of infinite progress. 'Surely', he wrote, 'when I set before me the condition of these times, in which learning hath made her third visitation, I cannot but be raised to this persuasion, that this third period of time will far surpass that of the Grecian and Roman learning — if only men will know their own strength and their own weakness both, and take, one from the other, light of invention, not fire of contradiction.'[1]

Unfortunately, as Bacon's life drew to its close, the fire of contradiction broke out again. In the revolution of Holland Grotius escaped from prison into lifelong exile ; in the Thirty

---

[1] F. Bacon, *Advancement of Learning*, in *Works*, ed. J. Spedding *et. al.* (1857–74), III, 476–7.

Years War Rubens in Antwerp lamented the collapse of the golden age ; and a little later the English disciples of Grotius at Great Tew would be broken up by what one of them, Clarendon, would describe as 'this odious and unnecessary civil war'.

Nevertheless, even the odious ideological wars of the mid-seventeenth century did not destroy the society of Europe. When they were over, the Republic of Letters was reconstituted, stronger than ever. The scholars and thinkers of Europe resumed their contacts. As Voltaire would write, ' Jamais la correspondance entre les philosophes ne fut plus universelle : Leibniz servait à l'animer.' [1] Leibniz, Locke and Newton were indeed the law-givers of the Republic, but its great propagandists, the men who gave currency to the name and popularity to the concept, were the two great rivals in Amsterdam, Bayle and Leclerc : Bayle, the sceptical Encyclopaedist, the 'Pyrrhonist' who looks back to Montaigne and Charron in the second of our two periods, to Erasmus — or at least to one aspect of Erasmus — in the first ; Leclerc, the Arminian disciple of Grotius, the editor of his *de Veritate Religionis Christianae*, who was also the admirer of Erasmus, the producer of the greatest edition of his works : an edition which a German publisher has thought worth reproduction *in toto* today.

The first major point which I wish to make in this essay is already, I hope, clear. To those who would say that the ideas of the European Enlightenment were hammered out in the strife of ideological revolution and civil war, it can be replied — and the men of the Enlightenment would themselves have replied — that, on the contrary, those ideas were worked out in periods of ideological peace and *rapprochement*, and were only interrupted and delayed, not furthered, by the intervening periods of revolution. Revolution may have shifted the balance of political or social power. It may have been necessary to preserve, here or there, the basis of intellectual advance. That is another matter. But on the substance of thought it had no discernible direct effect. The new ideas which were conveyed by devious channels through two centuries and which finally overturned the old orthodoxies of

[1] Voltaire, *Siècle de Louis XIV*, ch. xxxiv.

Europe were generated not in the heat of war or under the stress of revolution — that heat and that stress do not provoke new thought : rather they drive men back into customary, defensive postures, causing them to reiterate old slogans — but in the mild warmth of peace, the gentle give-and-take of free and considered international discussion.

Where then is the function of Calvinism : that Calvinism, that 'radical Protestantism', for which such large claims have been advanced and for whose claims, I have admitted, a *prima facie* case can be made ? The immediate answer is clear. Not one of the 'philosophers' to whom the men of the Enlightenment looked back, and whose names I have quoted, was an orthodox Calvinist. The doctrines of Calvin, as far as we can see, had no direct influence on any of the ideas which led to the Enlightenment. Whatever debt the philosophers of the eighteenth century might owe to Calvinist cities, Calvinist universities, Calvinist societies, we have yet to discover any evidence of obligation to Calvinist Churches or Calvinist ideas. Our problem, the connection between Calvinism and the Enlightenment, is a problem still.

III

How are we to resolve this problem ? Obviously, we can approach the answer only if we tread very cautiously. We must not hastily presume a logical connection where we can only demonstrate a local coincidence, however regular. Before basing any conclusions on that local coincidence, we must examine the local circumstances. This means that we must look at the separate Calvinist societies a little more closely than the confident political or sociological theorists have done. We must also look at them comparatively, remembering that Calvinism in one society is not necessarily the same as in another. One name may cover a variety of forms.

For international Calvinism was not an abstraction. Like any other international movement it was localized, and transformed by local forces, in a number of very different societies, and these societies had their own histories, their own internal tensions. There were European powers like Holland ; defensive federations like the cantons of Switzerland ; city-states like Geneva and La Rochelle ; isolated rural peninsulas like Scotland ; exposed and aggressive principalities like the Palatinate ; miniscule lordships or academic republics like Hanau, Herborn and Wesel, Saumur and Sedan. It is not enough to say that sixteenth-century Heidelberg, seventeenth-century Holland, Puritan England, Huguenot France, eighteenth-century Switzerland and Scotland — the successive seed-plots of the Enlightenment — were all Calvinist societies ; or at least it is not enough, having said this as a fact, to leave it as a demonstration. The societies themselves were too different, and also too complex in themselves, for such easy generalizations. The terms we have used are too loose. We must look more closely into both the one and the other. We must analyse the character of the societies and look behind the loose, general terms.

When we do this, we soon discover a very important fact. We find that each of those Calvinist societies made its contribution to the Enlightenment at a precise moment in its history, and that this moment was the moment when it repudiated ideological orthodoxy. In fact, we may say that the separate Calvinist societies of Europe contributed to the Enlightenment only in so far as they broke away from Calvinism.

This may be connected with a change in the character of Calvinism. For there is no doubt that such a change took place. Calvinism in the sixteenth century may have retained some traces of the intellectual distinction of its founder, some residue of the Erasmianism which lay behind it. But in the next century it is very different. Read (if you can) the writings of the great doctors of seventeenth-century Calvinism, the heirs of Calvin and Beza, Buchanan and Knox. Their masters may have been grim, but there is a certain heroic quality about their grimness, a literary power about their writing, an intellectual force in their minds. The successors are also grim, but they are grim and mean. Perkins and 'Smectymnuus' in England, Rivetus and Voëtius in Holland, Baillie and Rutherford in Scotland, Desmarets and

Jurieu in France, Francis Turrettini in Switzerland, Cotton Mather in America — what a gallery of intolerant bigots, narrow-minded martinets, timid conservative defenders of repellent dogmas, instant assailants of every new or liberal idea, inquisitors and witch-burners! But however that may be, the facts can hardly be denied. Once we look at the circumstances in which each of those societies I have named became in turn the home of the pre-Enlightenment, we discover that in every instance the new ideas which interest us spring not from the Calvinists but from the heretics who have contrived to break or elude the control of the Calvinist Church : heretics whom the true Calvinists, if they could, would have burnt.

But in order to illustrate this conclusion, let us look briefly and in turn at the Calvinist societies which I have enumerated, and the circumstances of their enlightenment.

First Holland. Here the facts are well known. The rise of liberal ideas in Holland, which was to make Leiden the seminary and Amsterdam the refuge of advanced thinkers in all the sciences, was made possible not by the Calvinist Church, but by its critics, its heretics : first the 'libertines', then the Arminians and their clients the Socinians. Every Dutch philosopher whose ideas look forward to the Enlightenment suffered persecution of one kind or another from the local Calvinist clergy. Fortunately, in the Netherlands, the Calvinist clergy never had complete power. The lay power, however precariously, was always supreme. Calvin himself might have Servetus, an early Socinian, burnt in Geneva, but Calvin's followers raged in vain against the followers of Servetus in Holland. When the French Calvinist Lambert Daneau, the disciple of Calvin and Beza, the greatest Calvinist doctor of his time, was 'called' to the ministry at Leiden in 1581, he soon discovered the difference between Dutch and Swiss Calvinism. He was told that the citizens of Leiden would no more tolerate the Inquisition of Geneva than the Inquisition of Spain ; and he returned in a huff to a more docile flock in rural Gascony. Wisely, the Arminians in Holland insisted on the supremacy of the civil power over the clergy. The civil power was their only protection against the fanatical *Predikants*. But at times of crisis, when the civil power was at bay against a foreign enemy and needed the support of the people, it was driven into alliance with the Calvinist Church. Such times were always fatal to the Arminians. In 1618 there was such a crisis, and it led to their immediate ruin. Their statesman Oldenbarnevelt was judicially murdered, their philosopher Grotius imprisoned and exiled. At the Synod of Dordt, a strict, repressive Calvinism was imposed on the Church of the United Provinces. However, the tyranny of the orthodox was not permanent; when the political crisis was over, the Arminians recovered their freedom and the Socinians — those 'most chymical and rational' of sectaries, as an Englishman called them [1] — throve under their protection. The universal oracle of orthodox Calvinism, Gisbert Voëtius, might denounce liberal ideas and new ideas of all kinds, and especially the ideas of Descartes, but the new philosophy was preserved and continued by Arminian patronage. From Arminius and Grotius, the spiritual and the secular disciples of Erasmus, the line of descent leads, through Episcopius, Limborch and Leclerc, unmistakably to the Enlightenment.

Exactly the same pattern can be seen in England. The struggle between the English 'Presbyterians' and the Independents in the 1640s, complicated though it is by changing political issues, is in one sense — the intellectual sense — a struggle between Calvinists and Arminians. The English 'Presbyterians', even their clergy, might not be good Calvinists as seen from Holland or Scotland, but at least they were better than the Independents. For the Independents were true Arminians — as indeed they were often called : believers in free will, in religious toleration, and in lay control of the Church. The victory of the Independents over the 'Presbyterians' may have been, in immediate politics, the victory of radicals over moderates, but in social matters it was the victory of the laity over the clergy, and therefore in intellectual matters the victory of lay ideas over clerical ideas. Scholastic Aristoteleanism — the old philosophy of the Catholic Church which Reformation and Counter-Reformation had alike refurbished and reimposed — went down in England not when

[1] Francis Osborne, *Advice to a Son* [1656], ed. E. A. Parry (1896), p. 112.

English Prynne and Scottish Baillie triumphed over Archbishop Laud, but when the Erastians like Selden — some of whom were 'Presbyterian' just as the Dutch Arminians were also Calvinists — refused to set up in England a 'presbytery' according to the word of God. It was then that the ideas of Descartes came into England, then that the ideas of Bacon triumphed, then that Oxford became the capital of the 'New Philosophy'.

It happened in Scotland too. In Scotland the Calvinist Church had succeeded in doing what it had not been able to do in England or Holland — what it could do only where the laity was weak and at the mercy of the clergy : that is, in relatively undeveloped rural societies like Scotland or New England, or in small, defence-less communities surrounded by a hostile world, like the Hugue-not Churches of France after 1629. It had stamped out all forms of dissent. First it had crushed Arminian deviation. That indeed had been easy, for Scottish Arminianism was a feeble growth. Its most famous, perhaps its only advocate within the Kirk, was John Cameron. He was soon forced into exile. Then, having crushed its heretics, the Kirk turned to do battle with its external enemies, the bishops. By the 1640s its triumph was complete. Its intellectual character in those years of triumph is clear from the copious correspondence of Robert Baillie, the most learned (and by no means the most illiberal) of the party, denouncing in turn lay control, toleration, free will, the 'Tridentine popery' of Grotius, the 'fatuous heresy' of Descartes and the 'insolent absurdity' of Selden. Baillie in Glasgow is an echo of Voëtius in Utrecht. But in the 1650s, with the English conquest, the Calvinist Kirk was broken, and for a few years a brief, partial flicker of Enlightenment hovered over its ruins. Unfortunately it did not last. There was no native basis for it, and when the foreign armies were withdrawn, the Kirk soon recovered its power and snuffed it out.[1]

A generation later it was the turn of the French Huguenots. In the sixteenth century the French Calvinist community had contained some of the most advanced and original thinkers in

[1] For this first flicker of enlightenment in Cromwellian Scotland, see my essay, 'Scotland and the Puritan Revolution', below, pp. 392–444.

France : Hotman, Duplessis-Mornay, Agrippa d'Aubigné, Bernard Palissy, Pierre de la Ramée, Ambroise Paré, Isaac Casaubon, Joseph Justus Scaliger . . . The list could be continued. Catherine de Médicis herself admitted that three-quarters of the best educated Frenchmen of her time were Huguenots. But after 1629, when the pride and autonomy of the Huguenots were broken, the independent laymen gradually disappear from among them, and French Protestantism, like Scottish Protestantism, is dominated by a clergy which becomes, with time, increasingly narrow and rigid : crabbed prudes and Puritans, haters of literature and the arts, stuck in postures of defence. There were exceptions of course ; but the great exception — the aristocratic Academy of Saumur — only proves the rule. For the Academy of Saumur, which shocked the Calvinist establishment by admitting Cartesianism into its teaching, was Arminian. John Cameron, the Scottish Arminian whom the Kirk of Scotland had expelled, had gone to Saumur and had there succeeded the formidable Dutch Calvinist Gomar. From that day onwards Saumur was the centre of Protestant enlightenment in France, an affront to good Calvinists everywhere.[1] As the *intendant* of Anjou wrote to Louis XIV in 1664, 'elle réunit tout ce qu'il y a de gens d'esprit dans le parti protestant pour le rendre célèbre';[2] and a later historian, looking back, can write that 'à la base de presque tout libéralisme protestant au 16ᵉ siècle, on retrouve Saumur'.[3] But Saumur was suspect among the Huguenots of France, and the other Protestant academies took good care to avoid such suspicion. There the laity remained obedient to the clergy, and the clergy obeyed the strict Calvinist rules of the Synod of Dordt.

From this subjection the French Protestant laity were ultimately released — little though he intended it — by Louis XIV. For the expulsion of 1685 — as the late Erich Haase has shown

[1] Compare, for instance, the sour remarks of Robert Baillie on Moïse Amyraut, the Arminian successor of Cameron at Saumur, whose 'fancies', 'vanity and pride' were 'troubling' the Churches of France (*Letters and journals of Robert Baillie* (Edinburgh, 1841–2), II, 324, 342, and III, 311, etc.).

[2] P. Marchegay, *Archives d'Anjou* (Angers, 1843), p. 127.

[3] Annie Barnes, *Jean Leclerc et la République des Lettres* (Geneva, 1938), p. 46. Cf. Joseph Prost, *La Philosophie à l'académie protestante de Saumur, 1606–1685* (Paris, 1907).

— was destined to be the intellectual salvation of the French Protestants. In exile, in sympathetic Protestant societies, they escaped at last from the rigid clericalism to which, as a persecuted minority in Catholic France, they had perforce succumbed. Among the Arminians and Socinians of Holland and the Latitudinarians of England they discovered a new freedom. So, leaving their self-appointed spiritual director, 'the Grand Inquisitor of the Dispersion', Pierre Jurieu, to castigate their backsliding and denounce them as Socinians or infidels, they followed the more seductive teaching of the Arminian Leclerc, the sceptical Bayle.[1]

A few years later a similar change took place in Switzerland. With the opening of the eighteenth century Switzerland began to replace Holland as the geographical headquarters of the Enlightenment. Balthasar Bekker, the Cartesian clergyman who was hounded from the Church of Holland for disbelieving in witches, was the last European figure of the native Dutch Enlightenment of the seventeenth century. Thereafter it was French-speaking Huguenots who re-created the Republic of Letters. And if they made its first capital in Amsterdam and Rotterdam, they soon made its second capital in Geneva and Lausanne. If the doctrines of Descartes had been received in Holland, those of Locke were received in Switzerland; and Switzerland would retain its supremacy for the rest of the century. When Gibbon decided to retire to Lausanne, his English friends thought him mad. How could a man who had enjoyed the polite society of London and Paris bury himself in a provincial Swiss city? But Gibbon knew Lausanne and he knew his own mind, which had been fashioned there. He never regretted his decision.[2]

But once again, when we look at the social background to this intellectual change, we find that this Swiss enlightenment has followed on an internal change, and that internal change is the defeat of Calvinism. In the seventeenth century the Calvinist Church in Switzerland had accepted the decrees of the Synod of Dordt. The Academy of Geneva had indeed suffered an Arminian

---

[1] Erich Haase, *Einführung in die Literatur der Refuge* (Berlin, 1959).
[2] See Gibbon's letter to Lord Sheffield in *The Letters of Edward Gibbon*, III, 58–59.

infiltration and had found itself threatened by the invading 'doctrine of Saumur'. But its resistance had been successful. Fear of Savoy had been to Geneva what fear of Spain had been to Amsterdam : it had given a reserve of power to the party of resistance, the bigots of the Church. The *Consensus Helveticus* of 1674 marked the triumph of the strict Calvinist party : it was the Swiss equivalent of the Synod of Dordt, and it was imposed on universities and academies throughout Calvinist Switzerland. The works of Grotius and all his disciples were banned, and the young Leclerc left the *cachot* of Geneva for the freedom of Saumur. By 1685 all the Swiss academies were in decline. Basel, once an international university, had become purely provincial. At Lausanne, jealously controlled by the oligarchy of Bern, the printing industry was dead and the canton de Vaud could be described as 'pays, sinon de barbarie, pour le moins du monde peu curieux et éloigné du beau commerce'.

From this intellectual stagnation Switzerland was raised by a new, and this time successful, Arminian revolt. In Geneva this revolt was begun by Jean-Robert Chouet, a Cartesian who returned from Saumur to Geneva in 1669. It was continued by his pupil J.-A. Turrettini. Thanks largely to the energy of Turrettini, the *Consensus Helveticus* was finally defeated in Geneva. From 1706 it was no longer imposed on the clergy ; and from that date Turrettini's exiled friend Jean Leclerc would date the enlightenment of Geneva. In the next generation Geneva, to the Encyclopaedists, was a Socinian city. The ministers of religion, wrote d'Alembert, have pure morals, faithfully obey the law, refuse to persecute dissenters, and worship the supreme being in a worthy manner : the religion of many of them is 'a perfect Socinianism'. This was a change indeed. The tables had been turned on history, and the Socinian Servetus had triumphed in the very capital of his grim enemy, Calvin.[1]

In Lausanne the same battle was fought, with a different result

[1] The suppression and final victory of Arminianism in Geneva is well described in Miss Annie Barnes' valuable work, *Jean Leclerc et la République des Lettres*. The Encyclopaedists' references to the Socinianism of Geneva — which caused a great stir in the city — are in the article 'Genève'. See also Francesco Ruffini, *Studi sui riformatori italiani* (Turin, 1955), pp. 444 ff.

and by different means. The battle there was more complicated because Lausanne was not, like Geneva, self-governing : it was a subject city, governed by the distant — and orthodox — oligarchy of Bern. Against that control the Arminians of Lausanne struggled hard. There was Daniel Crespin, the professor of eloquence, yet another product of Saumur, whose pupils were formally denounced for Arminianism in 1698. There was Jean-Pierre de Crousaz, Arminian and Cartesian, who had studied in Paris and Leiden and known Malebranche and Bayle. There was Jean Barbeyrac, the Arminian translator of Grotius, Puffendorf and Archbishop Tillotson. And there were others who, with them, sought to mitigate or evade the severity of the *Consensus*, its explicit condemnation of 'Pietism, Socinianism and Arminianism'. But while their colleagues in Geneva prevailed, the philosophers of Lausanne struggled in vain against an orthodoxy supported from without by the magistrates of Bern. Ten years after the victory of heresy in Geneva, Bern resolved to crush it in Lausanne, and when resistance mounted, the pressure was increased. Finally, in 1722, the oligarchs of Bern struck. They resolved to dismiss all clergy and teachers who refused to accept the *Consensus* in its strict sense, with its oath to oppose Socinianism and Arminianism. The liberal world was outraged. The kings of England and Prussia wrote letters of protest. But their Excellencies of Bern were resolute. They imposed their wishes. They broke the spirit of de Crousaz, now Rector of the Academy. And when protests continued to be raised, and Major Davel even threatened to lead a revolt against the domination of Bern, they issued a positive order forbidding further discussion of the subject. Orthodoxy, it seemed, had triumphed : the debate was closed.

And yet in fact, from that very date, the heretics had triumphed in Lausanne. The forms and oaths might be maintained for another generation, but their force was spent. The last antics of orthodoxy had made it ridiculous. As the young Gibbon wrote, whether through shame, or pity, or the shock of Davel's attempt, the persecution ceased, and if Arminians and Socinians were still denounced by the self-righteous, they suffered, from now on, only social discrimination. Intellectually they had won; and their victory inaugurated what a modern Italian historian has called the 'risveglio culturale losannese'. Long afterwards, looking back on the formation of his own mind, Gibbon would avow his debt to that cultural revival, and above all to de Crousaz, whose 'philosophy had been formed in the school of Locke, his divinity in that of Limborch and Leclerc', whose lessons had 'rescued the Academy of Lausanne from Calvinistic prejudice', and who had diffused 'a more liberal spirit among the clergy and people of the Pays de Vaud'.[1]

Finally, from Switzerland we return to Scotland again. There the brief flicker of enlightenment in the 1650s had been quickly extinguished. The Stuart Restoration and the 'Killing Times' had driven the Kirk back into postures of defensive radicalism — just as persecution by Louis XIV had driven the French Huguenots. The narrow bigotry of the Kirk, the messianic gibberish of the outlawed Cameronians, are the Scottish equivalents of the spiritual police system of Jurieu and the hysteria of 'the French prophets', the Camisards of the 'Desert'. But the peace imposed on the Kirk by William III had some of the effects of the peace formerly imposed by Cromwell, and the union with England in 1707, which opened new economic opportunities and new intellectual horizons to the Scottish laity, undermined the clergy in the same way in which exile in Holland and Switzerland had undermined the Huguenot pastors. Henceforth the Scottish laity would be, as Baillie had complained of the English in his time, 'very fickle and hard to be keeped by their ministers'. The liberalism which in the 1650s had rested on English regiments could now rest on a native Scottish base.

The solvent effects, first of the Orange Settlement, then of the union with England, were soon clear. Arminianism raised its

[1] The struggle between Arminianism and Calvinism in Lausanne is traced in the noble work of Henri Vuilleumier, *Histoire de l'Église réformée du Pays de Vaud sous le régime bernois* (Lausanne, 1927–33), III. See also Philippe Meylan, *Jean Barbeyrac 1674–1744* (Lausanne, 1957). The Italian historian is Giuseppe Giarrizzo, *Edward Gibbon e la cultura europea del settecento* (Naples, 1954), pp. 29–34. Gibbon's early essay is his preceptive 'Lettre sur le gouvernement de Berne' (*Miscellaneous Works*, II; edited also by Louis Junod in Université de Lausanne, *Miscellanea Gibboniana*, 1952, pp. 110–41). His remarks on de Crousaz are in his autobiography.

head again in the Scottish Church. By the Revolution Settlement of 1689–90 the Calvinist Church did indeed recover its formal structure. The bishops once again disappeared. The General Assembly, dissolved since 1653, was revived. The ejected ministers returned. But while the forms of the old Calvinism were thus restored, its internal strength was undermined. Episcopalian ministers were allowed to retain their livings simply by taking an oath of allegiance to the Crown. The covenants — the National Covenant of 1638 and the Solemn League and Covenant of 1643, the shibboleths of the strict Calvinists — were quietly dropped. Thus the Scottish Church too was set free from its Synod of Dordt, its *Consensus Helveticus*. In 1712 the Patronage Act, the work of the English Tories, put Scottish Church appointments effectively under educated lay patronage, and guaranteed the Church, at last, against the bigotry of the past century.[1] Twenty years later the strict defenders of the Covenants, long resentful of such backsliding, decided to secede from the Church on this issue. Having seceded, they showed the strength of their convictions by a solemn protest against the abolition of witch-burning. This 'Original Secession' was to be the first of a series of secessions which, by draining away the fanatics, strengthened the new, moderate, laicized party in the Kirk. By the time when foreigners looked in admiration to the Enlightenment of the north, the Scottish Kirk had been de-Calvinized : it was governed, for thirty years, by the Arminian historian William Robertson, the friend of Hume, Gibbon and Adam Smith.

Thus we now see that if the new philosophy was forwarded in successive Calvinist societies, it was forwarded, in each instance, not by Calvinism but by the defeat of Calvinism. Arminianism or Socinianism, not Calvinism, was the religion of the pre-Enlightenment. Calvinism, that fierce and narrow re-creation of medieval scholasticism, was its enemy : the last enemy which died in the last ditches of Holland, England, Switzerland, Scotland.

---

[1] For the civilizing effect of the Patronage Act, see the memorandum by the Rev. Alexander Carlyle quoted from the Carlyle MSS. in H. G. Graham, *Scottish Men of Letters in the Eighteenth Century* (1908), pp. 86–87. It was, of course, an anti-democratic Act. That does not prevent it from being liberal.

IV

Still, it may be objected, these 'heresies' are Calvinist heresies. Arminianism grew out of Calvinism. Socinianism was regarded by Catholics and Protestants alike as a radical movement, a deviation to the extreme Left. If the Calvinist thesis is untenable in the strict sense, may it not remain tenable in a modified sense ? Instead of 'Calvinism' may we not read 'radical Protestantism', Puritanism on the left wing of Calvinist orthodoxy ? Unfortunately even this modification is, I believe, untenable. It is untenable partly because such terms as Left and Right, however useful they may be in political history, have no meaning in intellectual history : ideas cannot be ranged, like political parties, in a continuous spectrum according to the energy or violence with which men are prepared to go in one of two directions. But even if such crude categories are admitted, it is still untenable because neither Arminianism nor Socinianism was in fact necessarily a radical movement.

Arminianism is generally regarded as a right-wing deviation from Calvinism. The Dutch Arminians were attacked by the Dutch Calvinists as opening the way to popery. Oldenbarnevelt was accused of appeasing Catholic Spain. Grotius was regularly denounced as a crypto-Papist. The constant cry of alarm of the Dutch Calvinists was that 'the Arminian was himself a disguised papist, a concealed Jesuit'.[1] Exactly the same was said of the English Arminians. 'If you mark it well', cried the Cornish Puritan Francis Rous in the last, tumultuary session of the early parliaments of Charles I, 'you shall see an arminian reaching out his hand to a papist, a papist to a Jesuit'. Crypto-popery was the regular charge made against the Arminian clergy in England and Scotland, the followers of Archbishop Laud.

It is true, historians have tried to separate English from Dutch Arminianism in order to admit the Anglo-Catholicism of the former while saving the Protestantism of the latter. Arminianism in England, they say, is a mere nickname : it was applied, almost accidentally, to a clerical party in the Anglican Church and does

---

[1] P. Geyl, *The Netherlands in the Seventeenth Century* (1961), I, 45.

not entail the same doctrinal content as in Holland; and in support of this they cite the *bon mot* of George Morley, who, when asked 'what the Arminians held', replied that they held 'all the best bishoprics and deaneries in England'. But this distinction between Dutch and English Arminianism is an arbitrary separation which does not survive closer scrutiny. In fact, English and Dutch Arminianism are closely connected. Grotius admired the Church of England of his time — the Church of Laud — above all other Churches: 'body and soul he professeth himself to be for the Church of England', a diplomatic colleague wrote of him; and he personally admired Archbishop Laud.[1] Grotius' English followers in religion were Anglicans: Lord Falkland and his circle at Great Tew — Chillingworth, Hales, Clarendon, George Sandys; Henry Hammond, the chaplain of Charles I, who was to be the chief propagandist of 'the Grotian religion' in the 1650s; Clement Barksdale, the royalist High Anglican parson who wrote the biography of Grotius and translated his works. Conversely, Laud himself, for all his clericalism, was liberal in theology: he was the patron of Chillingworth and Hales, the friend of Selden. And the Laudian bishops in Scotland, if we can see past the libels of the good Scotch Calvinists, denouncing them as monsters spawned in the foul womb of Antichrist, are found to be liberal, tolerant and enlightened men, true Arminians in the spirit of Grotius.[2] The most famous of Scottish Arminians, John Cameron, perfectly illustrates the indivisibility, the universality, of the Arminian movement. Like the Laudians he supported the introduction of episcopacy into Scotland and was attacked for his Arminian doctrines by the detestable Rutherford. But he remained a liberal within the Calvinist Church and when driven out of Scotland went to create the liberal tradition of Saumur, the saving spirit of the French Huguenots.

[1] See 'Testimonia de Hugonis Grotii adfectu erga ecclesiam Anglicanam', printed at the end of Leclerc's edition of Grotius' *de Veritate Religionis Christianae.* The diplomatic colleague was Lord Scudamore, English ambassador in Paris when Grotius was Swedish ambassador there: a strict Laudian who shocked even so good an Anglican as Clarendon by his refusal to communicate with the French Huguenots.

[2] See W. L. Mathieson, *Politics and Religion. A Study in Scottish History from the Reformation to the Revolution* (Glasgow, 1902).

The case of Socinianism is similar. Because the Socinians were attacked as the most outrageous heretics by orthodox Catholics and Protestants alike, they are often regarded as 'radical Protestants', on the extreme Left. But this is too simple a view. Socinianism in the seventeenth century was a heresy of the Right before it was a heresy of the Left — if indeed we can use such terms at all. It was regularly associated with Arminianism. In Holland only the Arminians accepted the Socinians into communion. In England Archbishop Laud and several of his bishops were accused of Socinianism.[1] So were the Laudian bishops in Scotland.[2] So were later Anglican bishops like Stillingfleet and Tillotson.[3] So was Grotius.[4] So were the disciples of Grotius : Falkland, Hales and Chillingworth in England ; Episcopius, Limborch and Leclerc in Holland. Indeed Arminianism and Socinianism are often interchangeable terms, at least as terms of abuse. Of course there may have been Socinians on the Left too — for Socinianism is only the application of secular, critical, human reason to religious texts and religious problems — and certainly, during the Puritan Revolution, both Arminianism, the Arminianism of John Milton, and Socinianism, the Socinianism of John Bidle, appeared as Puritan movements. But historically both had been movements within the Anglican establishment before they became movements in Puritan society ; and when the Anglican establishment was restored, they took their place in it again.

In general we are too prone to suppose that the Independency

[1] H. J. McLachlan, *Socinianism in Seventeenth-century England* (Oxford, 1951), p. 97. Cf. Bishop Goodman's complaint to Laud that Laud had raised to the episcopate men like Howson, Montagu, Curll and Mainwaring and 'some others whom you favoured and whom I suspected to be Socinians' (quoted in G. Soden, *Godfrey Goodman*, 1953, pp. 152–3). Sir Edward Peyton, in his *Divine Catastrophe of the House of Stuart* (1652), also accused the Laudian clergy of Socinianism.

[2] See, for instance, the attacks on John Maxwell, Bishop of Ross, Laud's principal agent in Scotland, in Samuel Rutherford's *Lex Rex* (1644), Preface. Rutherford accused Maxwell of 'popery, socinianism, tyranny etc.'.

[3] Stillingfleet was attacked as a Socinian by the Catholic convert Hugh Cressy (formerly Lord Falkland's chaplain) in his pamphlet, S[erenus] C[ressy], *Fanaticism Fanatically imputed to the Catholic Church by Dr. Stillingfleet* (1672) ; Tillotson in Charles Leslie, *The Charge of Socinianism against Dr. Tillotson considered* (1695), etc.

[4] E.g. in John Owen, *Vindiciae Academicae* (1655).

of the Puritan Republic was intellectually a radical movement. Once again this results from a confusion of political with intellectual terms. Because the Independents, the Cromwellians, were prepared to cut off the king's head, while the Presbyterians, the followers of Denzil Holles, wished to keep it on, it is easy to suppose that the former were more 'radical' than the latter. But this is not necessarily true, even in politics. After their radical gesture, the Independents showed themselves, in many ways, the more conservative party. They were the English party, who resented Scottish dictation in English affairs, and their ultimate ideal was an Elizabethan monarchy, with a moderate, lay-controlled Church, not a stadholderate and a theocracy. Once the Independents were established in power, they soon discovered their continuity with Anglican royalists. In Scotland, the old royalists preferred the regicide English Independents to the royalist Scottish Presbyterians, and in England Cromwell openly confessed that he preferred 'a royalist interest to a Scotch [i.e. Presbyterian] interest'. The execution of Charles I is to some extent, in the distinction between 'Presbyterians' and Independents, a red herring. Independency was not, in itself, a radical movement: it was the continuation, on a new political base, of a liberal tradition which had previously been embodied in Anglicanism, and which had to reassert itself against the illiberal Calvinism of the Scots.

Even in small matters this continuity can be seen. Those who see the Independents as Puritan fanatics, more extreme than the 'Presbyterians', tend to overlook the inconvenient evidence that contemporaries saw the position (at least outside politics) in reverse. They saw the 'Presbyterians' as the sour, Puritan party and the Independents as the gay, 'libertine' successors of the cavaliers. To Anthony Wood, the Presbyterians 'seemed to be very severe in their course of life, manners or conversation, and habit or apparel', constantly preaching damnation, whereas the Independents, clergy and laity alike, were 'more free, gay, and with a reserve frolicsome'; of a gay habit, preaching liberty. The Independent minister John Owen, for instance, when vice-chancellor of Oxford, 'instead of being a grave example to the university', went about 'in quirpo like a young scholar', with powdered hair, lawn bands and tasselled bandstrings, flowing ribbons, 'Spanish leather boots with large lawn tops, and his hat mostly cocked'.[1] In Scotland similarly the good Calvinist Baillie complained of the flamboyant elegance, lavish expense and courtly manners of his own hated rival, Owen's friend, the Independent Patrick Gillespie.[2] In Scotland, as in England, the Independents — or some of them — were the un-Calvinist, free, gay party : the heirs of the royalists.

Thus the Arminian–Socinian movement which, by breaking Calvinist rule in one society after another, released the forces of the new philosophy, was, if anything, a right-wing movement; royalist and Anglican in England and Scotland, 'crypto-Catholic' in Holland, 'libertine' in Switzerland. Nor is this in any way surprising. For in fact this movement is not an extension of Calvinism, as is so often supposed, nor a deviation from it, either to right or to left. It is an independent movement, with a distinct origin, a continuous tradition, and a pedigree longer than that of Calvinism. Indeed, Calvinism can be seen as an outgrowth of it, an obscurantist deviation from it, rather than *vice versa*. In order to see this, and to follow the two-hundred-years dialogue between the two movements, we must go back to the figure who stands at the source of both of them as of so much else : Erasmus.

V

If Arminianism is free will in theory, tolerance in practice, within a reformed, primitive, visible, Christian Church, Erasmus is the first Arminian ; and indeed the Dutch Arminians recognized the fact. So did their English disciples : Erasmus was the inspiration not only of Arminius and Grotius but also of Grotius' disciples at Great Tew. Equally if Socinianism is the application

---

[1] Anthony Wood, *Life and Times*, anno 1648, 1657, 1659 ; *Athenae Oxonienses*, ed. P. Bliss (1813–21), IV, 98.

[2] See below, pp. 423 ff. Owen declared his 'long Christian acquaintance and friendship' with Gillespie in his preface to Gillespie's posthumously published *The Ark of the Covenant Opened* ((1667).

of critical, solvent human reason to religious texts and to religious problems, within a similar Church, Erasmus is the first Socinian, and this paternity was recognized too. The Swiss and Italian *émigrés* who founded the Socinian movement in Switzerland and carried it to Poland — Castellio, Acontius, Lelio Sozzini himself — were disciples of Erasmus. Even in the narrow sense of the word, the sense in which its enemies used it, Socinianism derives from Erasmus. For the peculiar tenet of the early Socinians, the particular result of their application of reason to Scripture, was the rejection of the doctrine of the Trinity, and so of the divinity of Christ ; and although Erasmus had not exposed himself on this topic, any more than many later Socinians were to do, it was his textual scholarship which was the basis of their rejection. He demonstrated, with a cogency that was proof against his own later half-hearted withdrawals, that the only biblical text which could be used to support that doctrine was spurious. It can therefore be said that Sozzini and Arminius merely gave their names to particular developments of a philosophy which they had received from Erasmus. This philosophy preceded Calvinism as Erasmus preceded Calvin. It was violently attacked by Calvin, who assailed the believers in free will as 'libertines' and had Servetus burnt for rejecting the Trinity. Nevertheless, at certain times, it was subsumed in Calvinism and became a solvent force within it.

How Erasmianism was subsumed in Calvinism is easy to see. Erasmus himself preached his doctrines from the Right, to the Establishment. But he did not capture the Establishment, and in the generation after his death, his disciples had to reconsider their position. Either they must surrender to the Catholic Church which meant that they must give up their essential philosophy, or they must take up arms against that Church and, in so doing, accept radical leadership and the transformation of that philosophy. The choice was disagreeable, but could hardly be avoided — unless one were to seek a refuge outside the area of struggle, in distant Transylvania or anarchical Poland. The boldest spirits chose the second alternative. They decided to take up arms. Admittedly, in taking up arms, they had to surrender part of their philosophy, but it was better to surrender part than to surrender all. If they submitted to the leadership of a militant Protestant sect which, at that time, was still young and malleable, they might yet hope to control or influence it. At the very least they might preserve and reassert, after victory, the doctrines which, for the time being, must be muted. Submission to Rome, it seemed at that time, was quite different. Rome was old and strong. It did not bargain or compromise; and submission to it was total and final.

The militant Protestant sect to which the Erasmians naturally submitted was Calvinism. Calvinism might be, in many ways, fundamentally opposed to Erasmianism. Calvinism was intolerant, fundamentalist, scholastic, determinist, while Erasmianism was tolerant, sceptical, mystical, liberal. But Calvinism itself had Erasmian origins. Unlike Lutheranism, it presupposed a reformed, visible, primitive Church; it was also austere, scholarly, scientific; and in its earliest days it appealed to the same class in the same areas — the educated official and mercantial classes of Latin Europe. In submitting to Calvinism the Erasmians of Europe saw rather the common origin than the separate development of their movements. They were like those European Liberals who, in the 1930s, rather than surrender to Fascism, accepted Communist leadership of the Popular Front. Like these twentieth-century successors, they would soon find their relations with the Party uncomfortable, and afterwards — in happier times — they would seek the way out.

This slide of the Erasmians into Calvinism is easy to document. Wherever there was a centre of Erasmianism in the 1520s and 1530s — in the cities of France and Switzerland, the Rhineland and the Netherlands, in the princely Courts or noble households of Navarre, Transylvania, Poland — there we shall find a centre of Calvinism in the 1550s and 1560s. We can even watch the process happening. In the 1550s, when the Court of Rome seemed committed to blind reaction and all the works of Erasmus were put on the Index, the humanists of Europe were driven to the Left, driven into the arms of the only organization which seemed capable of preserving, at whatever price, the residue of their philosophy. It was then that the English humanists, fleeing from Marian persecution, accepted the leadership of Geneva ; then that the humanists of the Netherlands, persecuted under the *Plakaten*, turned to the Calvinism that was to provide the discipline of their later revolt ; then that the French humanists — the sceptical *littérateurs* of the days of François I — chose the road that would end, for many of them, with the massacre of St Bartholomew ; then that George Buchanan, who was one of them, would return at last to Scotland and become the intellectual leader of Calvinist revolution. Thanks to such men Calvinism, whose real social strength came from the urban artisanate, organized and disciplined by an indoctrinated clergy, could be said to have attracted the intellectual *élite* of Europe.

However, attraction is not absorption. This intellectual *élite* never formed the core of the Calvinist Church. Always the two intellectual elements of the Calvinist Church — the clergy who controlled its force and the humanists who merely attached themselves to it — remained separable, and often there was tension between them. The degree of tension varied with the structure of society around them. In monarchical countries with a developed, independent laity, the Calvinist Church could not prevail. Erasmian princes — Queen Elizabeth, William of Orange, Catherine de Médicis — might use the Church at times, but would always prefer to be independent of it, and looked to the laity to provide that independence. In petty principalities or city-states the Church would be proportionately stronger — especially if such states were politically weak and vulnerable and needed to draw on a reservoir of fanaticism. In such states the lay power would still seek to be independent of the Church. In Geneva there was a continuing struggle between the Venerable Company of Ministers and the City Council. In the Palatinate princely patronage was independent of the Church. But, in fact, in both societies, since they lived in fear of conquest, the Church exercised great power. In backward countries, like Scotland or Navarre, where an educated, independent laity hardly existed, the Church was without a rival : the prince had nothing to balance against it — unless, like James I or Henri IV, he had external patronage : the patronage of England or France. On the other hand, in eastern Europe, where an anarchical noble liberty prevailed, Erasmianism could still maintain itself independently of Calvinism — at least to the end of the sixteenth century. Hence Poland and Transylvania were the home of Socinianism in the second half of the sixteenth century.[1] Finally, the international Protestant universities preserved something of the liberty of the old communes. In great monarchies the universities might be brought to conformity with the established Church ; but where a university was a powerful international centre, it could be a centre of intellectual heresy. The great days of the Protestant University of Heidelberg were those in which it rose above the cramping orthodoxy of the Palatinate and was the western centre of Socinianism.[2]

This distinction between the intolerant, predestinarian, scholastic doctrines of the Calvinist clergy and the tolerant, sceptical rationalism of the Erasmians whom political necessity had joined to them must be emphasized if we are to understand the religious context of Protestant intellectual history in the seventeenth century. For the two movements were never completely fused. They never could be. Only the pressure of fear — the fear of Catholic subversion or foreign conquest or both — kept them united. It was this fear which had brought them together in the beginning. The same fear would bring them together again and again, whenever freedom had to be sacrificed to discipline, private criticism to common faith. But whenever that fear was suspended the two parties to the alliance naturally drew apart. In times of security why should the rational, sceptical, mystical heirs of Erasmus accept the leadership of intellectual reactionaries, scholastical bigots, blinkered Augustinians, Hebraic fundamentalists ? They could afford to stand on their own.

[1] See Stanislas Kot, *Socinianism in Poland* (Boston, 1957) ; A. Pirnát, *Die Ideologie der Siebenbürger Antitrinitarier in den 1570-er Jahren* (Budapest, 1961) ; F. Pall, 'Über die sozialen und religiösen Auseinandersetzungen in Klausenburg (Cluj) in der zweiten Hälfte des 16ten Jahrhunderts und ihre polnisch-ungarischen Beziehungen', in *La Renaissance et la Réformation en Pologne et en Hongrie (Studia Historica Academiae Scientiarum Hungaricae*, LIII, Budapest, 1963), pp. 313–28.

[2] C.-P. Clasen, *The Palatinate in European History 1559–1660* (Oxford, 1963), pp. 35–42.

Once this distinction is recognized, the relationship between Arminianism and Calvinism becomes much clearer. Arminianism is not a Calvinist heresy. Inherently, it has nothing to do with Calvinism. It is only accidentally connected with Arminius.[1] Essentially it is an independent movement which precedes Calvinism. Its apparent emergence out of Calvinism in Holland, Switzerland, Scotland, its appearance as a movement in the Anglican Church in opposition to the Calvinism of the Elizabethan clergy, is in fact merely the assertion of independence by an earlier tradition which had been temporarily merged with Calvinism.

It had been merged under the pressure of politics. The same political conjuncture which had first compelled the humanist Erasmians to join the Calvinist Church was to recur again and again. It was to recur in the 1580s, when the threat of Spanish conquest hung over the Netherlands and the Erasmians of Holland, in self-defence, would yield to the Calvinist *Predikants* whom many of them hated. At the same time, under the same threat, the English Calvinist clergy would become, for a time, the articulators of English resistance and, in that fortunate conjuncture, would attempt to impose their leadership on the Church. This was the time of the Marprelate Tracts and of John Field's attempt to capture control of the Church of England from within. In both countries, England and Holland, the Calvinists would be protected by that unscrupulous political adventurer, the Earl of Leicester, who was indeed the patron of 'radical Protestants' everywhere, but not necessarily, therefore, of original ideas. The same threat would create a similar alliance in France; but there the fact of civil war, and the nice balance of forces, would enable many of the humanists to preserve a middle position between the Churches. Those who in England and Holland were liberals within the Calvinist fold, in France might be Huguenots — but might equally be Catholic *politiques*. In either case, their loyalty to their religious party was conditional. When the external danger was removed, they would assert their independence.

[1] Thus in England Arminianism was first advanced by the French *émigré* Peter Baro, Lady Margaret Professor of Divinity at Cambridge, in 1595 — fifteen years before Arminius published his theses in Holland. See H. C. Porter, *Reformation and Reaction in Tudor Cambridge* (Cambridge, 1958), ch. xvii.

At the end of the sixteenth century that danger was removed. By 1600 the first assault of the Counter-Reformation had been successfully resisted, and the Erasmians no longer needed to submerge their identity within a disciplined party. So they re-emerged. But because they had once been submerged, they re-emerged with a difference, at least of name. Their continuous identity had been forgotten and they took, or were given, the names of their new leaders. Arminius in Holland seemed a heretic within the Calvinist Church, although in fact he did but reassert the old doctrines of Erasmus. Fausto Sozzini, through whom 'rational' theology came back to western Europe, seemed the founder of a new 'Polish' sect, although in fact he did but repeat the ideas of the Swiss and Italian disciples of Erasmus, displaced for a generation; and because that sect made itself known in Holland and disconcerted the clergy of the established Calvinist Church, it too seemed to be a Calvinist heresy. So Socinianism was described as a 'radical Protestant' movement, on the 'extreme Left' of Protestantism. But these terms are meaningless. Or at least, if they have meaning, it is only if we admit that Calvinism itself was a reactionary movement, a revival of the scholastic theology, providential history and Aristotelean science which Erasmus, Machiavelli and the Platonists of Florence had threatened to undermine.

So dawned the second phase of the Enlightenment, the golden 'Jacobean' age of Bacon and Grotius : a phase which was rudely interrupted as one society after another shrank into itself before the threat of renewed ideological war. In 1618 the fear of war, of Spanish and Catholic reconquest, came to Holland, and once again the Calvinist preachers, the propagandists of resistance, asserted their power. The Arminians were crushed, or recognized the greater danger and came willingly to heel. In other countries the same pattern was repeated, with local variations. If Grotius was imprisoned in Calvinist Holland, Bacon was posthumously puritanized in England. The advocates of the Puritan origins of science would puritanize him still. It was not till the end of the ideological wars of Europe — that is, till the 1650s — that liberal, rational ideas could begin to emancipate themselves, once again, from their alliance with Calvinism : that oppressive alliance which political necessity had forced upon them in order to escape the even more oppressive clericalism of the Counter-Reformation.

VI

But if Arminianism and Socinianism, the religious movements which led to the Enlightenment, thus looked back past Calvin to the days of Erasmus and the Pre-Reform, the days of an undivided Catholic Church, what of the other half of that Church, the half which remained Catholic ? For the Catholic Church also had its Erasmists. Not all of them surrendered unconditionally to the forces of the Counter-Reformation. Some at least had supposed, or hoped, that the critical, liberal spirit could be preserved within the Catholic Church : that surrender to the new dogmatism of the Council of Trent was a mere temporary necessity, and that afterwards they too could look back past the new orthodoxy to the ideas which it seemed to extinguish. In this they were perhaps mistaken, for the clericalism of the Counter-Reformation was more powerfully armed than the clericalism of the Protestant Churches. But we should not blame them for that. In their hatred of the excesses of the Reform — the vulgarity, the vandalism, the blind revolutionary spirit which it enlisted — they did not foresee the future. They did not calculate, in the 1550s, that the aggressive revolutionary, dynamic Calvinist clergy would gradually lose their grip while the Catholic clergy, the defenders of a weakened tradition, would gradually strengthen theirs.

So even in Catholic countries, beneath the forms even of Counter-Reformation orthodoxy, we can discover a persistent tradition of liberalism, waiting to reassert itself. It does not show itself in organized parties or distinct sects, like the Arminian and the Socinian parties in the Protestant Churches. The Catholic Church does not allow parties or sects : diversity of opinion within it must be expressed more vaguely, in 'movements'. But as a movement it is visible enough, at least in certain societies. Admittedly, it is difficult — though not altogether impossible — to see it in Spain and in the countries dominated by Spain : Italy, Flanders and Portugal. There the engines of clericalism were fully developed and were backed by a strong central power. It is equally difficult to see it in 'recusant' societies : Catholic communities living insecurely under Protestant rule. Such hunted minorities in Holland or England would be as narrow in their orthodoxy, as submissive to their clergy, as the Protestants of France under Louis XIII and Louis XIV. But in Catholic countries where there was no effective Inquisition and a strong, educated laity, able to influence their clergy, the tradition remains firm, even if submerged, even if disguised ; and when the pressure of social and ideological struggle is released it will soon break out.

The most obvious of such societies, at least in the first century of the Counter-Reformation, were France and Venice. In France the secular power was perforce tolerant of its numerous Huguenot subjects. In Venice the old republican independence was asserted and the Counter-Reformation was kept at bay. Consequently both France and Venice were natural centres of Catholic humanism. That humanism was not snuffed out by the Catholic reaction of the 1550s. It survived the anarchy of the Wars of Religion, and revealed itself openly in the years of reduced ideological tension which I have described as the second phase of the Enlightenment : the generation before the full impact of the Thirty Years War.

The great names in this period are obvious enough. If the years 1590–1625, in the Protestant world, are the age of Bacon and Selden and Grotius, in the Catholic world they are the age of Montaigne and de Thou, Davila and Sarpi. All these were recognized as precursors by the men of the Enlightenment. Montaigne was the heir to the scepticism of Erasmus, the father of that seventeenth-century Pyrrhonism which relaxed the dogmas of the Churches and the Aristotelean cosmology behind them.[1] De Thou, Davila and Sarpi are named by Gibbon as the

[1] On this subject, see especially Richard H. Popkin, *The History of Scepticism, from Erasmus to Descartes* (Assen, Netherlands, 1964).

second founders, after Machiavelli and Guicciardini, of 'philosophic history'. Davila is indeed the Machiavelli of the seventeenth century, the favourite reading of 'civil historians' and philosophic statesmen. De Thou, the most Protestant of Catholic historians — the founder, according to modern Catholic writers, of the persistent 'Protestant bias' in sixteenth-century French historiography [1] — was an admirer of Erasmus : indeed, his greatest crime in the eyes of the Church was that in his *History* he not only mentioned the forbidden name of Erasmus but described him as *grande huius saeculi decus*, 'the great glory of this century'. And as for Sarpi, how can we think of that generation without him ? At every turn we find ourselves faced by that indefatigable polymath : the Servite friar who corresponded with the Protestants of Europe in order to create a solid, non-doctrinal front against papal aggression ; the historian who sought to show that European history had taken a false turn at the Council of Trent ; the statesman who insisted, alone among Catholics, on the Socinian doctrine of the separation of Church from State ; the social scientist whose analysis of the economic power of the Church improves upon that of Selden, foreshadows that of Giannone, and was hailed by Gibbon as 'a golden volume' which would survive the papacy itself, 'a philosophical history and a salutary warning'.[2]

Most of these 'Catholic Erasmians' of the early seventeenth century were heretics within their Church, just as the Arminians were heretics in the Protestant Churches. De Thou, in spite of a determined rearguard action, saw his work condemned by Rome in 1609. At his death his last volume was preserved from destruction only by the devotion of his secretary, Pierre Dupuy, who sent the manuscript abroad to be published in Geneva. The devotion of his heirs would have burnt it. Sarpi, of course, was the hated enemy of the papacy, and his great work was smuggled to England for publication : it was never published in a Catholic country till the eighteenth century. Even Montaigne, whose Pyrrhonism could be and was used as a means to defend tradi-

---

[1] Cf. Lucien Romier, *Le Royaume de Catherine de Médicis* (Paris, 1925), p. xxxii.
[2] Gibbon, *Decline and Fall of the Roman Empire*, VII, 99.

tional Catholicism, did not survive unscathed : his essays were finally condemned in Rome in 1676. And if the greatest religious thinker of seventeenth-century France, Cardinal Bérulle, the founder of the Oratory, contrived to combine the ideas of Erasmus and Montaigne with the Catholicism of the Counter-Reformation,[1] his disciples, the French Oratorians, soon found themselves in difficulty.

For the Oratorians, in the second half of the seventeenth century, would be the heretics within the Catholic fold. In Saumur the Catholic Oratory would compete with the Huguenot Academy in teaching the ideas of Descartes, condemned by the orthodox of both Churches. The Oratorian Malebranche would reconcile Cartesianism with Catholicism. The Oratorian Bernard Lamy — another Cartesian of Saumur — would draw the young Leclerc from Calvinism to Arminianism. And above all, there would be the greatest of seventeenth-century biblical scholars, the Oratorian Richard Simon, who reintroduced Socinian rationalism into the study of Scripture.

Richard Simon was a devout Catholic. If he demolished the sacred text of the Bible, he did it, no doubt, for good Catholic purposes. He wished to turn the tables on the Protestant controversialists who had demolished the Fathers and fallen back on the Bible as the sole source of truth. But he demolished it all the same, and the Trinity to boot. For he too, like Erasmus and Socinus, rejected the famous verse, 1 John v. 7, on which the doctrine of the Trinity was held to depend. For his critical method Simon looked back to Erasmus. His immediate models were the Protestant scholars Scaliger, Buxtorf, Cappel and Bochart. And he provided material for Voltaire. No wonder the orthodox — Protestant as well as Catholic — hated him. No wonder Bishop Bossuet, the paladin of Catholic orthodoxy, the defender of the monolithic Roman (or rather, Gallican) tradition against the multiple, changing heresies of Protestantism, was haunted to his death by the thought of this infamous priest. For

---

[1] For Bérulle, whom Mr Popkin describes (*History of Scepticism*, p. 178) as 'perhaps the most important religious thinker of the Counter-Reformation in France', see especially Jean Dagens, *Bérulle et les origines de la restauration catholique* (Bruges, 1950).

Simon's work, published by Protestant printers in Amsterdam and sent to the bonfire by Bossuet in Paris, showed irrefutably that the supposed monolith, for all its superficial smoothness and apparent strength, was itself no less complex, no less uncertain, no less variable than the enemy which beset it. The grandiose synthesis of established Counter-Reformation Catholicism was worm-eaten with heresy — Socinian heresy — too.[1]

Thus throughout the seventeenth century the Erasmian tradition — to use a convenient phrase — survived in the Catholic as well as in the Protestant Church, and by the end of the century it was challenging the established orthodoxy there too. Under different names it was undermining or transforming the Aristotelean certainties which had been restated and reimposed by Catholics and Protestants alike. Ultimately it would undermine even the new system which, for a time, had seemed to threaten both Churches, but which had gradually been absorbed into the state-Catholicism of France and had supplied it with a new articulation and a new defence against Pyrrhonism : the system of Descartes. Giannone would turn from Descartes to de Thou, Montaigne, Bacon and Newton.[2] Voltaire would reject Descartes for Bacon, become the prophet of Locke and Newton — both Socinians in religion — and draw on the work of English Quakers and deists, French Oratorians and Jesuits : for the Jesuits too, for a brief time, were 'heretical' in the eyes of the Church, critics attenuating doctrinal difficulties, anthropologists preaching a religious relativity which would lead them into trouble and scandal in the great affair of Chinese ceremonies.[3] Gibbon's intellectual progress typified the pre-history of the Enlightenment. First, he would succumb to the majestic system of Bossuet :

---

[1] For the Oratorians, see Haase, *Einführung in die Literatur der Refuge*, pp. 66, 379–80 ; for Richard Simon, Henri Margival, *Essai sur Richard Simon et la critique biblique au XVIIe siècle* (Paris, 1900) ; also Henri Hazard, *La Crise de la conscience européenne 1650–1715* (Paris, 1935), pt. ii, ch. iii, iv.

[2] P. Giannone, *Vita scritta da lui medesimo*, ed. Sergio Bertelli (Milan, 1960), pp. 22–23, 36–41 ; [L. Panzini] *Vita*, in P. Giannone, *Opere postume* ('Italia' [i.e. London], 1821), pp. 149–50 ; Giuseppe Ricuperati, 'Le Carte Torinesi di Pietro Giannone', *Memorie dell' Accademia delle Scienze di Torino* (Turin, 1962), pp. 23–27.

[3] For the Jesuit influence on Voltaire, see Réné Pomeau, *La Religion de Voltaire* (Paris, 1956).

'the English translations of the two famous works of Bossuet, bishop of Meaux, achieved my conversion', he would write, 'and I surely fell by a noble hand'. Then, following the example of the Socinian Chillingworth and the Pyrrhonist Bayle, whose 'acute and manly understandings' had been entangled in the same sophistries, he returned to his native Protestantism and was finally re-educated in Lausanne by Arminian teachers and the works of emancipated Huguenot scholars of the Dispersion.[1]

In all this, where is Calvinism? Where is 'radical Protestantism'? Except as enemies of the Enlightenment they are nowhere to be found. Their part, it seems, is no more positive than that of the Dominican and Franciscan inquisitors in the Roman Church — except that their repression was, happily, less effective. Indeed, where Calvinism was strongest — in Scotland — we find the seeds of Enlightenment not so much in its Arminian deviationists, whom it was able to suppress, as in its open enemies, who hid from it in secluded corners or fled to safety abroad. For the Scottish Enlightenment — that wonderful, unexplored subject which Scottish historians have disowned in order to reiterate old party war-cries about the battle of Bannockburn and the dubious virtue of Mary Stuart — perhaps owed more to Scottish Jacobites, even to Scottish Catholics, than to Scottish Presbyterians: to the Jacobite physician Archibald Pitcairne, denounced as a deist or atheist and more at home in Leiden than in Edinburgh; to the Jacobite scholar William Ruddiman secluded in his protective library; to the episcopalian north-east captured by the mysticism of Antoinette Bourignon; to the Catholic lairds who nourished heretical ideas in isolated castles and peel-towers and the Catholic hedge-priests who visited them. The founder of critical history in Scotland, Thomas Innes, was an *émigré* Catholic priest in the service of the Pretender. The chevalier Ramsay, precursor of the encyclopaedists, began as one of the mystics of

---

[1] In his *Memoirs of my Life and Writings* Gibbon declares his debts to his intellectual predecessors. It is interesting to observe how many of the writers who influenced him — like Bayle and Leclerc, Jacques Basnage, Isaac de Beausobre, Jean Barbeyrac, Jean-Pierre de Crousaz — were exiled Huguenots.

the north-east, became the secretary of the Catholic Quietist Madame Guyon and ended as a Catholic deist, tutor of the young Pretender. The 10th Earl Marischal, friend of Frederick the Great, patron of Rousseau, was an *émigré* Jacobite. David Hume was a Jacobite till 1745 ; his friend Lord Kames remained one thereafter. And without these, what is the Scottish Enlightenment ? [1]

VII

Thus, when we look into the religious origins of the Enlightenment we do not discover them in any one Church or sect. They are to be found in both Churches and in several sects. What is common to the men who express such ideas is that all of them are, in some sense, heretical : that is, they either belong to dissident groups within their Churches or are themselves regarded as unorthodox. The orthodox Churches — Catholic, Lutheran, Anglican, Calvinist — look askance at them.[2] Moreover, the heretical tradition which they share is not only independent of the Reformation from which it is so often supposed to have sprung. It precedes the Reformation ; and the Reformation, though it may at first have liberated it, has soon become a repressive movement, positively fragmenting and obstructing it. The intellectual tradition of scepticism, mysticism, critical scholar-

[1] For some sidelights on these Jacobite and Catholic influences, see A. D. MacEwen, *Antoinette Bourignon, Quietist* (1910) ; G. D. Henderson, *Mystics of the North East* (Aberdeen, Spalding Club, 1934) and *Chevalier Ramsay* (1952) ; Franco Venturi, *Le origini dell' Enciclopedia* (Milan, 1962), pp. 16–26 ; and, for Innes, *Registrum de Panmure*, ed. John Stuart (Edinburgh, 1874).

[2] I have not concerned myself with Lutheranism in this essay, but I believe that the same general point could be made in respect of it, viz. : that it was 'heretical' Pietism, not orthodox Lutheranism, which opened the way to the Enlightenment in Germany. The rigid structure of clerical Aristoteleanism was undermined and destroyed by the Pietists Spener and Thomasius ; the Pietists were attacked by the orthodox as Pelagians (i.e. Arminians), Papists and Socinians ; and the great Pietist defence of heresy, Gottfried Arnold's *Unparteyisiche Kirche- und Ketzerhistorie*, afterwards inspired the greatest figure of the German Enlightenment, Goethe. The Pietists, like the Arminians and the Socinians, looked back behind the (Lutheran) orthodoxy of the state Church to Valentin Weigel and Sebastian Franck and, through them, to Erasmus, the neo-Platonists and the Rhenish mystics ; cf. A. Koyré, *Mystiques, spirituels, alchimistes* (Paris, 1955).

ship, lay reason, free will, which was united in Erasmus was broken up and driven underground by the ideological struggles of the sixteenth and seventeenth centuries. What had once been a general movement within a united society, acceptable in the courts of princes and in the cathedrals of the established Church, became, under the impact of successive ideological struggles, a number of separate heresies, labelled with sectarian names and equally condemned by all right-minded members of the several religious establishments. In times of ideological peace, olympian minds like those of Grotius or de Thou or Bacon would seek to reunite these ideas, to restore to them their original respectability, and to develop them further. Once again princes and higher clergy would listen to them. But the return of religious war gave power to the radicals of orthodoxy ; to the Calvinists who condemned Grotius in Holland, to the friars who condemned Galileo in Italy. The movement which might have been reunited was once again splintered : what might have been the orthodoxy of a united society became again the heresies of divided Churches. The eighteenth-century Enlightenment, when it came, would be a reunion of all the heretics, the reintegration of a movement which religious revolution had arrested and transformed, but could not destroy.

And yet, when we have said this, we have not said all. The ghost of Calvinism cannot so easily be exorcised. For if Calvinism was intellectually retrograde and repressive, a positive, vindictive enemy of enlightenment, politically it nevertheless performed an essential service. It is not enough to say that the Enlightenment would have come sooner had there been no ideological war in the sixteenth and seventeenth centuries. The fact is that there was such war ; and once we accept that fact, we have to admit that Calvinism played an important, perhaps a vital part in it. It gave to the Netherlands the spiritual force which transformed an aristocratic resistance into a national revolution and created a new political phenomenon in Europe. It gave to Scotland the power to assert and preserve its national identity. It gave to the city of Geneva the power to resist covetous enemies. Without that resistance the Counter-Reformation might well have triumphed in Europe, and although we may admit that the Erasmian tradition survived even under the heavy weight of the new Catholicism, we have to admit also that its survival was very precarious and that without the resistance and example of Protestant Europe, it might have been extinguished. Certainly this was the view of contemporaries. We cannot overlook the general view of the humanists of the mid-sixteenth century to whom the choice seemed to be either total surrender of the intellect to Catholicism or merely partial surrender to Calvinism. The discipline of Calvinism could be seen as the temporary discipline of necessary war; that of Counter-Reformation Catholicism seemed the permanent discipline of a police-state. And certainly it was in the societies in which the Counter-Reformation had not triumphed that intellectual independence was soonest resumed.

This conviction of contemporaries that Calvinism, however intellectually reactionary, was the necessary political ally of intellectual progress is shown most clearly by the attitude of the Roman Catholic precursors of the Enlightenment. Jacques-Auguste de Thou was a good Catholic who lived and died in the profession of his faith. But he was also, as he continually observed, devoted to historical truth, and historically he saw the Huguenots as the defenders of Erasmian reform and progress. For this he was denounced in Rome. To avoid condemnation he adopted every device, every compromise, every concession — except the only one which would have served him. He refused to retract his opinions. Consequently he was condemned. The drama of de Thou's long-drawn-out battle with Rome, the whole tenor of his *History*, a 'Protestant' history by a Catholic writer, and the evidence of his correspondence with his intimate friends in the Calvinist party — Jerome Groslot de Lisle, whose father had perished in the massacre of St Bartholomew; Isaac Casaubon, who had fled to England to escape the *convertisseurs*; Georg Michael Lingelsheim, the tutor and councillor of the Calvinist Count Palatine — all this shows that, for de Thou, even Catholic enlightenment depended on the help of the Calvinist resistance.

Even more vivid is the evidence of de Thou's great contemporary, Paolo Sarpi: the Catholic friar who led the intellectual resistance of Europe, and the political resistance of Venice, against the aggression of the Counter-Reformation. Sarpi's whole life made him an ally of the Protestant world, and there is no need here to document the details of his alliance with it. But one fact deserves special mention. Soon after the Synod of Dordt, Sarpi wrote to the Dutch scholar and poet Daniel Heinsius declaring his own position in the religious controversies of Holland. That position, at first sight, surprises us. For Sarpi gave his support not, as we should expect, to the Arminians, the party of liberal Calvinists who were the natural allies of liberal Catholics, but to the Contra-Remonstrants, the extreme Calvinists, the persecutors of Grotius, the bigots of Predestination. On merely intellectual grounds this action is unintelligible. It assumes significance only if we see it in a political light. On the eve of renewed ideological war, the greatest Catholic historian recognized that the extreme Calvinists, the party of uncompromising, unconditional resistance, were the essential allies of all those Catholics who sought to preserve the intellectual freedom so nearly smothered by the Council of Trent.[1]

Politically, therefore, Calvinism may well have been necessary to the intellectual progress of Europe in the seventeenth century. This we may concede, just as we may concede that politically the Whig party was necessary to the securing of English liberty in the same century. But there is a difference between political and intellectual truth. The fact that Whig resistance broke Stuart despotism does not mean either that the Whig theories of the constitution and of liberty were intellectually right or even, in themselves, progressive. Nor does it mean that such theories, of themselves, entailed the consequences which followed the victory of the party professing them. Similarly, the fact that Calvinist resistance was necessary to the continuation and development of an intellectual tradition does not entail any direct or logical connection between them. A philosopher, in a time of crisis, may have to put on a suit of armour. To that suit of armour he may

[1] See Boris Ulianov, 'Sarpiana: la Lettera del Sarpi allo Heinsius', in *Rivista Storica Italiana*, 1956.

owe his life, and his capacity to go on philosophizing. But that does not make the armour the source of his philosophy. Indeed, while it is being worn it may well impede free speculation, which can be resumed only when the battle is over and it has been put off. The virtue of Calvinism, in respect of the Enlightenment, may perhaps be reduced to this. As a suit of armour it proved serviceable in battle, and though more uncomfortable to wear, proved easier to discard than the archaic, ornamentally encrusted chain-mail which protected, but also stifled the philosophers of the rival Church.

Index

Abano, Peter of, medieval physician, 131, 133

Acontius (Giacomo Aconcio), Italian Reformer, 220

Agobard, St, Bishop of Lyon, 92

Agrippa, Henry Cornelius, 130, 132, 133, 146, 179

Alba, Pedro de Toledo, 4th Duke of, 23, 147

Albigensians, their connection with witchcraft, 103–4, 116, 118, 127, 144, 175, 183–4

Alciati, Andrea, 130, 131n, 133

Alembert, Jean d', 211

Alexander IV, Pope, 103

Alexander VI, Pope, 110

Allen, Francis, regicide M.P., 335

Alsace: witch-craze in, 106, 169; diabolical peculiarity in, 95n; unaffected by Edict of Nantes or its Revocation, 44

Alsted, Johann Heinrich, millenarist, 47n

Amadeus VIII, Duke of Savoy (Pope Felix V), 'eldest son of Satan', 104

Amyraut, Moise, 'Arminian' Huguenot, 209n

Anabaptism: German, 41, 143

Ancre, Pierre de l', an enchanting persecutor, 112, 130n, 139, 153, 159, 171, 180n, 189–90

Anglican Church: sound on witches, 142n

Anti-semitism, compared with witch-hunting, 100

Apocalypse: its dubious authorship, 129

Aquinas, St Thomas: his magisterial ruling on *incubi*, 96; advantages of ignoring him, 185n; mentioned, 178, 184

Arboga, Swedish iron-mine, 11

Argyll, Marquis of, *see* Campbell

Aristoteleanism, compatible with demonology, 123, 184; except in Padua, 131, 134, 186; undermined by Erasmian sceptics, 227, 230

Arminius, Jacobus, 224 and n, 225; Arminianism a refuge for intellectual Calvinists, 28; opposed to witch-beliefs, 170-1; forwards the Enlightenment, 200-35

Arnold, Gottfried, German Pietist, 182n, 232n

Arnold of Brescia, 41

Aubigné, Agrippa d', 209

Augustine of Hippo, St: a father of the witch-craze, 92, 96; a hammer of the Manichees, 127n, 184, 185n

Bacon, Francis, Lord Verulam, Viscount St. Albans: on the General Crisis, 73, 76, 83–85; his New Philosophy, 199–202; the philosopher of social reform, 224–36 *passim;* reserved on witches, 130n, 180–2; posthumously puritanized, 225; mentioned, 230, 233

Baillie, Robert, A.M. (Glasweg.), a busy Scotch minister: 205 208, 213, 219

Bannockburn, a Scotch war-cry, 231

Barbeyrac, Jean, 212

Barksdale, Clement, a Grotian parson, 216

Barnes, Annie, 209n, 211n

Baro, Peter, Arminian professor in Cambridge, 224n

Basson, Thomas, English Arminian printer at Leiden, 171

Bavaria: disgusting orthodoxy of, 144n; witch-craze in, 139; killed by a Theatine monk, 123

Baxter, Richard, 168

Bayle, Pierre: on witchcraft, 152, 180; mentioned, 196–7, 201, 203, 210, 212, 231

Beast, logarithms invented to work it out, 47n; discovered by Rev. Francis Potter, F.R.S., 173 and n

Bedford, Jacquette, Duchess of, tried as a witch 1470, 128

——Earl of, *see* Russell, Francis

Beghards, 41

Bekker, Balthasar, Cartesian Dutch minister, 173–5, 180, 182, 210

Belzebub, a big black man, 124

Benedict XII, Pope, 103

Benoist, Elie, Huguenot historian, 10

Bernard of Como, inquisitor, 104

Bernardino of Siena, an anti-semitic saint, 109

INDEX

Erastus, Daniel, professor of Heidelberg, 146, 178, 181n
Ewen, C. L'Estrange, 116n, 162n, 163n
Ewich, Dr. Johann, 132, 141n, 147 and n, 179, 192
Eymeric, Nicolas, inquisitor-general of Aragon, 110

Farnese, Alexander, Duke of Parma, 16, 24
Febronianism, 43–44
Fèbvre, Lucien, 101n, 122
Feiling, Sir Keith, xiii
Ferrari, Antonio (Galateo), 130
Ficino, Marsilio, 43n, 132, 134, 161
Field, John, Puritan organizer, 224
Flade, Dietrich, rector of Trier University, burnt as a witch, 150
Fontaine, Françoise, servant-girl seduced by Devil, 125
Forner, Friedrich, suffragan Bishop of Bamberg, 157
Franche-Comté, salt-mines of, 11
Francis Xavier, St, 59
François I, King of France, 48, 61, 146, 198, 222
Fraticelli, persecuted by Pope John XXII, 108
Frederick Henry, Prince of Orange-Nassau, 49
Frondes, the, 46, 51, 81, 83, 195
Fugger family, of Augsburg, 21, 22, 30, 32

Galilei, Galileo, 42–43n, 170, 171, 173
Gardiner, S. R., 245, 320n, 358n
Geer, Louis de, 'the Krupp of the seventeenth century, 8, 9, 11, 13–17, 19, 22
Giannone, Pietro, 195–6, 228, 230
Gibbon, Edward, 95, 196–7, 200–1, 210, 212–14, 227–28, 230–1
Gillespie, Patrick, Principal (and 'poisoner') of Glasgow University, 219
Gladstone, W. E., 4n
Glanvill, Joseph, F.R.S., sceptic and demonologist, 168, 180
Gloucester, Eleanor Cobham, Duchess of, tried as a witch 1441, 128
Gnostics, 127n
Gödelmann, J. G., professor at Rostock, 111, 151, 160, 164
Goldast, Melchior, 141n
Goldschmidt, L., 22n
Gomar, Francis, quarrelsome Calvinist doctor, 199, 209
Gondomar, Diego de Sarmiento, Conde de, 69–70, 77–78
Goodman, Godfrey, Bishop of Gloucester, 62, 64, 84n
Graham, Henry Grey, 214n
Grandier, Urbain, 160
Granvelle, Antoine Perrenot, cardinal, 49, 61, 62

Great Tew, Lord Falkland's house at, 203, 216, 219
Grenus, François, Swiss capitalist, 13, 14, 18
Greve, Johan (Graevius), 170, 171, 173
Grillandi, Paolo, 124
Grimm, Jakob, 116n
Groote, Nicolas de, entrepreneur in Cologne, 19
Gross, Henning, a witch-hunting bookseller, 151, 154n
Grotius, Hugo: heir to Erasmus, 130n, 219; assigns power to lay magistrate, 170–1; opposes Mosaic law, 170–1; silent on witches, 180, 181 and n; a religious reunionist, 201; persecuted in Holland, 207, 233, 235; accused of popery, 208, 215; and Socinianism, 212; his works banned in Calvinist Switzerland, 211; his English disciples, 203, 219; an honorary Anglican, 216; edited by Leclerc, 203; translated into French by Barbeyrac, 212; mentioned, 91, 197, 225, 227
Gruter, Jan, 202
Guicciardini, Francesco, 198, 200, 228
Guise, Henri, Duc de, 66
Guizot, F. P. G., 3, 193
Gustavus Adolphus, King of Sweden, 7
Guyon, Madame, 125, 232
Haan, Dr Georg, chancellor of Bishop of Bamberg, burnt as a witch, 157
Haase, Erich, 209
Habsburg, dynasty: their financiers in Thirty Years War, 11–13, 40
Hales, John, of Eton College, 216–17
Hammond, Henry, chaplain of Charles I, 216
Hanseatic League, 12-13, 16
Hansen, Joseph, archivist and historian, 98–99, 185
Harrington, James, author of Oceana, 51, 196
Harvellier, Jeanne, of Verbery, a witch, 124
Harvey, William, 170
Hatton, Sir Christopher, 256
Hauber, Eberhard David, 174n, 189n
Heidelberg: a centre of Calvinism, neglected by sociologists, x; its university commended for critical spirit, 191 and n; a centre of Socinianism in sixteenth century, 223
Heinrich Julius, Duke of Brunswick: a really good German, 112; a learned persecutor of Jews and witches, 154–155, 167n
Hemmingsen, Niels (Hemmingius), Danish witch-doctor, 137n, 164
Henri II, King of France, 48–49
Henri III, King of France, 15; attacked as a patron of witches, 136, 147n

240

216, 229; Catholic oratory at 229
Savonarola, Girolamo, 110
Savoy, Christina, Duchess of, 13
—— dukes of, 104, 197
—— home of witches, 104, 152 and n
Saxe-Weimar, Bernard, Duke of, 10
Scaliger, Joseph Justus, 91, 209, 229
Schönborn, Johann Philipp von, Prince-Bishop of Würzburg and Elector of Mainz, ends witch-persecution, 160
Schöneburg, Johann von, Elector of Trier, hammer of Protestants, Jews and witches, 149–50
Scot, Reginald: his *Discovery of Witchcraft* refuted by public bonfire, 148–9; translated into Dutch, 170–1; mentioned, 112n, 155, 166, 172, 174–5, 179, 192
Scotland, witches in, 120–2, 138, 141, 163n, 188, Enlightenment in, 205, 208, 213–14
Scriberius (Pieter Schrijver), Dutch historian, 171
Scribonius (Adolf Schreiber), medical advocate of cold-water test for witches, 141n, 178
Scudamore, John, Lord, Charles I's ambassador in Paris, stuffy towards Huguenots, 216n
Selden, John: his reserve on witches, 130n, 180–1; his 'Platonic' views on Nature, 181n; his Erastianism exasperates Professor Baillie, 208; mentioned, 216, 227–228
Servetus, Michael, Socinian heretic, burnt by Calvin, 206, 220; his posthumous revenge, 211
Shakespeare, William, effortlessly aristocratic, 56, 60, 72
Sigismund, Archduke of Austria, perplexed by witch Bull, 130
Simon, Richard, biblical critic, 197, 229–30
Sixtus IV, Pope, authorizes Spanish Inquisition, 108, 114
Smectymnuus, collective noun for a posse of Presbyterian clergy, 205
Smith, Adam, 197, 214
Socinianism, the religious philosophy of the Enlightenment, 206–31
Socinus, *see* Sozzini
Soldan, Wilhelm Gottlieb, 98, 116n
Sombart, Werner, 4, 20, 21, 23
Sozzini (Socinus), Fausto, 225
—— Lelio, 27, 220, 229
Spain, Inquisition in, 108–9; witches in, 110, 113
Spee, Friedrich von S.J., poet and critic of witch-craze, 158–61, 166, 171–5, 179, 192
Spener, Philipp Jakob, German Pietist, 182n

Spiering brothers, Dutch entrepreneurs in Sweden, 9, 15–16
Spina, Bartolomeo, Inquisitor, 104, 133
Spinola, Cristóbal Rojas de, Catholic reunionist, 201
Sprenger, Jakob, Dominican inquisitor, co-author of *Malleus Maleficarum*, 101, 105
Stapleton, Thomas, English Catholic *émigré*, 189
Stereotypes, social: witches and jews, 111–15, 150; others, 165–8; they depend on general context, 177–8; how formed and unformed, 182–92
Stertzinger, Ferdinand, Theatine monk, 123
Stillingfleet, Edward, Bishop of Worcester, accused of Socinianism, 217
Strafford, Earl of, *see* Wentworth
Strasbourg, an island of sense, 129n, 142
Streicher, Julius, Nazi Jew-baiter and pornographer, 165
Sully, Maximilien de Béthune, Duc de, 10
Sundborg, Bertil, 164
Sung dynasty, efflorescence of Chinese science under, 38n
Sweden: immune from the witch-craze?, 188; Swedes suppress it in Germany, 160, 182; but succumb at last, 163–4
Switzerland: its prosperity created by immigrants, 18, 20, 23; a home of witchcraft, 101–8, 137–8, 143, 152, 167; seed-plot of the Enlightenment, 205, 210–13
Syncretist movement in Thirty Years War, 164, 178n

Taborites, radical of Bohemian revolution, 41, 55
Tacitus, P. Cornelius, 127n
Tallemant family, Huguenot bankers of Richelieu, 9
Tanner, Adams, S.J., 158–9
Tawney, R. H., ix, 7
Templars, Knights, accused of witchcraft, 128
Theresa, St (Sta Teresa de Jesus), 125
Thomasius, Christian, opposes torture and witch-craze, 174–5, 182; and Aristoteleanism, 232n
Thorndike, Lynn, jun., 98, 131
Thou, Jacques-Auguste de (Thuanus), 201–2, 227–30, 233–4
Thyraeus, Peter, S.J., 139, 151
Tillotson, John, Archbishop of Canterbury, 200, 212, 217
Tilly, Johann Tzerclas, Count, 156
Torture, judicial, its history and relation to witches' confessions, 117–23

73   12 11 10 9 8 7 6 5